THE VULNERABLE IN INTERNATIONAL SOCIETY

The Vulnerable in International Society

IAN CLARK

OXFORD
UNIVERSITY PRESS

OXFORD
UNIVERSITY PRESS

Great Clarendon Street, Oxford, OX2 6DP,
United Kingdom

Oxford University Press is a department of the University of Oxford.
It furthers the University's objective of excellence in research, scholarship,
and education by publishing worldwide. Oxford is a registered trade mark of
Oxford University Press in the UK and in certain other countries

First Edition published in 2013
Impression: 1

British Library Cataloguing in Publication Data
Data available

ISBN 978–0–19–964608–1 (Hbk.)
978–0–19–964609–8 (Pbk.)

Printed and bound by CPI Group (UK) Ltd, Croydon, CR0 4YY

Preface

This book follows in a long line of my other studies on 'international society' (Clark 2005, 2007, 2011). In writing them, I had become increasingly aware of one big issue lurking in the background. While it is mostly explicit in the literature that international society makes a difference from the 'state of nature', it is left largely implicit whether and how that difference is a positive one. Certainly, international society did not emerge with any unequivocal approbation from those earlier works. But is it actually possible that the difference it makes could be negative instead? It was in order to confront this issue directly that I embarked on this examination of what might strike some readers as the dark side of international society. At the very least, such an undertaking will provide a more rounded and balanced account, and serve as an antidote to any crude perception that international society is wholly benign, and should be considered largely soft and cuddly. Doing so from the perspective of 'the vulnerable' seemed to offer a particularly rich terrain for further exploration, and in this expectation it has not disappointed.

Although this is a relatively short book, it has incurred some very large debts. The first is institutional. I express my gratitude to the Department of International Politics and Aberystwyth University for releasing me on a year-long sabbatical through 2012. At the other end, I am similarly indebted to the School of Social and Political Sciences at the University of Melbourne for hosting me as a Visiting Fellow during that period. I owe a particular debt to Robyn Eckersley, who was instrumental in setting up this arrangement. I am particularly indebted to the University of Melbourne Library for its excellent resources.

The arguments in the book have benefited considerably from their exposure to critical scrutiny in a number of seminars, and I record my appreciation to those who organized them: Colin Wight and Paul Fawcett of the Department of Government and International Relations, Sydney University; Tim Dunne and Heloise Weber of the School of Politics and International Studies, University of Queensland; Bina Fernandez of the School of Social and Political Sciences, University of Melbourne; Roderic Pitty and Mark Beeson of the Department of Political Science and International Relations, University of Western Australia. I am most grateful also to a number of individuals who have commented on earlier drafts of parts of the book, and/or who have pointed me towards important sources: Robyn Eckersley; Toni Erskine; Mervyn Frost; Hannah Hughes; Ian Hurd; Claire Loughnan; Adam Kamrad-Scott; Tony Lang; Andrew Linklater; Cian O'Driscoll; Gerry Simpson; and

OUP's anonymous readers. As always, Dominic Byatt at OUP has given the project the immense benefit of his enthusiasm and support.

Less formally, I wish to record my appreciation of two wonderful Fitzroy cafes (Southpaw on Gertrude Street and Scent of a Flower on Victoria Parade); their excellent coffee, and above all their highly sociable staff, did much to sustain my writing on a daily basis. On a more personal note, the year was greatly enriched by the proximity of, and close contact with, our lovely Australian family. As ever, I am deeply indebted to Janice for making our stay in Melbourne such a special one, as well as for her own direct assistance and contribution in bringing the project to completion.

I.C.
Melbourne

Contents

List of Abbreviations   viii

Introduction   1

1. What Have the Vulnerable Ever Done for International Society?   13

2. Political Violence and the Vulnerable   37

3. Climate Change and the Vulnerable   62

4. Human Movement and the Vulnerable   84

5. Global Health and the Vulnerable   106

6. The Moral Problem of the Vulnerable   128

Conclusion: What Can International Society Do for the Vulnerable?   152

References   165
Index   187

List of Abbreviations

ABM	anti-ballistic missile
AOSIS	Alliance of Small Island States
BASIC	Brazil, South Africa, India, and China
BAU	Business as Usual
CBDR	common but differentiated responsibilities
COP	Conference of the Parties
ES	English School
FCTC	Framework Convention on Tobacco Control
G8	Group of Eight largest economies
GHG	greenhouse gas
GHG	global health governance
IDP	internally displaced person
IHL	international humanitarian law
IHR	International Health Regulations
IPCC	Intergovernmental Panel on Climate Change
IR	international relations
LDCs	least developed countries
MSF	Médecins Sans Frontières
POW	prisoner of war
SALT	Strategic Arms Limitation Treaty
TRIPs	Agreement on Trade-Related Aspects of Intellectual Property Rights
UNDP	United Nations Development Programme
UNEP	United Nations Environment Programme
UNFCCC	United Nations Framework Convention on Climate Change
UNHCR	United Nations High Commissioner for Refugees
UNRRA	United Nations Relief and Rehabilitation Administration
WHO	World Health Organization
WMO	World Meteorological Organization
WTO	World Trade Organization

Introduction

During June 2012, Médecins Sans Frontières (MSF) reported on a complex emergency in Mali under the heading 'Refugees in a Vulnerable Situation' (MSF 2012). People were being driven to flee the violence in the north of the country that had broken out between government and rebel forces. Some sought refuge within Mali, while others had crossed into neighbouring countries, such as Niger and Burkina Faso. Many now faced acute health problems, as well as lack of food in a region described as already experiencing food insecurity as a result of changing climate and rainfall patterns. So why were these people vulnerable? At first glance, their 'vulnerable situation' seems straightforwardly a compound of four sets of material conditions: violence, climate, movement, and health. But what exactly was it that had made them 'vulnerable' in this way? Is it sufficient simply to refer to that set of descriptive conditions as a full and adequate explanation of the 'facts' of their situation? This book explores another way of thinking about those issues. Its focus is indeed upon the vulnerable, but it seeks to provide a much richer account of that situation in which some people come to find themselves.

International relations (IR) has accorded the vulnerable less systematic treatment than they deserve, and in this it is quite unlike a number of other academic disciplines. Concepts of vulnerability are now prominent in the study of a range of topics like disasters, migration, and climate change, and appear widely throughout those social sciences where physical and social systems are seen to interact. For instance, there has developed a general tendency when investigating the impact of seemingly 'natural' disasters to focus additionally upon their social determinants: 'a natural hazard does not always result in a disaster. It only does so when the hazard hits in a context of social vulnerability' (Gemenne 2010: 29). This notion of 'social vulnerability' is absolutely central to what follows, and its objective is to find a way to integrate this approach more effectively within IR. In the spirit of that intellectual ambition, this is a book that explores the international societal determinants of some of the seemingly 'natural' harms that befall humankind. Accordingly, it is about various categories of people: the vulnerable. It is about who they are, and what makes them so within a number of specific policy settings that currently trouble the international order: political violence, climate change, human movement, and global health.

It addresses those issues from one distinctive perspective: international society. It is not, however, simply about how the vulnerable are viewed *through* the eyes of international society, as if standing apart merely as some passive observer. Instead, its core argument is that vulnerability takes such forms as it does, and is allocated in particular patterns, *by* the very nature and embedded norms of international society, very much engaged as an active participant. While the principal focus is indeed upon the vulnerable, at the same time international society is its subject, and the vulnerable are fashioned as its object. In short, what follows is an inquiry into what will be called the international social practice of the vulnerable, and the ethical issues that are intrinsic to that practice. While international society is a common enough subject of study, this book differs in looking at it from this original perspective.

This serves a wider purpose. The underlying concern of this study is to highlight the profoundly insecure ethical bases upon which the current international order rests. However, to establish this case, it does not set out its own normative theory, nor develop its own critique of the international order from that starting point. Instead, it explores the morally contested terrain already occupied by international society, and demonstrates how a number of contemporary problems are characterized above all by deep moral fissures that militate against their satisfactory resolution. Such moral contestation is endemic in international society precisely because its own actions stake out a moral position, at least implicitly, and even if only with temporary sanction. Moreover, the central claim is that many of these moral clashes revolve around notions of the vulnerable. Accordingly, to reach a full assessment of the obstacles to international order, we should begin first of all with a better understanding of the vulnerable, and why they represent such a major challenge to international society.

As such, the book offers a reflective and synoptic overview of some of the major issues in contemporary international order, and of some of the most pressing challenges that currently need to be addressed. It contributes to our understanding of international society by interrogating it from the original perspective of the vulnerable; it adds to our appreciation of disparate forms of vulnerability by placing these within the unifying theme of international society. In these ways, it provides an integrated perspective on problems that are all too often discussed in isolation from each other. Rather than deal with them individually in a series of disconnected essays, this book seizes upon their unifying characteristic, namely the situation of the vulnerable, and how this comes to be conditioned by the rules and norms of international society. It brings out the many tensions and contradictions in how the vulnerable are regarded: some enjoy priority claims for protection, while the exposure to harm of other categories is seemingly tolerated, and often made even more deeply entrenched, by international society's own legitimating social practices.

THE PROBLEM

The question to be investigated is this: if there are in other contexts significant social impacts on vulnerability, does this apply also in the setting of international society and, if so, how are these impacts produced and what are their consequences? Standard definitions tell us that to be vulnerable is to be 'able to be wounded; able to be physically or emotionally hurt; liable to damage or harm' (*New Shorter Oxford English Dictionary*). In those senses, it might be thought, we are all equally vulnerable, as this simply depicts the universal human condition. However, what we must ask in addition is what aggravates this 'ability' to be hurt, or generates this 'liability' to harm, and crucially for the following argument, why is it that some *become* more vulnerable than others? That is to say that vulnerability is neither a wholly pre-existing condition, nor is it evenly and universally distributed. The most revealing questions are then what makes it possible in the first place, and why it comes to be distributed in the way that it is. The main focus of this study will be exactly on these degrees of differentiation in vulnerability, rather than on the extent to which we experience it in common. It responds to a complaint, made some two decades ago in a major rethinking of 'natural' disasters, that there was then 'a serious lack of analysis of the linkages between vulnerability and major global processes as root causes'. This neglect was thought all the more deplorable, given the emerging consensus at that time that 'we need to look at social factors that increase vulnerability' (Blaikie et al. 1994: 30–1). Such a social perspective, on a global scale, is what is offered here through the specific medium of international society.

This differentiation in the allocation of vulnerability might be regarded as simply an observable fact, embedded in physical conditions, as the above definition seems to suggest: the extent of any liability to damage or harm is something that can be empirically assessed, as an objectively existing dimension of any given situation. For example, the driver of a car that proceeds the wrong way up a motorway is vulnerable to a markedly greater degree than are most other drivers. Moreover, to any observer, it seems straightforwardly possible to determine the proximate source of this particular vulnerability, and to do so in an apparently empirical way: those driving on the wrong carriageway are more vulnerable than those who are not. However, what this example also reinforces is that this heightened exposure to risk results from a failure to comply with social rules that are otherwise in force, and in this way the rules are themselves a necessary part of the causal story: while there are always risks attached to driving, the vulnerability would not exist *in this form*, absent society's rules. Vulnerability, to this extent, is attached not simply to an agent doing something that is inherently risky, but derives crucially and additionally from the fact of doing something 'wrong'. In this way, society's norms and rules are immediately implicated.

This has an important corollary. The reason why this is so central to the following argument is that vulnerability, thus understood, denotes also a key moral category, not just an empirically descriptive one: it is not only that certain people *are* vulnerable as part of the natural order of things, but that they are *made* vulnerable by the norms and values embedded in social arrangements. Since this may result in harm to them, vulnerability must be considered a prime site of normative concern. So much is this so that the concept does indeed appear to enjoy a widespread—almost universal—appeal as a central moral category. Part of the reason is that it is very close to our ideas of 'affectedness' to harm by others, present in 'every social morality' (Linklater 2011: 91; Harris 1980). Any idea that so powerfully combines an empirical exposure to harm, along with an almost universally accepted moral principle, is one deserving of our close attention, especially in the context of IR. Given this rich potential, the book seeks to rescue the vulnerable from their neglect by IR, and to bring them into its mainstream.

How then should we begin to think about this relationship between international society and the vulnerable? It is possible to offer a preliminary range of answers to this question along a hypothetical spectrum. At one end, it might be thought that a main objective of international society is to reduce vulnerability, and to do so as best it can, in some kind of impartial way. If the institutions of international society serve any real purpose, it must surely be to mitigate the inconveniences of international life, and protect its members from avoidable harm. In this version, international society serves as a benign force, even if not always highly effective in achieving this objective. At the other extreme, it could be objected that the category of those exposed to vulnerability is not already self-defining or objectively pre-existing, and becomes formed only in the context of any one social order. In this way, vulnerability cannot precede, but arises only within, any particular institutional order: vulnerability is *ex post*, not *ex ante*, and has to be understood as immanent within a specific order. In this version, international society's role might be considered much more malign. In the former, the problem of vulnerability is thought already fully to exist, and the task of international society is to mitigate it; in the latter, vulnerability is wholly and directly attributable to the artifice of international society.

Is international society to be cast as the hero or villain in our story? As is so often the case, international society can instead be taken to depict a *via media* (C. Brown 2010: 40–52). In between those two extremes, it is proposed instead that—while neither wholly the solution nor wholly the problem—international society manifestly does make a difference: it impacts outcomes by contributing its own distinctive configurations of vulnerability. This is a study of how these distributions emerge, and how they affect the quality of human life as a result. Political geographers have concluded of 'natural' disasters that 'social systems themselves generate unequal exposure to risk by making some groups of people, some individuals, and some societies more prone to hazards than others' (Cannon 1994: 14). Specifically, it is claimed that 'environmental crises are not experienced equitably', but instead that 'vulnerability . . . is a factor of social relations', and this leaves 'some people more vulnerable than others' (Johnston 1994b: 8). If so, can this same logic be applied to international society, and how does this particular social system generate 'unequal exposure to risk'?

There are, of course, some potential objections to treating international society as any kind of purposeful agent in this way. These will be considered in detail in Chapter 1. What is this thing called international society? It is not straightforwardly obvious that it can act, make choices, and have causal impacts on the lives of people. Nonetheless, if we consider it as a really existing social structure, with its own shared norms and institutions, then it does provide the framework within which its members interact: at one level, this lends it the capacity to 'socialize' its members in distinctive directions; at another, and even more fundamentally, it can be claimed that it 'constitutes' the particular identities of those members. These ideas are commonplace, as we shall see, in English School (ES) theory, as well as in much constructivist IR writing more generally. However, whereas there is a widespread assumption that much of this socialization works to mitigate human adversity, the focus of this study is instead upon a less obvious consequence of this social practice of the vulnerable: how international society legitimates social norms and institutions that have the capacity, in effect if not explicitly in intent, to contribute to a particular distribution of human harm.

As such, the book draws our attention to one of international society's more negative characteristics. It is for this reason, and just as importantly, that some of the major problems of contemporary international order must be understood as inherently moral. This is because their essence is already bound up with international society's own practices: the manner of its own identification of the vulnerable articulates an evolving position that invites subsequent moral challenge and contestation. While there has been much normative IR writing about the specific problems discussed in these pages, the concept of vulnerability offers a unique and hitherto unexploited way of integrating them within one common framework. In short, it would certainly be shallow and misleading to suggest that all the problems identified in the following discussion should be laid at the door of international society, and this is assuredly not the thrust of the argument. Nonetheless, what certainly can be said, at a minimum, is that the way international society conceives of, and responds to, those problems does have its own impact upon the resulting *relative distribution* of risk. As such, international society is not always the author of the underlying problem but, in the way that it intervenes, it certainly becomes the author of its moral consequences: the latter are embedded in those outcomes it has already helped to influence, no matter how benign or otherwise its overall intentions in the matter.

THE ARGUMENT

In its disparate activities, international society treats the vulnerable as seemingly knowable *categories* of people, subject to various *conditions* that render
their exposure to harm particularly acute. In this way, it views the vulnerable
as largely given, and responds to them as it purports to find them: *they* are the
problem to be addressed. However, key to this study is the alternative suggestion that the vulnerable become fully known only as a result of their framing
by international society: in this way they are also, and just as importantly,
defined by an overall *concept* of the issue area that inevitably has profound
moral implications. In imposing on each individual policy problem its own
concept, its own preferred categories for dealing with it, and its own understanding of which conditions underlie it, international society in effect influences outcomes and so appears as a moral agent—*its* own characterization of
the vulnerable, in turn, gives rise to moral problems further down the line.
This ensures that it cannot avoid the consequences of its own impositions, and
so the politics *within* international society necessarily derive from those moral
stances it has already adopted. To deal effectively with the vulnerable entails
therefore a deeper engagement with those moral issues associated with the
very concept of the vulnerable that it has introduced.

How does this happen? In effect, the normative preferences of international
society generate distinctive patterns of vulnerability. That there is some direct
relationship between individual orders and the vulnerabilities that arise within
them is sufficiently self-evident to be irrefutable. For example, the very fact
that war is generally accepted as an institution of international society makes
this point: international acceptance of war necessarily leads to toleration of
socially condoned forms of vulnerability, and these become an inescapable
consequence of war's social purpose. This has immense significance for how
we think about IR. It also establishes an urgent normative perspective as a
feature of how international society itself works: if society wills the institution
and the normative foundations on which it rests, it shares also in the allocation
of vulnerability that flows necessarily from it. In short, this book is about what
has been described as 'the power hierarchies that explain unequal vulnerabilities to harm and the uneven distribution of security, and which invariably
lead to perceptions of injustice' (Linklater 2011: 6–7).

As this brief summary makes clear, there are several key links in the logical
chain of the following argument overall: the salience of *both* power hierarchies
and evolving norms in their joint expression through international society;
how these frame the approach to dealing with major problems confronting
international order; the resultant socially legitimated distribution of vulnerability; the pervasive sense of injustice to which this frequently gives rise; and
hence the intrinsically moral nature of so many key problems that face

international society today. Since the vulnerable become so *in* international society, rather than in any wholly pre-existing sense, it is equally obvious that it is the author of those particular moral dimensions it has already inscribed in the vulnerable.

In this respect, it will be argued, the book strikes a note similar to E. H. Carr's *The Twenty Years' Crisis* (Carr 1939 [2001]). This highly influential work engaged with a series of then contemporary issues, but in such a way as to raise perennial questions about international life more generally. In some ways, the present study echoes elements of his approach, but from the distinctive perspective of vulnerability. To be absolutely clear, it is not for a moment suggested here that Carr was some kind of proto-theorist of the vulnerable, as he most certainly was not. However, what Carr did do, in his own fashion, was to grapple with the abiding problems in the relationship between power and morality in international affairs (Cox 2000; Molloy 2009). Accordingly, the specific relevance of Carr is that vulnerability can be seen as one especially effective way of bringing these two concepts into direct relationship, since social vulnerability emerges in relations of differential power, and for that reason is also the source of an important moral claim. In that way, the discussion unfolds as an extended essay on the capacity of international society to frame the vulnerable, on the normative problems to which this gives rise, and why both of those dimensions therefore need to be considered in tandem. This is a continuation of a theme already prominent in my general argument about legitimacy (Clark 2005: 25), but has particular force in this context.

As such, the argument will revisit Carr's position, and his own attempted compromise: 'Political action', Carr enjoined, 'must be based on a co-ordination of morality and power' (Carr 1939: 125). In practice, this seemed to mean that 'those who profit most by that order can in the long run only hope to maintain it by making sufficient concessions to make it tolerable to those who profit by it least' (Carr 1939: 215). That tension in his analysis replicates the tension explored in this book. All international orders claim to rest on universal principles, but actually serve to protect the interests of the stronger parties (Carr 1939: 101). In the case of Carr, the puzzle this left behind was that his prescription seemed wholly inconsistent with his explanatory analysis, and so seemed to suggest that no satisfactory reconciliation between power and morality was possible.

The discussion offered here re-presents that analysis, grounded specifically in the notion of vulnerability. This position immediately acknowledges the connection between the *effects* of a particular social order and the moral challenges to which its stability is subject. The powerful—of many kinds and at multiple levels—are implicated in those vulnerabilities that have been produced. Unsurprisingly, it is those hitherto prevailing concepts framing the vulnerable that become open to subsequent challenge and revision. This process as a whole is referred to here as international society's practice of the vulnerable. Since it is about a specific relationship between the powerful and the vulnerable, as mediated through international society, it needs necessarily to be understood in moral terms.

THE OUTLINE

In its six main chapters, the book initially establishes the theoretical framework, then investigates it in relation to a set of four policy issues, and finally engages in a thematic treatment of the distinctively moral problems represented by vulnerability. In this way, it views the subject of international society through the distinctive lens of 'the vulnerable', while simultaneously making sense of the latter as the consequence of international society's routine workings.

In each of the policy cases, we encounter a multiplicity of defects and shortcomings in the functioning of a variety of international regimes, charged with responsibility for the management respectively of violence, climate change, human movement, and global health. In all these areas there are striking inconsistencies, and operational failures. This, by itself, may not be sufficient to make them subject to moral disapproval by the participants, or to create problems that require moral redress as an inherent part of their solution. What makes these problems distinctively moral is precisely that they can be understood only in terms of a socially patterned vulnerability. As a concept, this term is then fully intelligible only insofar as we recognize its moral provenance: to speak of the vulnerable, as international society so regularly does, is already to speak a normative language.

The introductory chapter outlines this framework of vulnerability, and develops the central argument. By definition, international society does not cater adequately for the vulnerable: the latter are those who find themselves insufficiently protected by it. This is a vital perspective. It treats the vulnerable both as an empirical object (but one that has been already socially crafted) and at the same time as a normative subject, and directly challenges any formal distinction between the two modes of analysis (Price 2008; Reus-Smit and Snidal 2008). This makes it central to any rounded understanding of international society, and of the problems it currently faces. The principal elements of the framework required for this argument are the *concepts*, *categories*, and *conditions* of the vulnerable, as set out in Chapter 1.

There follow the four case studies. As will be demonstrated, each of these reveals the manner in which international society has contributed its own social distributions of vulnerability. It has done so by how it has conceived of each of these problem areas, and above all by its imposition on each of distinctive sets of categories. It treats the vulnerable as if they can be identified as already existing classes of people, grouped by category and defined by the conditions that face them. In combination, these are taken as a map of the world of really existing exposures to risk and hazard. In so doing, however, international society also imposes a profoundly moral framework that becomes the site of subsequent contestation. Each of the cases explores that moral domain by a critical examination of international society's concepts and categories, their ethical significance, and the controversies to which they have subsequently given rise.

Historically, those impacts can be illustrated by a focus upon one key constitutional moment in the life of each of these policy domains. Accordingly, as one part of the historical review, the case studies look closely at a set of important foundational agreements and conventions, and the concept of vulnerability that animated and emerged from each in turn. In the case of political violence, we turn to the Geneva Conventions of 1949 and their subsequent Protocols of 1977. With regard to matters of human movement, a similarly defining moment is to be found in the 1951 Refugee Convention, and the Protocol of 1967. As regards global health, the creation of the World Health Organization (WHO) in 1948 offers another key moment of this kind, and its constitution contains a specific understanding of what vulnerability means in this context. Since climate change emerges considerably later as an object of international policy concern, the intervention of international society in that case is best captured by the UN Framework Convention of 1992. Each of these moments articulates some kind of consensual view of international society, while simultaneously giving expression to the power differentials between its various stakeholders. These established the parameters within which subsequent moral contestation was to be conducted.

The first case confronts international society's general stipulations about protection and vulnerability in the context of violence. These emerge principally through its adoption of various concepts of political violence (such as war) and the sharp contrast that it draws between this and others (such as insurgency or terrorism). It then deploys its own categories, such as those of combatants and civilians, and so begins to generate a social map of vulnerability, in accordance with its own preferred concept. In this manner, international society establishes those categories that demand our protection, while consigning others to their fate. What these various reflections demonstrate is how the rules deployed by international society apply differently to various potential categories of the vulnerable. In the face of multiple challenges at the present time, international society is struggling to come up with an adequate, and internally consistent, set of responses. In short, the chapter uses the framing of vulnerability to explore the terrain that lies between differing concepts of violence, on the one hand, and the various categories of the vulnerable that result from them, on the other.

There is much common economic background applicable to the next three cases on climate change, human movement, and global health. Arguably, within the present international economic order (under the market and capitalism), we are all exposed to varying degrees of vulnerability: that is how markets work, and recent financial upheavals remind us of the full extent of our possible exposure. Nonetheless, if vulnerability is again universal at one level, current arrangements also result in distinctive patterns of vulnerability, as the recent acceleration of global economic disparities demonstrates. For some social theorists, risk is the defining quality of the present moment (Beck 1992), and the global economy is manifestly a risky business. However, the important issue for this study is how that risk is socially mediated, and hence distributed. In all of the following cases, there is a highly revealing dialogue between the 'universality' of vulnerability as posited in theory, and the very specific allocations of it in social practice.

Chapter 3 addresses climate change, and nowhere are the themes of the book more clearly on display. The very complex politics in this area (both domestic and international) are essentially about how emerging and prospective vulnerabilities are to be distributed, and on which principles. Clearly, although climate change manifests itself through seemingly 'natural' processes, its causes—as well as its mitigation—extend deeply into the existing social, economic, and political orders. In consequence, while we all may well be vulnerable to climate change, the most immediately vulnerable are those who international society has helped to locate in the front line. It has been estimated, for example, that the 100 states most vulnerable to the impacts of climate change are themselves responsible for approximately only 3 per cent of global greenhouse gas (GHG) emissions. This asymmetry between the distribution of risk and causal responsibility for its production already attunes us to some of this political ecology.

What this reinforces is that, in the environmental context, people are vulnerable not just to 'nature' but to the decisions of powerful others, and international society is one such highly important medium. While climate is commonly presented as a classic demonstration of universal vulnerability, its particular allocations are just as striking. Moreover, the full significance of this lies in the fact that the response to climate change is, in turn, integral to all of the other policy cases discussed in the book. Climate change will have pronounced effects on the forms, level, and distribution of economic activities, will become a major determinant of relative access to food and water, will shape global patterns of health, and pose critical challenges for human movement. For these reasons, it is the distribution of vulnerability that takes us to the very heart of the politics surrounding this issue: any and all future international climate orders will have diverse impacts on that distribution. In its own construction of the problem, international society has again imposed its own highly influential categories: climate change thus far has been principally conceived of as an issue between developed and developing states, and the resulting distribution of responsibilities and vulnerabilities has been largely presented in those terms.

The third case turns to the social vulnerability associated with human movement. Historically, human movement has always been driven by powerful economic motives and, while some international orders have been largely permissive, others have been much more restrictive. In the nineteenth century, the order actively encouraged the movement of goods, capital, and people. In recent decades, it has generally been found much more convenient to move jobs and money to people than vice versa, and the legal and political restrictions on human movement have become more pervasive at the same time as the regulation of capital movements has been greatly relaxed: ours is an age of 'wall building' with respect to people, while other types of wall have been steadily dismantled (W. Brown 2010: 20–4). Successive international social arrangements, in their distinctive fashions, have thus over the decades choreographed the human movement of the vulnerable in different ways.

The international political order of the states system has both stimulated, and greatly complicated, 'natural' movements of any kind. Refugees are demonstrably the product of this particular order and, as has been suggested, 'are the human reminder of the failings of modern international society' (Haddad 2008: 3). While refugees are at first vulnerable to the original conditions that give them cause for flight, they then confront a double jeopardy in their subsequent exposure to the decisions of powerful others about whether or not to admit them for protection. International society approaches the vulnerable through its own preferred categories, such as refugees, migrants, illegal migrants, and the internally displaced. Groups of people are thus rendered vulnerable not just by the immediate conditions of their movement (as in the recent events in Mali), but additionally by the categories through which international society chooses to process them.

It should not be thought, however, that only those humans actively engaged in movement are vulnerable. Historically, these movements have also created immense vulnerabilities for those at the receiving end, and it has been international society's past intervention, largely in favour of the former against the latter, that has been so decisive in this regard. The movements to the new worlds displayed graphically the impact of international society on the distribution of vulnerability: the international order at that time provided legal entitlement to 'civilized' settlers to occupy lands already inhabited by the 'uncivilized'. This resulted in the displacement of millions of indigenous peoples: 'The same system of international law that has promoted norms of sovereignty and human rights has also been complicit in European processes of conquest and colonialism' (Havercroft 2008: 112).

The final policy case considers global health. Structures of global health seek increasingly to protect those vulnerable elsewhere to the spread of epidemics, by keeping 'in quarantine' those already suffering from disease, while at the same time selectively allowing the movement of trained health professionals to staff health facilities in developed countries. Once again, the vulnerabilities of some are catered for by the manufacture of deeper configurations of vulnerability elsewhere.

More specifically, international society—especially through its own international organizations—has encouraged particular ways of thinking about the problems of global health. For the most part, it has promoted a biomedical approach that, by itself, can be insensitive to its social dimensions. Through its trade and investment regimes, over which it has regulatory tutelage, it has made access to affordable medicines highly restrictive, and has done little to promote research into those very illnesses that afflict the majority of humankind. The resultant social map of vulnerability in terms of global health compounds the existing risks to ill health, as it accurately reproduces those deformities of international society elsewhere, even if many specific outcomes have not been explicitly 'intended'.

If the case studies reveal the workings of power, expressed through the norms and institutions of international society, and the role of dominant states within them, the final chapter returns to a focus on the inherently moral dimensions of the problems that currently beset the world. Accordingly, this thematic chapter provides a more explicit statement of what will have already been demonstrated in the cases, namely that international society constructs particular patterns of vulnerability—they represent to this extent its impacts on alternative vulnerabilities. This invites, finally, a fuller exploration of the topic of vulnerability in connection with power and ethics. The objective is not, however, to set out a fully systematized ethical position, either as an end in itself or as some kind of siren call to political action. It is to restate a position that will already have run through the preceding policy cases, and so provide a fuller understanding of the essentially moral nature of the problems that we face: in this way, the empirical and normative will be seamlessly blended. The ethical dimension is not some *post hoc* gloss that we might optionally be called upon to provide, but instead is an integral part of the problem that needs to be addressed. It is certainly in those terms that the problems are cast from the perspective of the participants.

By the end, the book comes full circle. It starts from the question about what the vulnerable have ever done for international society. The answer, in short, is that the vulnerable are its incidental scapegoats and blind spots; they are the symptoms of the politically convenient ways in which it has managed its own affairs, and how the hidden costs of those arrangements have been transferred to others in a multiplicity of harmful ways. But the vulnerable are not wholly excluded by international society. While they represent its own handiwork, they also remain within its gates, and serve as a constant reminder of the moral casualties of its own normative order. As such, it is appropriate that, in the conclusion, the book returns to what international society can do for the vulnerable: what are the implications of understanding the vulnerable in this way, and what insight does this provide into the nature of international society?

1

What Have the Vulnerable Ever Done for International Society?

The brief of this book is not the vulnerable *and* international society, taken as two discrete subjects brought momentarily and contingently together, but rather the vulnerable *in* international society, stipulating a constant empirical and moral conjunction between the two. This point can best be made by analogy with my previous studies of international legitimacy (Clark 2005, 2007, 2011). While legitimacy is an inherently normative concept, the object-ive of those works was not to construct a normative theory of legitimacy to serve as some exogenous standard by which to evaluate international society. Instead, and explicitly, they were attempts to analyse legitimacy as a *social practice* within international society. To that extent, they took the form of an empirical review of how that practice had evolved historically, and how it now operated in contemporary circumstances. At the same time, these surveys would make no sense at all without reference to the norms that were embed-ded in that practice, and how the content of these norms, as well as the balance between them, had moved over time. International legitimacy, I argued, reflected the shifting equilibrium between the norms of legality, morality, and constitutionality (Clark 2005).

This study is similar in its combination of the empirical and the normative, focused in this case on the concept of vulnerability: it traces a social practice of the vulnerable. It likewise eschews establishing any exogenous standard, with respect to which vulnerability is to be diagnosed, and its remedial require-ments addressed. Neither does it set out its own moral theory of vulnerability as such. Its brief instead is an exploration of the endogenous practice of vulnerability within international society: how has it been conceptualized; which of its forms have been prioritized; and how has it been proposed that it be redressed? As a result, what are the moral deficits that international society can be observed to experience? These questions will be answered not from any Archimedean position, but from an analysis of international so-ciety's own expressed values. Critically, its practices make direct appeal to a variety of norms—often conflicting and competing, and certainly changeable over time—in asserting its sundry claims to how the vulnerable should be identified and treated.

This method of exposition is important for two reasons. Firstly, the book is primarily interested in vulnerability as a social condition; secondly, it starts from the premise that the practices around it are inherently normative, even if there are ways in which we can study them in a sociologically 'empirical' way. Accordingly, the evidence that will be adduced in support of claims to the morally problematic nature of international society's allocations of vulnerability is not derived from some external standard of moral evaluation, independently established in this work. Instead, the moral contestability is an inherent dimension of what is called here the social practice of the vulnerable. To the extent that temporary conjunctions allow for legitimated social allocations of vulnerability, these are predicated on moments of consensus sufficiently strong to endow any one such allocation with a provisionally accepted status. These can be found, for example, in a number of those constitutional moments that, as will be presented in the following cases, were to lead to the establishment of specific managerial regimes. It is precisely this provisional moral plausibility that tends thereafter to become the subject of the most intense contestation. In this way, international society's practices of the vulnerable become central to the management of international order, and its potential for stability. The essential first step is to submit the nature of international society to closer scrutiny.

THE ENGLISH SCHOOL (ES) AND INTERNATIONAL SOCIETY

International society is the subject of this book, and it appears as a powerful agent in the construction of the vulnerable. How does it manage to do this? Can such a seemingly abstract theoretical concept exercise such a profound influence over the lives of people? When international society acts, who is it that acts in its name? Is it actually no more than the most powerful states within it? The worry these questions express, at base, is that any pretence that international society has the capacity to shape the vulnerable depends on unacceptable assumptions about its homogeneity, and ends with hopeless reification. International society is at most a field of action, some might object, rather than any kind of actor in its own right.

Nonetheless, the idea of its potent social effects is very much implicit in general understandings of international society, and if this were not so it would be much less interesting to IR. However, on the face of it, there are a number of potential difficulties with any such suggestion. First, it could be held instead that it is the members of the society who act, rather than the society itself: international society is at most the shadow play of the agency of states. In support, this is implicit in Hedley Bull's oft-cited definition whereby the states *form* a society, *conceive* of themselves as bound by it, and *share* in the workings of its common institutions (Bull 1977: 13). In this account, all the active verbs pertain to the state members, not to international society as such. From this, it is but a small step to the related proposition that when international society appears to act, it does so only at the behest of the strongest: 'international society is a purposive entity', Morris maintains, 'the normative content of which is, to a significant degree, determined by the great powers of the day' (Morris 2005: 280). Of course, similar debates about agency, and whether institutions enjoy any kind of autonomous capacity to act beyond that of their individual members, are to be found around specific international organizations, such as the UN Security Council (Hurd 2007).

Secondly, there is the even more fundamental objection that international society is a theoretical concept, rather than something that possesses agency of any kind. This point is most clearly conveyed in accounts of international society that regard it as merely an 'ideal type' (Keene 2009; Navari 2009b: 5–6). It is, on this conception, 'not a society of states *out there* in the world, but rather an ideal-type', and as such a tool employed by analysts (Linklater and Suganami 2006: 53). It may operate in the minds of (some) IR theorists, but can scarcely do things in the real world of international relations. In this version, any suggestion that international society distributes vulnerability is no more than a theoretical obfuscation. These objections can be considered in two stages: in what sense is it appropriate to regard international society as an agent at all; and in what sense might it be thought to be a moral agent specifically?

In common with much social theory, the argument in this book is grounded in the general belief that social structures do have an 'agency' all of their own, at least in one specific sense (Friedman and Starr 1997; Wight 2006): without any such belief, the notion of international society could not play the powerful role that it does in English School (ES) theory. While international society is assuredly no reified single agent, at any one moment in time it has real-life effects *as if* it were. It is simultaneously an agent and a field of action. In Geoffrey Stern's fitting analogy, it represents the 'orchestra', not just the individual players (Stern 2000: 9). Crucially, then, we cannot fully separate out the actions of the individual members from the activity of the society as a whole, and to this degree it does make sense to talk of international society having a view of, say, revolutions, over and above the attitudes of any of its individual member states (Armstrong 1993).

It is largely through the umbrella concept of 'socialization' that international society is most commonly believed to 'act', and this has been defined generally as 'the comprehensive and consistent induction of an individual into the objective world of a society' (Berger and Luckman 1966: 120; see Giddens 1987: 61; Crothers 1996: 4). 'A central tenet of the English School', Dunne reminds us after all, 'is the belief that the agents are socialised by the structure' (Dunne 1998: 10). One of the results of this is the way in which international society 'homogenizes' its members (Halliday 1992). This is a pervasive theme in ES discussions (Alderson and Hurrell 2000: 69). It is echoed more widely also in constructivist arguments that give ideational structures a quasi-causal force in 'constituting' agents, and in related under-standings of the co-constitution between agents and structures (Wendt 1999; Copeland 2006: 3). While it may appear wholly counter-intuitive that, as free-standing rational actors, all states would collectively agree to form an inter-national society that might do positive harm to some of them, their behaviour is more readily understandable as that of actors constituted in specific ways by international society (Frost 2009).

But does it make sense to treat international society as a moral agent, as seems to be implied in this book? This topic is normally approached as part of the wider issue of collective or institutional moral agency (Erskine 2003a). Here it is routinely asserted that moral agency requires mentality, moral purpose, and the potential for moral rationality or deliberation (S. Miller 2010: 32), and on this basis it is widely preferred to restrict notions of moral agency to human beings; for the same reason international society would be immediately disqualified. Nonetheless, even moral 'individualists' tend not to dismiss 'collective' agency altogether, albeit remaining generally sceptical of assigning it to institutions as such (S. Miller 2010: 153). Within IR, however, assignment of degrees of agency and responsibility towards a variety of insti-tutions has been much more commonly and openly acknowledged (Erskine 2003b; Lang 2003).

Even so, it is one thing to contemplate the moral agency of institutions, but possibly quite another to acknowledge the same of something much less formal and organized, namely international society. For instance, Erskine clearly differentiates between those institutions that 'can conceivably be con-sidered agents' and those 'institutions of international society' that presumably cannot, let alone international society *in toto* (Erskine 2003b: 5). Most directly relevant to this discussion then is Chris Brown's explicit assessment of the capacity of international society to act in a moral way. In his exploration of the issue, he reaches the somewhat diffident conclusion that 'those who posit the existence of an international society that can act morally in world affairs are not wholly mistaken', albeit that the values and norms on which it acts are 'limited in range and scope' (Brown 2003: 64). Although Brown's is no ringing endorsement, neither is it any absolute rejection of the possibility. In the same way, and in this limited sense, we do find a number of other attributions of 'moral agency' to international society (Bellamy 2005b: 10), even if it is seemingly the states that possess the 'moral purposes' in the first place (Reus-Smit 1997, 1999): they do so because they are constituted in that way. In short, international society becomes the repository of some values, and it is only with reference to those embedded norms that we can then begin to explain the 'coordinated shifts' in state identity and interests (Finnemore 1996: 2–3): even if individual 'virtue ethics' are absorbed into international society, the latter in turn constitutes the requirements for appropriate ethical behaviour on the part of individuals (Gaskarth 2012).

Any such attribution of moral agency might then, in turn, be further extended into an argument for explicit assignment of responsibility to international society for its own acts of commission and omission with respect to the vulnerable. The following argument stops short of doing so, however, as this would require it to espouse its own normative theory. Instead, it suffices for the present discussion to show that a perception of how those responsibilities come into play, as held on the part of the participants, is intrinsic to the politics of international order. Accordingly, whereas Brown is primarily interested in whether or not international society can act for moral *reasons*, this book is more modestly interested in exploring the moral *consequences* of those normative practices in which it is already inescapably engaged. International society has agent-like moral effects whenever it adopts collective stances on certain issues; simultaneously, it is a heterogeneous field of moral action, as its component parts seek to shape and reformulate those stances. There is no need to reduce international society to either one of those elements: it expresses both unity and diversity at the same time.

One of the clearest ways in which this can be demonstrated is through what is called here the social practice of the vulnerable. Central to this is a form of politics that depends on such assignments of agency and responsibility by the participants. In this sense, international society is associated with the 'constitution' of what has been described as 'dispersed practices' that do routinely invite explicit forms of ethical judgement (Frost 2003b: 84, 96). Accordingly, where the following discussion refers in shorthand to international society distributing vulnerability (in a seemingly intentional, purposeful, and causal way), the reader may at those points wish to have in mind this more complex process, and prefer to substitute the language of international society's constitution of the vulnerable, following upon its pervasive socialization of those who operate within its domain.

In sum, international society 'acts', or possesses 'agency', to the extent that it becomes constitutive of its members, a claim that is generic to most constructivist theory. In this way, it 'does' a large number of things: it polices its own rules of rightful membership, including its terms of recognition (Fabry 2010); it generates, and reinvents, its own rules of rightful conduct (Scheipers 2009); it diffuses norms that can have a revolutionary impact on gender roles (Towns 2010); it has the ideational resources to translate material facts (war, balance of power, great powers) into institutions and legitimate practices; it can become a bearer of duties, encouraging the establishment of protection regimes (Cronin 2003), including the possibility of a Responsibility to Protect; and in these terms it makes sense to describe it as 'morally backward' (Keal 2003), as well as to explore the evolution of *its* norms in relation to, for instance, humanitarian intervention (Wheeler 2000).

It is perfectly possible to make such claims while simultaneously recognizing the diversity within international society and the 'deformity' in the setting of its norms and rules (Hurrell 2007: 10, 305; see also Harbour 2003: 69). One dimension of this deformity certainly includes what 'the strong impose upon the weak', but it encompasses much more than this alone, if we are to take 'the idea of international society seriously' (Alderson and Hurrell 2000: 70). This picks up once again, from a slightly different direction, the notion of 'hierarchy' in international society (Dunne 2003; Clark 2009). While the suggestion that there can be hierarchies within the 'anarchical' society had long appeared contradictory, there is now widespread acceptance in the literature that such legitimated hierarchies do in fact occur (Hobson and Sharman 2005; Donnelly 2006; Lake 2007, 2009; Clapton and Hameiri 2012). From this perspective, the social practice of the vulnerable can be regarded as one example of the kind of hierarchies that can be found in international society: although these demonstrably rest on gross inequalities, the interest of this study is in how they are both legitimated and contested around the vulnerable in particular.

It is therefore not the case that international society holds any homogenous or constant views on the normative foundations of its activities. On the contrary, these are subjects of profound contestation. Nonetheless, international society— through its own institutions and constitutional provisions for the management of specific issues—does occasionally reach moments of sufficient consensus to give expression to legitimated norms and regimes for dealing with the vulnerable as it sees them. At these moments, it does indeed display a capacity to act. Specifically, they permit it to assign 'special responsibilities' to individual actors, thus endowing them with important social powers (Bukovansky et al. 2012: 20). More generally, they provide the overall normative framing for those issues that international society feels called upon to manage. These are always likely to be unstable equilibrium points, expressing some temporary conjunction between the potency of generally held norms and the relative degrees of support they happen to enjoy, taking place within specific distributions of material power. In this respect, international society (viewed as a macrocosm) displays the very same tension in the relationship between 'legislation' and 'deliberation' as is found in the Security Council (viewed as a microcosm) (Johnstone 2008; Vos 2011): that latter body can 'act' in introducing new international law, but at the same time reflects an imperfect deliberative process.

While these moments depend on pragmatic compromise, their equilibrium also rests on some kind of moral plausibility, at least for the time and in the circumstances in which they occur. These are highly fluid conditions. In one context, this process can be illustrated by the example of the adoption of anti-slavery by Britain in the early nineteenth century. This represented a happy confluence of a norm with a powerful set of norm entrepreneurs, both located in an overall favourable distribution of material power (Clark 2007). This enabled slaves to be redefined by international agreement in 1815 as vulnerable, and hence in need of protection, at least insofar as the trade in them was concerned. Importantly, we can infer, they were not 'vulnerable' prior to the declaration issued at Vienna.

Accordingly, if international society is the repository of its members' collectively shared norms (at any one moment), there is no contradiction in claiming that it can have real-life impacts on the distribution of exposure to harm that is patterned in accordance with those norms. It 'does' so precisely through the interaction of its members that constitutes international society (Alderson and Hurrell 2000: 23), and their constitution or socialization by it in turn. However, and critically for this study, these distributions do periodically enjoy some kind of legitimacy, and are not altogether coerced or imposed. Even in this most inauspicious domain of the vulnerable, it is striking to discover that practices of legitimacy continue to pertain. Above all, this is one rich paradox of this study.

Any attempt of this kind to locate the vulnerable in the context of international society might, at first glance, appear counter-intuitive. The whole point of this ES perspective is to argue that international society generates norms and institutions thought to mitigate the otherwise 'anarchic' international condition (Butterfield and Wight 1966; Bull 1977; Dunne 1998; Bellamy 2005a). How then can it be claimed that international society performs such a perverse or apparently dysfunctional task as framing and prioritizing various forms of vulnerability? Surely, it might be thought, international society is intended instead to bring about benign effects through its Grotian softening of the international state of nature (Bull 1966; Bull, Kingsbury, and Roberts 1992), and hence to express itself through the more progressive developments in international life, such as international law and diplomacy. Any such one-sided notion is sadly misleading, however, since international society must be understood to encompass the full range of its formations, whether benign or malign in consequence. 'To believe in the importance of a common framework of rules and social norms', Hurrell rightly attests, 'does not imply that power, coercion, and conflict do not play a major, often dominant, role in international relations' (Hurrell 2007: 38). International society, in short, does not simply 'socialize' the positive, but can also be seen to develop practices around those other aspects of international politics, including some of its endemic deformities. Indeed, many of these have routinely become 'institutionalized', and this is similarly the case with its practices of the vulnerable.

One possible way of explaining this perverse outcome could then be by stressing the bifurcated nature of the order pursued by international society. In his critical interpretation, Edward Keene pointed to one missing dimension in standard accounts of the evolution of international society, and of its norms. While, as was commonly recognized, it had historically practised a norm of toleration within its European heartland, and was to this extent protective of differences between states, in its approach to cultures outside it had instead adopted a norm of civilization that promoted the assimilation of others into European preferred frameworks, while providing explicit sanction to the expansionist activities of a motley collection of its own colonizers (Keene 2002). The results of this expansion were, of course, disastrous for existing indigenous societies, and it was European international society that had aided and abetted this incursion: 'the expansion of Europe resulted in a progressive erosion and denial of the rights of indigenous peoples' (Keal 2003: 35). This critical literature draws our attention powerfully to that 'intimate relationship between international society and domination' (Dunne 2005: 74–5). And so in institutionalizing pluralism within Europe, international society simultaneously set in place elsewhere a specific form of vulnerability to European normative frameworks. It is impossible to recognize the one without acknowledging also the logical consequence for the other.

The argument could then be made that the specific sense in which the vulnerable are *in* international society is that certain peoples are subject to the normative rules of that society, but at the same time are not properly *of* it: historically, there was to be no practice of toleration towards those on the outside, nor yet were they to be allowed any latitude to follow their own devices. It is tempting, therefore, to account for the negative features of international society largely as a result of this deep-seated bifurcation. However, this is not the argument presented here. Instead, the following critique is more fundamental and general: the social practice of the vulnerable has been a characteristic of international society across all its dimensions, with respect to full insiders, not only those on the outside. Vulnerability has not been dumped exclusively on those beyond the pale, although certainly those peoples have received much more than their fair share of any such dumping. But even those fully 'in' and 'of' international society have likewise experienced the distributive impact of its socially generated vulnerability.

In this way, the remit of international society should be construed in very broad terms indeed, and it becomes accordingly less perplexing to admit the possibility of a normatively constructed practice of the vulnerable in that society. Just as international society has made those other institutions of war, balance of power, and the great powers into what they have become, so it has shaped the practice of the vulnerable in its own image. It has sought to provide normative regulation for various forms of vulnerability, thereby configuring and prioritizing different versions of it. Hurrell is absolutely right to emphasize the deformities in international society, and among these he singles out 'the choices taken by institutions and states as to whose security is to be protected' (Hurrell 2003: 41): this selective provision of security is but the flip side of the production and toleration of other forms of vulnerability. As such, this is yet another way of saying that international society creates and allocates particular distributions of vulnerability. Vulnerability, then, has been very much a construct of international society, and this book traces how these constructions have developed, and charts the many clashes to which they now give rise.

Why should we assume that these vulnerabilities are the creation of *international* society, rather than of a conglomerate of deformed *domestic* societies (Miller 2007: 260)? This is a dichotomy that constantly plagues all discussion of attempts to ameliorate the lot of specific peoples exposed to harm. Where are the obstacles to such improvement to be found? Are they international or domestic? Are human rights universal, and is it therefore a requirement that they are protected through international instruments? Or are they instead the creation of individual societies, and must each society be left to determine in its own way what is appropriate for that community? This is the very stuff central to debates between solidarists and pluralists (with reference to ES theory), just as it is the critical difference between cosmopolitans and communitarians (with reference to international normative theory more generally). In this way, as we shall see, cosmopolitans and communitarians differ fundamentally, less about the central importance of vulnerability, and more with respect to its causal conditions and the tolerability of its current distribution.

The other side of the coin is then what is believed to be the root cause of this distribution. As regards world poverty (and the exposure to vulnerability that results from it), there has been a deep-seated argument as to its intrinsic causes, and about the obstacles to effective economic development, for more than half a century. For many, especially in the 1960s and 1970s, the problem was identified as resulting from the failures of an inherently exploitative interstate economic order, and the various injustices and inequalities to which this gave rise. By the 1980s, however, and under pressure from the economically dominant states, the focus had shifted to the internal conditions in developing countries, and particularly towards the governance deficits from which they were claimed to be suffering (Foot 2003: 4–5). This transition had been captured first in the push for a New International Economic Order, and in the developed countries' subsequent determined resistance to it. These development debates, and contestations over the economic order, were explicitly concerned with alternative framings of vulnerability. For the poor developing countries, vulnerability was considered a product of the international rules of the game, as imposed by the most powerful states. As such, it was caused, and could be redressed, only by international arrangements. From the alternative perspective of the wealthy developed states, vulnerability was portrayed as resulting from internal deficiencies in poor countries, and this now became the prime site for remedial action. To the extent that this argument was temporarily resolved de facto by the new forms of neo-liberal regulation, as enforced through international financial institutions, it can certainly be said that the economically powerful had the last word on this topic, whatever the intrinsic merits of the two opposing positions. For that particular moment in time, the power-norm issue was resolved into a new equilibrium point. The imposition of political conditionality, with respect to good governance, that accompanied this economic restructuring ensured that vulnerability came to be widely perceived as a domestic, much more than an international, problem. What this demonstrates so strikingly is the capacity of international society successfully to frame vulnerability, even in the very act of denying its own agency and responsibility. By its very nature, however, this outcome represented a fragile consensus, and was immediately open to further challenge. Crucially, this took the form not of an extra-social power challenge to the satisfied on the part of the revisionists, but instead of an intra-social moral challenge over which conception of the vulnerable international society should feel bound to endorse. Before addressing the full significance of this claim, we must first consider how the vulnerable become so *in* international society.

WHO ARE THE VULNERABLE?

This book makes no conventional contribution to normative international theory, in the sense of presenting straightforwardly its own ethical position on the vulnerable. Neither, however, is it a purely empirical investigation into the risks of exposure to a variety of putative harms. What is absolutely central to the unfolding argument is that the 'normative' and the 'empirical' dimensions of vulnerability in international society are fully connected, so that there can be no meaningful discussion of one in separation from the other (Reus-Smit 2008). This is fundamentally because such a 'dualism' is already deeply embedded in the very nature of international society, and in the frameworks it has chosen to set in place.

We therefore need to approach the subject in this integrated way, with due attention given both to exposure to physical and natural hazards, alongside recognition of the normative ideas that condition international society's understanding of them. Vulnerability provides the perfect point of entry into this analysis precisely because it, too, shares this 'dualistic' form. It manifestly refers to a set of physical, material, or 'natural' hazards, such as those arising from an earthquake or a tsunami. At the same time, it also captures the social vulnerability that arises from those 'ideational structures' that map onto that exposure, and particularly from their manifestations in the decisions of other powerful agents, as expressed through the normative frameworks of international society. Typically, in other disciplines, scholars of the environment absolutely accept the necessity of such an integrated approach, recognizing that 'the concept of a social-ecological system reflects the idea that human action and social structures are integral to nature and hence any distinction between social and natural systems is arbitrary' (Adger 2006: 268; see also Dryzek 2005: 9, 12).

Accordingly, a diverse range of social and natural science disciplines have been trying to 'understand vulnerability in a holistic manner in natural and social systems' (Adger 2006: 272). Even if some hazards are natural, 'disasters are generally not', since what makes particular populations 'unsafe' is their place in the social order (Cannon 1994: 13; Bankoff 2003: 12). This perspective began to take a firm hold in the 1980s (Hewitt 1983), and was further consolidated in the 1990s (Blaikie et al. 1994; Varley 1994). On this basis, there have been subsequent attempts to develop a 'vulnerability science', on the grounds that it is 'both physical place and social conditions that expose some social groups to the potential for greater harm' (Tierney 2006: 111). Its relevance for IR is that it is precisely in this interface that the essence of vulnerability as an international condition is fully to be discovered.

For that reason, we cannot regard vulnerability entirely as some empirically pre-existing state of affairs, abstracted from society's norms and rules. In addition, its social dimension is of salient importance to how vulnerability is constructed, mitigated, prioritized, and distributed within any particular international society. To put it slightly differently, while vulnerability may appear as a wholly objective circumstance, this is so only to the extent that social mediation is already part of the 'real' world that confronts vulnerable actors. Powerfully at work as a conditioning factor in bringing this about is what has been called the 'human ecology of endangerment' (Hewitt 1997). When Katrina struck New Orleans, people were obviously exposed to the force of the hurricane and its resulting flooding, but just as importantly were rendered vulnerable, in differential degrees, by an existing social topography, since 'poorer households tend to live in riskier areas in urban settlements' (Adger 2006: 271; Daniels, Kettl, and Kunreuther 2006). It was those 'social logics' that 'exposed the most vulnerable segments of the society' to Katrina's destructive impact (Gray 2005: 89–90). Moreover, it is this often hidden social dimension—the shaping by social practices, institutions, and collective decisions—that brings out the inherently normative nature of the problem. In consequence, this book tries to answer one key question: how does international society contribute to this 'human ecology of endangerment'?

Here, what is stressed is how 'vulnerability is generated by social, economic, and political processes that influence how hazards affect people in varying ways and differing intensities' (Blaikie et al. 1994: 5). As a result, while accepting natural events as risks or 'triggers', this approach 'puts the main emphasis on the various ways in which social systems operate to generate disasters by making people vulnerable' (Blaikie et al. 1994: 11). This has parallels with the perspective at the heart of Amartya Sen's famous diagnosis of famine where, he argued, people could face starvation for reasons other than any shortage of food (Sen 1981, 2010: 390). Whatever the underlying physical realities, risk conditions are further mediated through complex social processes that, in turn, have the capacity to become the principal drivers of specific vulnerabilities, and hence of their allocation to particular categories of people.

In this case, any objective assessment of risk is filtered through political perceptions that place the current condition of international society at the centre of its field of vision. This is fully justified since the 'objective' conditions of health and disease, for example, entail the activities of a multiplicity of actors operating throughout the international system (Davies 2010: 1169). Social determinations of vulnerability then tend, for example, to privilege certain risks to global health above others, and to distort the international agenda in such ways that the interests of more powerful agents come to be prioritized (Davies 2010: 1175). This is just as apparent in the relative ability to adapt to those new risks, including differential levels of access to international systems of regulation and control: 'adaptive actions often reduce the vulnerability', it has been pointedly suggested, 'of those best placed to take advantage of governance institutions' (Adger 2006: 277). These outcomes can be re-inforced by the structural power of international health agencies, such that 'while it is recognized that globalization has resulted in a world that is more vulnerable to both infectious and non-infectious diseases alike, it appears that attempts to secure the world's population against them still appear to prioritize the national security demands of the global North' (T. Brown 2011: 324). This notion that the distribution of vulnerability is in large measure social lies at the heart of this book.

What this seems to say is that, however 'natural' or 'physical' the risks of suffering various types of harm might appear, what renders some people vulnerable is this extra layer of the social and normative. On that basis, it could be suggested that we make a sharp distinction between risk and vulnerability. However, there are two different ways in which this might be done. Firstly, in some of the risk literature (Kunreuther and Useem 2010), there is already a presumption that risks 'really exist', and that the social dimension is more important with respect to what should be done in response to them. This is thought, for instance, to be the key feature of Ulrich Beck's seminal analysis of risk society (Beck 1992), in which he regards 'risks as empirical realities', while 'social and cultural factors come into play only when one decides what risks to address and how to address them' (Clapton 2011: 282–3). However, this strict dichotomy has been roundly challenged elsewhere: 'Even if risks are rooted in material conditions, the way in which these are approached and understood will be normatively conditioned' (Clapton 2011: 287). If so, the central arguments of this book about vulnerability are equally applicable to risk. Accordingly, it is unnecessarily problematic to suggest that risk is wholly 'objective', in contrast to vulnerability that is 'socially constructed'. Secondly, then, a more promising alternative route is to suggest that risk and vulnerability share in common both 'natural' and 'constructed' dimensions. If they are then to be distinguished, it cannot be straightforwardly on the basis of their extra-social existence. Instead, it is proposed that risk applies to the hazard and its likelihood of occurring, whereas vulnerability specifies in particular those sectors of society that are most exposed to it. In other words, risk focuses on the malign event (and its likelihood of occurrence), while vulnerability draws our attention to the people most likely to experience it (by their differential degrees of exposure): risk denotes the subjects likely to induce harm, whereas vulnerability is focused on their human objects. How and why international society allocates particular distributions of vulnerability then becomes a matter of profound moral concern to all the regimes that international society has developed for the management of the most pressing international problems.

The same point can be made with reference to the heightened levels of interdependence, regarded by many as a distinctive characteristic of the recent phase of globalization (Hurrell 2003: 36–7). Vulnerability has been defined specifically as one key characteristic of interdependence and, in this technical sense, tells us something important about that interdependence. This interpretation was first elaborated in Keohane and Nye's classic study of the subject (Keohane and Nye 1977). In that treatment, they distinguished between 'sensitivity' and 'vulnerability'. While the first is a measure of exposure, the latter adds a second significant consideration, namely the availability of alternative policies, and the cost at which these alternatives might be implemented. 'The vulnerability dimension of interdependence', they suggested, 'rests on the relative availability and costliness of the alternatives that various actors face' (Keohane and Nye 1977: 13; Wendt 1999: 344). To this extent, vulnerability is one important measure of power in a situation of interdependence. By way of illustration, they pointed to the impact of the violence of radical movements in the late 1960s, arguing that the 'vulnerability' of various societies was accordingly dependent 'on their abilities to adjust national policies to deal with the change and reduce the costs of disruption' (Keohane and Nye 1977: 15). The availability and affordability of other options, for that reason, remains central to any assessment of vulnerability.

In short, vulnerability is created not simply by a straightforward relationship between an actor and the risk to which it is exposed, but is constituted fully by its other resources and ability to adapt to new circumstances. This combination of elements can be found in the recent analysis of climate change, where vulnerability has emerged as a central concept. Accordingly, in its own work, the Intergovernmental Panel on Climate Change (IPCC) considered there to be three principal constituents of vulnerability: 'Vulnerability is a function of the character, magnitude, and rate of climate variation to which a system is exposed, its sensitivity, and its adaptive capacity' (IPCC 2001: 1.4.1). This takes the physical exposure to hazard or risk, and adds to it those two dimensions already identified in Keohane and Nye's discussion of interdependence, namely sensitivity and adaptability. The last, as we have seen, is heavily influenced by costs, as well as by the availability of social capital and resources, including such things as governmental capacity. In this way, we commonly understand the vulnerability of a particular country to climate change to be a function not just of its geographical and meteorological circumstances, but of its general capacity to adapt. While this might seem immediately to highlight economic, technological and other material resources, it should be considered more widely to encompass societal capital, not least the ability to make favourable use of existing international regulatory frameworks and other instruments of international society. This brings us full circle to a rounded understanding of vulnerability that is both produced by a social condition of interdependence and also amenable to mitigation, largely through the successful exploitation of the normative resources of international society, at least on the part of those best placed to take advantage of available governance systems and organizations. In all these areas power still matters, and for that reason international society remains a potent source of the social determination of vulnerability.

One way in which we might think about its impact is by analogy with an argument found about the role of law in determining responsibility. Contrary to the conventional wisdom that a prime function of law is exactly to legalize the allocation of responsibility, Veitch (2007) sets out the claim that, in doing so, it also establishes a wider terrain of irresponsibility, and usually with respect to even greater issues of human suffering. Accordingly, it will be suggested here that international society, by seeking to establish formal regimes of protection—on violence, climate, movement, and health—actually establishes large areas of vulnerability at the same time. Moreover, the latter is a necessary part of the very same process that determines the former. In the same way that law (indirectly) legitimates irresponsibility, international society legitimates practices of vulnerability that have the effect of adding to the sum of human suffering, or at least of influencing its relative distribution.

How does this argument develop? Veitch claims that 'legal institutions are centrally involved in organising irresponsibility'. They do so because these institutions, and particularly their 'practices, concepts and categories', function in such a way as to 'facilitate dispersals and disavowals of responsibility'. Moreover, they do so 'in consistent and patterned ways' (Veitch 2007: 1). Veitch's concern is with those 'large-scale harms' which are, of course, exactly what the vulnerable become exposed to. Accordingly, if we substitute international society for legal institutions, and replace responsibility/irresponsibility with protection/vulnerability, his argument is closely akin to that set out in this book. It is not that international society sets out intentionally to cause harm to people, nor to undermine its own regimes of protection. However, its operation of these regimes, sometimes selectively, serves to open up—as a necessary corollary—other areas of vulnerability. Following Veitch, as we shall see, it does so largely through adoption of its own 'practices, concepts and categories'.

Again, to prevent the following cases being read like a straightforward conspiracy thesis, this reminds us of the much more nuanced process that is at work. States acting through international society do not necessarily decide to create regimes of harm. To illustrate this point, Veitch appeals to Adam Smith's invisible hand as a suitable metaphor, and suggests that law works in a similar fashion. While Smith's version serves to produce a social good, Veitch's variant produces harms, but not in any straightforwardly malevolent way. The reason for this is his denial that law operates on the basis of 'centralised decisions' or 'actual consensus', and likewise his insistence that there 'is no individual or collective intention through which responsibility is dispersed' (Veitch 2007: 73). That is nonetheless its outcome overall. It is this very process of disaggregation that ensures that 'when seen from *the perspective of the experience of suffering*' there will be no possible 'aggregation that would reconnect that experience with its causes' (Veitch 2007: 73). This is integral to the way contemporary society deals with risks in which 'the *politics* of the definition of risks become a crucial feature of attempts to acknowledge or alleviate them' (Veitch 2007: 115). So, also, is it with irresponsibility in international society, and its resultant politics of the determination of risk: the outcome is discrete categories of the vulnerable, for the creation of which nobody seems responsible, except nature itself. International society may, from time to time, agree on the contours of various regimes of protection. The consequence of this is the simultaneous creation of large areas of heightened exposure to harm.

How then should we begin to think about vulnerability, and how are we to identify those who are vulnerable? The basic definition, as we have already seen in the Introduction, expresses it in terms of a liability to suffer damage or harm. If vulnerability is the shorthand expression for this liability, then there are as many types of vulnerability as there are forms of potential harm. There are nonetheless some general characteristics of vulnerability that can helpfully be analysed at the outset, in order to establish the framework of this book. First, we might consider the vulnerable in terms of those categories of people who, in relation to certain harms, are thought to be at exceptional risk. For example, as one possible *category* of the vulnerable, we might think of civilians or non-combatants who find themselves in the way of war or political violence. Similarly, there are the categories of gender (the exposure of women to war or economic deprivation), or of children (to war, hunger, or disease), or of migrants (perhaps less effectively protected by international or domestic laws). As we shall see in the cases, international society predominantly interprets the vulnerable as instances of such categories, and seeks to impose them on its solutions to various specific problems.

Secondly, we might think about the vulnerable in terms of the particular conditions that contribute to their exposure. A *condition* of vulnerability identifies the specific issue area, or the combination of issues, that is the immediate source of the harm. From this perspective, the vulnerable become so specifically in connection with particular events or processes, such as natural disasters, climate change, war, terrorism, economic inequality, global health, and so on. As a result, a migrant or a refugee may be deemed to fit in the relevant category, but it is the specified conditions that place this category in its meaningful context of prospective harm. A refugee may be considered vulnerable as belonging to a particular category, but that exposure may be exacerbated by a range of different conditions, such as those arising from climate, health, or political violence. Accordingly, any particular category of people may be exposed to risk by one or more specific sets of conditions, acting independently or in combination. To grasp the identity of the vulnerable fully, we therefore require information under both of these headings. These first two approaches to classifying the vulnerable are relatively straightforward.

Thirdly, however—and much less obviously—the vulnerable can be fully identified only by some underlying *concept* of the issue or problem that confronts them. Absolutely key is this underlying concept that sets out how the problem is to be defined, and the limits set by the framework within which it is to be resolved. Insofar as this concept is a construct of international society, it is this concept that makes vulnerability a part of its own internal relationships. This captures the moral reality of their vulnerability, and is separate from either the aforementioned category or conditions. For instance, it was suggested above that we might intuitively think of civilians as a category of the vulnerable exposed to the risks of war. Within international society's operative concept of war, however, it is formally combatants alone that are strictly vulnerable. That is to say they bear a *social* liability to be killed that is quite distinct from any actual risk faced by civilians.

A world of difference in vulnerability thus separates the descriptive category from the moral concept. As a concept, vulnerability does much more than provide simply an empirical description, but begins to open up the nature of the moral problem: it attunes us to a possible social claim. In common usage, the term 'vulnerable' is routinely coupled with other attributes of this kind, in such a way as to suggest an additional insight into the nature of vulnerability itself, or at least to help orient us normatively towards it. Frequently, the vulnerable are described as one half of a pairing, along with the likes of the 'weak', 'dependent', 'poor', 'powerless', or 'innocent'. These should be seen not just as empirical descriptors (as with categories and conditions), but more potently as highly significant moral qualifiers, and hence as part of an overarching concept of the vulnerable.

In the cases below, what will emerge sharply is international society's preference for imposing its own concepts and categories of the vulnerable, all of which are subject to various aggravating conditions. For instance, in the case of political violence its most potent instrument for dealing with the vulnerable is its concepts of the different forms of violence: war, civil war, terrorism, and so on. Such concepts, it must be stressed, while presented as empirical classifications, already draw upon deep assumptions about the moral realities of the vulnerable, and certainly have moral effects in the distributions of vulnerability that they tolerate and sanction. They do so primarily through a set of relevant operational categories. For instance, in the case of political violence, and under a concept of war, the principal categories have been combatants and civilians, and their respective exposure to risk is governed as much by prevailing social concepts as by any brute physical realities on the battlefield.

As such, international society establishes a set of norms—and in some instances facilitates a legal regime—around a particular legitimated distribution of vulnerability. This relationship between the concept and its associated categories tends to be fundamentally unstable over time, and hence the vulnerable become a major site of moral contestation: the dominant concept is challenged, along with the proper scope of its categories, and this undermines the justifications for any one assignment of vulnerability in preference to any other.

Much the same will become apparent in the other three cases. As regards climate change, international society has imposed its own structure on the problem through its dominant conception of how it is to be understood and approached. At the same time, international negotiation has taken place between the two categories of the developed and developing countries, and the entitlements and responsibilities distributed to each category respectively. For the most part, these categories have been deployed as a way of evading the full moral force of the issue: international society has adopted the categories, but has largely shied away from the moral concept that underpins them. However, the use of the language of 'responsibility'—pervasive in the climate regime—already suggests that these empirical categories convey significant normative relationships. As a result, these concepts and categories have become the site not just of political wrangling between two contingent groups of countries, but of a profound moral contestation about the normative identity of the vulnerable in the face of climate change. In the case of human movement, international society has conceived of the issue as one that is now a *problem*, and subject to legal control within the remit of international society, even if it has strongly resisted creating a regime for management of the issue as a whole. Operationally, it deals with that problem through its highly influential categories of migrant, illegal migrant, refugee, internally displaced person, and so on. With regard to global health, the problem has been conceived as one of how to establish effective barriers or quarantines to prevent the transmission of pathogens across borders; as a challenge that is essentially biomedical, rather than socio-economic, in its nature; as a matter that remains subject to the potent norms of international trade; and as a field in which the priorities for research into, and treatment of, disease have been profoundly shaped by its dominant categories of infectious versus chronic. In all these ways international society has brought to its activities its own conceptions of the problem and its own operational categories for addressing it, and in doing so has created what is deemed to be socially acceptable allocations of the vulnerable. These are all now subject to moral contestation in ways that challenge the effectiveness of these regimes overall. They are exposed because the purported empirical categories and conditions seemingly elide the normative concepts that underpin them, but in ways that continually open them up to new challenges.

Why is the moral dimension so important, and how does it infect the empirical classifications that international society chooses to deploy? The point can most effectively be made with respect to the generic notion of 'innocence' that widely pervades all of those cases. For example, what is the connection between vulnerability and innocence? It appears that we are morally more troubled about vulnerability in some contexts than in others, and that is why so many international problems become so greatly exacerbated. At stake in their resolution is an inchoate feeling that some liabilities to harm are more 'undeserved' than others. This is not a judgement we make from the outside, as observers, but is a crucial dimension of the internal negotiation of this set of problems, as perceived through the eyes of the participants. This empathetic feeling is often conveyed by appealing to a notion of innocence (meaning literally 'doing no harm'), with the strong corollary implication that the vulnerable—if indeed innocent—should not have any harm inflicted in return: they do not deserve to be vulnerable. Moreover, this sense of the innocence of some is especially troublesome insofar as the particular distributions of vulnerability are understood to result from the activities of international society itself. It is this direct juxtaposition of the seeming innocence of the vulnerable alongside international society's role in framing their social exposure that is the source of the normative problem.

Intriguingly, these *concepts* of vulnerability become attached to different *categories* of the vulnerable in different *conditions*, and this combines the empirical and normative dimensions in a highly potent mix. In the context of war, typically the characterization of the vulnerable as innocent has been developed predominantly through use of the category of non-combatants, thought to enjoy a special moral status. In the context of climate change, the category of the innocent—that is those deserving our considered mitigation and redress, since they have not themselves inflicted any harm—includes those countries with historical records of very low levels of greenhouse gas (GHG) emissions, or conspicuously the category of future generations, as they can be considered quintessentially innocent. In this context, it is noteworthy that Gardiner locates the 'perfect moral storm' of climate change precisely in its 'potentially severe injustice to *innocent and vulnerable* others' (Gardiner 2011a: 47, emphasis added). Are the innocent and vulnerable then separate categories, or are they associated attributes of the same category, such that innocence becomes semantically one part of what we mean by the vulnerable? In particular, does the depiction of the vulnerable as innocent provide a moral qualifier that makes clear why this form of vulnerability is so unacceptable and why it should be redressed wherever possible? These issues may be troublesome for moral philosophy, but in what sense do they have the potential actually to disrupt the international order?

E. H. CARR AND THE MORAL ISSUE

This section sketches the wider implications for international order of the preceding argument. It soon becomes clear that vulnerability is deployed and responded to in different ways in different contexts; because this is so, it is best viewed as a single integrated topic under the purview of international society as a whole. Decisions taken to alleviate any one form of vulnerability can have the direct consequence of creating another, and possibly more severe, version elsewhere. To this extent, vulnerability tends not to be eradicated, but rather to be moved around.

Why then should we prioritize a concern for the vulnerable in addressing international society? What have the vulnerable ever done to merit such special consideration? The answers to these questions require three central arguments. First, issues of ethics are not some separate activity over and above the quest for international order, but are an intrinsic part of that quest: they are deeply embedded in the essential practices of international society, and lie at the core of the contestations to which that society is routinely subject. Secondly, this becomes particularly apparent when we look at the condition of vulnerability: vulnerability is not some external and wholly autonomous condition that international society seeks to control, but is inherent in the nature of the political choices that it is led to make. To this extent, as in many of its other activities, vulnerability is to some degree what states make of it. Thirdly, the wide range of possible forms of vulnerability is profoundly interconnected. As a result, it is imperative that we think about them in an appropriately holistic and integrated manner—to consider and address one type of vulnerability in isolation will lead to loss of this crucial insight.

For all these reasons, E. H. Carr provides a convenient point of entry into the discussion. His overarching concern was with the instability of the interwar, and the ensuing post-1945, international order. In both *The Twenty Years' Crisis* (Carr 1939 [2001]) and his subsequent *Conditions of Peace*

(Carr 1942), he detailed its various shortcomings and failings. While not explicitly addressing the vulnerable, he nonetheless made a case for international planning, and hence for intergovernmental intervention, at least in Europe (Molloy 2003: 290–1). Strikingly, he insisted that the central failure of this period had indeed been a moral one. This finding may seem surprising, given the widespread tendency to present him as the epitome of the view that morality is the creation of power (Crawford 2002: 83). Contrary to his stereotypical portrayal, others remind us that Carr's 'central imperative was an ethical one' (Rich 2000: 212; see generally, Evans 1975: 78, 81; Jones 1998; Nishimura 2010: 9), and he was at pains to highlight 'the bankruptcy of political programmes which were devoid of ethical content' (Dunne 2000: 227). He affirmed this judgement unequivocally in his 1942 book: 'The essential nature of the crisis through which we are living is neither military, nor political, nor economic, but moral. A new faith in a new moral purpose', he maintained, 'is required to reanimate our political and economic system' (Carr 1942: 110; see Molloy 2003: 290).

But what was the nature of this moral crisis? For Carr, it inhered in the clash between the status quo and revisionist powers, and the unwillingness of the former to accede to demands for legitimate change. It was in this spirit that he decried the stance of the peacemakers of 1919: 'Let injustice persist' was their apparent watchword, 'rather than that the sacred rights of the existing order should be infringed' (Carr 1942: xvi). As he saw it, this deficiency placed a special onus upon the satisfied powers, since it fell to them above all to engage in 'give and take' and to demonstrate a willingness 'not to insist on all the prerogatives of power' (Carr 2001: 151–2). This 'give and take' was a process that only the custodians of the existing international order could initiate.

The key issue, of course, was what should be considered reasonable concessions in this process, and this was the point at which Carr's argument conspicuously faltered. His own relativist methodology seemingly precluded any universal conception of what was 'reasonable' in this context (Bull 1969: 628). More fundamentally, Morgenthau had already berated Carr on the grounds that he had 'only the vaguest idea of what morality is', and accordingly could offer 'no transcendent point of view' (quoted in Molloy 2003: 294) on the problematic relationship between power and morality. What this suggests is that Carr was wrong to depict the moral issue exclusively in terms of the collision between satisfied and dissatisfied powers. To be sure, this clash did indeed give rise to its own moral problems, but not all divergence between the status quo and revisionist powers is to be captured in moral terms: Germany had no convincing moral claim to 'take' all of Czechoslovakia and Poland, and the status quo powers had no moral obligation to 'give' these concessions.

Accordingly, Carr was mostly right, but for the wrong reasons. He was correct to attribute the international crisis to its moral fault lines, but wrong to imagine that these coincided neatly with the failure to reconcile the interests of the satisfied and dissatisfied. The present argument, then, accepts Carr's general suggestion that the major problems of contemporary order have their source in moral concerns, but distances itself from the specific manner in which Carr formulated that claim. As an alternative, therefore, this book places the notion of vulnerability at the heart of its argument, and substitutes relations of vulnerability for the status quo/revisionist problematic found in Carr's original account. Not all requirements for maintaining the status quo are morally deplorable, nor are all revisionist demands equally justifiable: what is crucial is how either impacts on the treatment of the vulnerable, as this represents the central international normative problem of our age. For that reason, this book revisits Carr's argument from the distinctive perspective of the vulnerable. Critically, this is appropriate because the major moral problems of vulnerability inhere in these very relationships that make up international society in the first place: it is an attribute of those relationships, rather than some objective condition wholly external to them.

When Hedley Bull provided his own retrospective assessment of Carr's *The Twenty Years' Crisis*, he concurred that the moment was indeed ripe 'to restore the moral or normative element' in the study of international relations, and recommended that we do so by 'recognizing the role actually played by values and rules in international society' (Bull 1969: 632–3). His complaint, on the other hand, was that Carr had become so fixated by the self-interests perpetuated by ruling groups of powers that in the end he 'jettisons the idea of international society itself' (Bull 1969: 638). Restoring this idea, it follows, is the first step towards a more convincing analysis, but is incomplete unless we place the moral problem of the vulnerable at its heart.

A focus on vulnerability is not the only way to make sense of international society, but it does provide one very compelling, and hitherto neglected, point of view. As against the international society perspective advocated here, it might be protested instead that, like the poor, the vulnerable are always with us: categories of people are vulnerable because of objective circumstances over which neither they, nor anyone else, has any control. What sense, then, does it make to lay these problems at the door of international society? However, this objection misses the crucial point: vulnerability is not some wholly objective condition of this kind, but is also a function of the social frameworks in which it is located, and is to this extent amenable to the power exercised by others with a capacity to act and make decisions. Carr had already given expression to this complaint: 'the belief that certain facts are unalterable or certain trends irresistible commonly reflects a lack of desire or lack of interest to change or resist them' (Carr 1939: 113). For this reason, people are vulnerable not just to 'nature', but moreover to the impacts of powerful human agency, as reflected in existing social norms and institutions. This book's title therefore conveys the core argument that it is the dependence of the vulnerable on the decisions of others, as reflected in the frameworks of international society, that compounds the difficulty of so many of the most challenging problems of contemporary international order. Above all, this is what lends these problems their especially recalcitrant quality—and gives them their ethical edge.

It is for this reason that Carr's position captures so well the spirit of this inquiry. 'Carr's call for a science of international politics that engages the empirical and the normative', it has been said, 'is thus inextricably linked to his belief that effective political action is mindful of both power and morality' (Reus-Smit 2008: 56). His critique of the interwar period rested not just on the mistaken policies that had been pursued (the neglect of power by a generation of utopians), but on his urgent sense of a more deep-seated failure of moral understanding that had resulted from the hubris of power. It is his insistence that there is a necessary place for both power and morality—'reality' and 'utopia' in his preferred terminology—in the construction of international society that is vital for the argument that is to follow.

As a result, this position will now be staked out within the distinctive terrain of notions of the vulnerable. Vulnerability arises in a multitude of different conditions, but what makes it so vexing is the normative content with which it is so richly infused. So, for example, classically vulnerability is a theme found in all discussions of war and violence. However, the problem of vulnerability in this context takes on its special significance precisely because it is framed by the 'moral reality of war' (Walzer 1977: 15), and from an acceptance that war 'is an inherently normative phenomenon' (Hurrell 2007: 39). While this much is commonly recognized, it has been much harder to appreciate its logical consequence—that there is also an associated 'moral reality' of vulnerability. Hedley Bull noted that in the Hobbesian analysis of the state of nature among individual people there existed an equality of vulnerability, and this is what made that original condition so unbearable. Things were not quite the same in international society since 'Great Powers have not been vulnerable to violent attack by small powers to the same extent' (Bull 1977: 50). In this way, and by the mediation of the institutions of international society, the conditions of vulnerability have been socially choreographed, with variable consequences for different groups of people: there have been winners and losers from international society's arrangements.

These social configurations of violence, and their resulting vulnerabilities, have tended to reflect the interests of the strongest political agents, and, despite Bull's chastising of Carr for not taking the notion of international society seriously enough, Bull himself ended up acknowledging that the 'system of rules will be found to serve the interests of the ruling or dominant elements of the society more adequately than it serves the interests of the others' (Bull 1977: 55). For a long time, these dominant elements have been the state members of international society and the regimes of sovereignty that they have articulated. States, and especially strong states, have thereby sought to set the terms of international vulnerability as they would prefer them, but in their endeavours to do so they have been endlessly challenged and resisted by other political forces (Devetak 2005: 244). Much of this process of contestation has been conducted through moral argument, and this has been an important element in bringing about change (Crawford 2002: ch. 2).

Arguably, states now find themselves less able to impose those terms than in the past. They no longer have a totally free run in international society, as the emergence of the powerful regime of human rights since 1945 has so clearly attested. That is to say that international society has been progressively encroached upon by global civil society, or by what I have referred to elsewhere as its encounter with world society (Taylor 2005; Clark 2007). If so, this has immense implications for international society, and just as much for the types of vulnerability that it can promote and sustain.

There is one further issue that needs to be noted. The implicit suggestion running through these arguments is that vulnerability is inherently associated with weakness, or lack of capability. And yet the question that must be posed is whether this dichotomy between power and vulnerability is quite so clear-cut and straightforward. Power for some can certainly create vulnerability in others, but material power by itself is no absolute guarantee of invulnerability. The events of 11 September 2001 provide one example of this puzzle. In his exploration of the conditions underlying contemporary terrorism, Philip Bobbitt confronts the stark paradox of 9/11 with respect to its meaning for the United States. 'It is because America is so very vulnerable', he insists, 'and at the same time so ubiquitously and overwhelmingly powerful that twenty-first century global terrorism has arisen' (Bobbitt 2008: 400). Others have been struck by this very same theme in their reflections on the significance of 9/11. To Judith Butler, the great shock represented by those attacks was to America's own sense of invulnerability: 'The United States was supposed to be the place that could not be attacked, where life was safe from violence initiated from abroad' (Butler 2004: 39). To Benjamin Barber, the United States had been '[i]nsulated from the old world by two centuries of near mythic independence', but in the aftermath of 9/11 found itself 'stunned today by a sudden consciousness of vulnerability' (Barber 2003: 15). In this case, vulnerability burst forth all the more starkly as it arose against a backdrop of hitherto serene levels of security and omnipotence: vulnerability was not the opposite of great power, but seemingly its close accompaniment.

What does this tell us about the nature of vulnerability? If vulnerability is distributed by the frameworks of international society, and if we are to suppose that these reflect principally the preferences of the dominant states, what explains the failure of international society to prescribe against the vulnerability to which the United States succumbed after 9/11? In exploring this question, we are led to consider the social basis of vulnerability, and the many overt challenges that have been presented to its regulatory endeavours over the centuries. A study of the vulnerable in international society tells us much about the nature of vulnerability, but it provides just as telling an insight into the character of international society itself: while inequities in power do certainly play a major part in the social practice of the vulnerable, we confront the paradox that material power by itself provides no absolute guarantee of immunity to exposure.

CONCLUSION

It is in the combination of these three classificatory schemes of the vulnerable—concept, category, and condition—that we see how the normative dimension comes overtly into play. Although many categories of people might be liable to harm, there are contexts in which we privilege the claims of some because we understand that they are otherwise incapable, on their own, of alleviating their adverse circumstances: they are not just exposed, but powerless to adapt to changed circumstances. We often inject additional evaluations into our understanding of the specific sense in which people are vulnerable: it is not their 'fault' that they are vulnerable, and in consequence it is the 'responsibility' of others to take remedial action. Above all, our appreciation of the exposure to risk is coloured by an understanding that social circumstances have contributed to this outcome, and these circumstances require our special attention and consideration. To understand fully the notion of vulnerability and the range of its moral ramifications, we need therefore to weave together, along with consideration of the relevant descriptive categories and conditions, some reference to the moral concepts that come so strongly into play. These arise to the extent that vulnerability is a quality emerging from the dynamic relationships within international society, and especially from its core asymmetries in power at any one moment in time. The vulnerable are a moral problem for international society precisely because they hold up a mirror to its own workings.

We may or may not all subscribe to any principle of this kind, but it is sufficiently compelling to ensure that the current practices of international society cannot remain immune from its critical influence. Contestations framed around these fundamental concerns—however inchoately they might be articulated in practice—continue to lie at the heart of international society and its evolving attempts to refashion its own instituted hierarchy of vulnerabilities, each with its own degree of consensual tolerability. In the cases that follow, this general theme will be explored in the specific contexts of violence, climate, movement, and health. Since one of the most pervasive characteristics of international society throughout its history has been toleration of resort to certain concepts of violence, governed by its own categories operating in specified conditions, it is with that case that the survey can now begin.

2

Political Violence and the Vulnerable

Of the many risks to which people are exposed by international politics, the most prominent, enduring, and seemingly most 'natural', is from its accompanying range of political violence: the international, by definition, puts people in harm's way, since violence is by all accounts its *ultima ratio*. Moreover, in this instance, vulnerability takes on an especially acute form, as the liability to harm includes potentially a threat to life.

However, a moment's reflection suggests that the precise manner in which the impact of this violence is distributed, as well as the varying degrees of protection raised against it, is as much the work of political artifice on the part of international society as any part of the natural order of things. Without its conscious manipulation, this allocation would undoubtedly display quite different patterns: the vulnerable might simply be the weakest or the defenceless, whoever they are, or indeed could be considered a universal category. As against this, and in contrast to war, it has been said that terrorism produces 'general vulnerability', and that it is its logic alone that 'steadily expands the range of vulnerability' (Walzer 2004: 51–2). The puzzling question this raises is why 'general vulnerability' should be peculiar to terrorism, and not the natural condition in the face of all forms of political violence. Why, in practice, is vulnerability to all political violence not universal in this way? Why is it distributed in the way that it is?

The discussion in this chapter develops in the following stages. It begins by identifying the specifically social dimensions of vulnerability in relation to violence, and how these have come to be codified in international law, and in the Geneva Conventions in particular. It then shows how international society's dominant conception of legitimate violence is now challenged by other concepts, at the same time as it is further eroded by some of international society's own practices in this area: examples from counterterrorism and humanitarian intervention will be used to illustrate the point. Central to these developments has been the undermining of key assumptions about the equality of belligerents that had hitherto sustained the dominant concept, along with its associated operational categories of combatants and non-combatants. This analysis is offered as a way of unravelling the central puzzle that international society formally allocates vulnerability to combatants, but has then behaved in ways that have seemingly placed civilians at even greater risk. The outcome is that the social vulnerability with regard to violence is substantially undermined in practice in ways that now expose the rationale for civilian protection to even greater moral contestation. Fundamentally at stake is this underlying concept that seeks to make moral sense of that discrimination between combatants and civilians in the first place.

POLITICAL VIOLENCE, SOCIETY, AND NATURE

The main theme of this chapter is that vulnerability, in this context, denotes a 'social liability' to be killed, and that international society has been a principal determinant of its allocation. We find one highly revealing illustration of this logic in the argument advanced by Michael Walzer. His claim is that the scope of violence is governed by the 'war convention', and this sets limits to what can be done in the name of 'reason of war'. The latter, he pointedly suggests, 'can only justify the killing of people we already have reason to think are *liable to be killed*' (Walzer 1977: 144, emphasis added). His precise wording here is certainly striking: this 'liability to be killed' evidently amounts to an acute form of vulnerability. Moreover, as a matter of state practice, this liability extends only insofar as it corresponds to appropriate instances of violence—those designated as war—or in more recent parlance, as instances of international armed conflict. The status of proper targets is thereby determined by the overall concept of the political violence, and people 'only become combatants in the strict sense in a conflict of the right kind, that is, the State of War as defined by legal and moral convention' (Finlay 2010: 312). Moreover, and crucially, what we see plainly here is that the 'legality of killing combatants in war is thus dependent on the laws and customs of international society' (McKeogh 2011: 588). Combatants are made socially vulnerable by the way international society conceives of war as the only appropriate form of violence.

What creates such a liability, and on what basis might we think that some people have it and others do not? Walzer's claim assuredly advances more than just some statistical likelihood of occurrence, and thus represents more than a conventional risk assessment, in that term's usual meaning. As such, any appraisal of this kind can scarcely rest on a naturalistic condition, since in that situation it is meaningless to suggest that anybody enjoys any greater or lesser liability than anyone else. If anything, it might be thought that, since they are largely defenceless, civilians as a category are more 'naturally' prone to be killed than anyone else. Instead, as Walzer elaborates, 'what is involved here is not so much a calculation of probability and risk as a reflection on the *status* of men and women whose lives are at stake' (Walzer 1977: 144, emphasis added). This is the crucial step. At this juncture, the argument shifts away from calculations of risk, seemingly determined by natural circumstances—actuarially, are those in their forties more at risk on the battlefield than those in their twenties?—and emphasizes instead 'artificial' degrees of exposure, determined by a social calculus about status. To say this much, of course, is just to open an argument, rather than to close it. As we shall see, there can be many subsequent disagreements about what precisely gives rise to this liability: does it apply to those who are 'morally liable to be killed', or rather only to those who 'may otherwise kill you' (Shue 2008: 100; see McMahan 2008: 21)? The identity and scope of the vulnerable then depend critically on which of these specific justifications is deemed persuasive.

This specific argument is fully captured in one discussion of so-called asymmetric conflicts. It explores 'how the idea of civilian vulnerability expands' in that setting, in ways that 'violate the principle of noncombatant immunity'. As this claim already makes clear, the relative degree of vulnerability, rather than reflecting some universal logic intrinsic to all uses of force, varies rather in relation to the application of a social category to which the putative target is said to belong. Moreover, this category is defined by degrees of actual involvement in the infliction of violence, in such a way that 'any scale of direct and indirect participation has significant ramifications for the idea of vulnerability' (Gross 2010: ix, 43). What this suggests, in turn, is that vulnerability is subject to a sliding scale, derived from a social calculus: first, in correspondence with the social status of non-combatancy, and secondly in relation to socially agreed ways of determining what counts as direct participation in the actual application of force. It depends both on a social category, and how its boundaries are understood and implemented. To this extent, vulnerability is not straightforwardly a function of any exposure to the unmediated risks of violence.

What does this tell us about vulnerability in this context? This case study immediately presents a striking paradox for the general argument. As will be demonstrated, international society principally determines the allocation of vulnerability through its promotion of the two cognate principles of civilian immunity (those deemed not vulnerable) and 'combatant non-immunity' (those deemed liable to be killed, but simultaneously not liable to be prosecuted for killing within the laws of war) (Nathanson 2010: 89). Accordingly, the normative framework of international society ideally seeks to distribute vulnerability away from civilians, and to confine it to combatants alone. Unhappily for this normative scheme, the actual practice during the past century has marched steadily in the opposite direction, such that the statistical likelihood of civilian to combatant deaths had, by the 1990s, edged close to a ratio of 10:1 (McPherson 2007: 529). For this reason, we are now told that the hard choice is no longer simply between civilians and combatants, but instead lies in '[d]etermining which civilians are vulnerable' (Gross 2010: 154): it is no longer whether, but which, civilians are at risk. What sense are we to make of this conundrum that the social allocation of vulnerability appears so radically out of line with the exposure to the actual risks of violence? To answer that question we need to explore the full complexity of this social practice of the vulnerable with regard to political violence.

At its most fundamental, international society has a powerful say in what counts as violence in the first place, and what does not. This has given priority to an essentially statist account (Fullinwider 2003: 23). Inherent in state-making was not just its monopolization of the external uses of force, 'but the elimination or neutralization . . . of private international violence' (Devetak 2008: 11; see Rodin and Shue 2008b: 13; Johnson 2011: 9). Thus arose that 'intimate' relationship between the state and violence insofar as, in Weber's terms, the state came to be regarded as the 'sole source of the "right" to use violence' (Lassman and Speirs 1994: 310–11). This concentration of violence in state hands engendered a degree of domestic pacification but, as John Keane reminds us, 'states are positively dangerous instruments of pacification' (Keane 1996: 26). It allowed them not only to turn their violence against their own citizens without fear of international interdiction; elsewhere, it has arguably further allowed them to act forcibly against the 'stateless'—historically as in colonial occupations, and currently in what has been described as a 'frontierland . . . of state violence against refugees' (Pickering 2008: 108). Above all, it has been able to superimpose a wealth of 'state-centred categories and narratives on the organization . . . of violence' (Skurski and Coronil 2006: 1–2).

The principal way in which international society has sought to influence these activities is by formally differentiating between various concepts of violence, and so imposing its own preferred regulatory scheme on resort to it. It does so because it necessarily condones resort to some forms of violence as part of its normal political workings, and so eschews any radical disjunction between politics and violence (Frazer and Hutchings 2011). However, only selected forms of violence receive its sanction, and those do so because they are broadly compatible with its basic norms and serve to reproduce them: typically, 'the practices of political violence', as described in the works of major political and military theorists, 'embody, rely on, constitute and reinforce the distinctions between social and political, private and public, inside and outside that sustain the state as a political entity' (Frazer and Hutchings 2011: 67). If some of those concepts have been developed mainly in theory, they have at the same time become deeply entrenched in a number of international society's own practices, and are replicated in many aspects of international law. In a variety of ways, its preferred manifestations of violence have thus come to be normalized as an aspect of international life.

In this hierarchical scheme, different concepts of violence—of which war is only one—entail different systems of regulation, and this significantly shapes exposure to their impacts. At its most basic, international society makes the difference by the calibrated language it uses to describe the different forms this violence can take, and hence to convey the normative orientations to be adopted towards them respectively: some are to be condoned, while others are to be proscribed. As a result of this elaborately nuanced vocabulary, diverse allocations of harm and exposure are potentially created. This is demonstrably so with regard to those specific terms of art such as war, guerrilla war, irregular war, civil war, rebellion, insurgency, terrorism, intrastate conflict, interventionism, and so on. Of all its various classifications, none more powerfully reflects the imprint of international society than its pervasive distinction, embodied in the Geneva Conventions and elsewhere, between international and non-international armed conflict.

All these concepts describe forms of political violence, but each has potentially differential impacts on various classes of people. This is because of the specific normative framing that is introduced by each of these terms, and the associated practices that are translated from them into rules governing actual military conduct on the ground. In consequence, international society renders some categories as the vulnerable, while seeking to remove other categories, in some degree, from harm's way. Historically, international society has been a highly proactive author of such conceptions, while an array of actors—many within its own ranks—has sought to resist and reframe its impositions, with varying degrees of success. This ambiguity—unity in diversity—is a general characteristic of international society, and reflects its periodic ability to act, even while simultaneously its consensual norms remain open to further challenge.

Alongside its fundamental concepts, the laws of armed conflict specify the categories and conditions that surround their operationalization, thereby determining when and where certain classes of people are to be considered legitimate targets of violence, and which are not. In doing so, international society has established a normative hierarchy of violence that reflects its own values and interests: this, in turn, has become a major focus of contestation for those who would resort to other forms, not sanctioned by the interstate system. What emerges from this patchwork of regulation, and its supporting normative ideas, is a terrain that renders many vulnerable to, in the words of one critic, 'morally acceptable slaughter, suffering and chaos', for the reason that they are '"unintentional", "collateral" or "necessary"' (Burke 2004: 332). In what it thus condones, international society adds appreciably a social dimension to existing exposures to risk. It is in this world of imperfect regulation—in the grey area where normative preferences meet military pragmatism—that international society's making of the vulnerable can most readily be discerned.

None of this is natural, however much early just war theorists assumed that regulation of warfare derived from 'natural' law. In the 'natural' condition, those vulnerable to violence would tend to be weaker individuals, or groups, whoever and wherever they might be. In his own analysis, Hedley Bull drew upon the work of H. L. A. Hart, and derived the conventions associated with war directly from the supposed move *away* from this natural condition: 'because of human vulnerability', in one interpretation of Bull's reasoning, 'there must be rules restricting the use of violence' (Vincent 1990: 44). In short, war already represents a significant departure from naturalistic violence insofar as it is governed by its own separate body of rules and conventions: nature's universal vulnerability, correlated with physical weakness, is transmuted instead into particular vulnerabilities, associated with social status and divisions of labour. Early just war theorists, for example, excluded as permissible targets those in certain occupations. Hence, while generic risk from violence may be part of the human condition, the concept of war seeks not only to limit that exposure, but to channel it in socially accepted directions. As a result, the original state of nature becomes radically reconfigured by the political artifice of the state, and by the supporting actions of international society. While many, including Rousseau, have since lamented the resulting international 'state of war' as simply replicating that original state of nature (albeit in a much more severe version), this new state of war must be understood as embodying an importantly different concept of violence from the one that it had displaced.

From an ES perspective, the fundamentals of this argument are expressed through the notion that war is an institution of international society. That is to say that one particular version of political violence is accepted as war, and this type is distinctive. The very transformation that is wrought by it constitutes powerful evidence for the existence of international society. This violence is to be undertaken by legitimate actors, and for approved ends, and when these conditions are met it can serve the general purposes of international society, including the enforcement of international law and the maintenance of the balance of power. For these reasons it can fairly be thought of as an institution. But what does this imply? At the very least, it means that this concept of violence called war is characterized by its own norms and rules (Bull 1977: 186). These are imposed by international society because violence represents a potential threat to it, but also because—in its guise as regulated warfare—it can yet play a 'positive role in the maintenance of international order' (Bull 1977: 188). Crucially, the institution of war imports its own practice of the vulnerable with regard to violence.

The condition of war is additionally thought to be different from other resorts to violence, precisely because those who are party to it are institutionally called upon to enforce its limitations, and can be held to account for any violations. Hence, so it is often argued, non-state violence *is* different, because its participants are not accountable in the same way. This is, of course, now only a half-truth at best. The other side of the coin of extending the protections of international humanitarian law (IHL)—as we shall see—to non-international armed conflicts has been that such non-state actors are obliged equally to respect it (Estreicher 2011–12), and there are now instruments to hold them in some measure legally to account for any failures to do so. For the moment, however, the key point is that different concepts of violence were believed to pertain in the state and non-state realms respectively, in large measure because of differences in their assumed potential capacity to adhere to its regulation.

Accordingly, to make sense of this idea that some people specifically are 'liable to be killed', appeal is made to those meaningful concepts and categories that differentiate between types of violence, and proper and improper targets of war. The argument is demonstrated at two interacting levels: first, there are distinct categories of the vulnerable, expressed through the language of proper targets, and gradations in the liability to be killed; secondly, these make sense only in the context of some underlying concept that plausibly differentiates between various types of violence. While, to date, the moral argument has largely been focused on the former, given the exposure of civilians to contemporary military technology, it will be suggested that the more fundamental seat of moral controversy is in fact engendered by the latter.

What, then, accounts for the discrepancy between the social vulnerability to violence and its seemingly 'natural' incidence? The unfolding argument will reveal why this apparent contradiction is not quite as puzzling as it might initially seem. Central to the analysis is the simultaneous, and interconnected, disturbance of a prior condition of supposed equality (between belligerents), on the one hand, and of the consequent challenges to the previously assumed inequality (between targets), on the other. Essential hitherto to the regulation of political violence has been a prevailing concept based on the equality of belligerents, such that in war both sides are subject to the same code of conduct, irrespective of the merits of their involvement in the conflict: the laws of war apply equally, whether or not one side was deemed at fault. Moreover, since war was considered to be an interstate activity, this equality was logically guaranteed by the very sovereign equality thought to attach to all states, both in peace and in war. This equality was further complemented by the doctrine of non-equality in the proper targets of warfare, namely the principle of discrimination between combatants and non-combatants. Again, for this to be applied, it was necessary for there to be a stable and sharp separation between the two. During the course of the twentieth century, those equilibrium points around both the equality and the inequality have become gradually destabilized, and for essentially the same reasons in both cases. The challenge to equality in the former respect has opened up the prospect of yet greater equality in the targets of violence as well. Briefly, this argument can first be placed in its historical context.

HISTORY, VULNERABILITY, AND CONCEPTS OF POLITICAL VIOLENCE

Historically, the major attempts at discrimination in targets of violence have been logically supported by international society's insistence on a prior distinction between war and other concepts of political violence, and more recently between international and non-international armed conflicts. The main purpose of the institution of war, accordingly, has been to confer a monopoly on legitimate resort to violence upon states alone. Thereby it has purported to socialize understandings of vulnerability into one dominant pattern, as a necessary precondition for application of some important types of regulation. As a result, rules of war have been enforced by state authorities, just as they could be agreed internationally between them. The main beneficiaries since the nineteenth century have been the regular members of the armed forces, who could potentially be treated with greater civility both on and off the battlefield, and eventually also civilians on all sides, who could increasingly be given some degree of legal protection.

In all these matters, international society has proceeded by way of formulating its own classifications: it has established its own meaningful categories of people in conditions of violence, but has made the degree of respect for these categories conditional on the concept of violence in which they were located. Of the many classifications, two in particular have been especially influential in determining the distribution of vulnerability: the discrimination between combatants and civilians (categories); and the distinction between international and non-international armed conflicts (concepts).

As a military practice and as an ethical theory, discrimination in warfare has a venerable history. However, we are told that the distinction between combatants and civilian populations 'had found acceptance as a self-evident rule of customary law in the second half of the nineteenth century', and this principle was restated in the Hague Conferences of 1899 and 1907 (Kalshoven 1973: 31–2). What is critical here is the manner in which this discrimination was thought to derive from the essential nature of international armed conflict: as such, it was the underlying concept of war that specified, in turn, those who were vulnerable in accordance with it. A very clear example of this relationship is provided in Francis Lieber's classic 1863 'Instructions for the Government of Armies of the United States in the Field'. That code proceeds by way of an impeccable syllogism:

> Public war is a state of armed hostility between sovereign nations or governments . . . [There has developed] the distinction between the private individual belonging to a hostile country and the hostile country itself. The principle has . . . acknowledged that the unarmed citizen is to be spared in person, property and honor as much as the exigencies of war will admit. (Quoted in Kalshoven 1973: 46)

From this concept of war, the relevant categories for its prosecution necessarily emerge, and the limitations on its conduct are logically entailed. We should, at the same time, note also the highly significant qualifying phrase—'as much as the exigencies of war will admit'—inserted at the end. This permissive principle 'set the tone' (Slim 2007: 18) for the future accommodation struck between military necessity and non-combatant immunity.

However, the codification of the laws of war throughout this period had devoted virtually all of its attention to the category of the combatant, at the expense of the civilian. With regard to the latter, the culminating point was not reached until the 1949 Geneva Conventions, particularly part IV, which 'is the first treaty devoted exclusively to the protection of civilians in time of war' (Meyer and McCoubrey 1998: 58; Roberts and Guelff 2000: 299). This was very timely, given the ghastly civilian experience during World War II which, according to international lawyer Hersch Lauterpacht, had 'reduced to the vanishing point the protection of the civilian population' (quoted in Hayashi 2007: 110). In response, the Geneva Convention Common Article 3, as well as Convention Four, set out detailed protections 'according civilians unprecedented status' (Cardenas 2010: 3). Under their terms, the two categories of civilian and combatant are mutually exclusive, and the 1949 Geneva Conventions describe a civilian negatively, in opposition to a combatant (Van Engeland 2011: 30). The category of civilian is not itself legally defined.

These categories were reaffirmed in the 1977 Protocols to the Geneva Conventions. For instance, Protocol 1, Part IV, Article 48 recorded its Basic Rule that 'the Parties to the conflict shall at all times distinguish between the civilian population and combatants . . . and accordingly shall direct their operations only against military objectives' (Roberts and Guelff 2000: 447). Article 51 prohibited also 'threats of violence the primary purpose of which is to spread terror among the civilian population' (Roberts and Guelff 2000: 448).

The other crucial distinction addresses the concept of violence in which its operational categories are embedded: the decisive separation here had become that between international and non-international armed conflicts. Until the middle of the twentieth century, the laws of war effectively applied only to the former (Roberts and Guelff 2000: 22). Importantly, the reason they did not apply to internal armed conflict was precisely because of the supposed legal 'inequality' between the parties. This mattered so much because this 'difference of fact cannot fail to be reflected in the law which international society is prepared to lay down for the two situations' (Kalshoven 1973: 14). Accordingly, this point is central to the present argument. What international society determined at Geneva in 1949 was that it 'rejected the notion that all of the laws of war should apply to internal conflicts' (Roberts and Guelff 2000: 481), and there was much resistance in the drafting to some of the proposed extensions. The concern, as typically expressed by the British delegate, was that it would implicitly legitimize insurgents 'whose right to wage war could not be recognized' (Cullen 2010: 32). That said, the conference certainly did move well beyond any notion that observance of the Conventions be restricted to states alone, engaged exclusively in interstate conflicts. Its Common Article 3, referring to internal conflicts, deliberately employed the terminology of the 'parties to the conflict', not just States parties (Roberts and Guelff 2000: 24). Nonetheless, it remained the case that the perceived inequality of the parties was deemed decisive in determining the kind of rules that must be observed (Cullen 2010).

The 1977 Protocols went even further in extending legal protections in the case of non-international conflicts, and this proved to be deeply controversial (Solis 2010: ch. 4). However, what is most important to stress is that the basic distinction between two alternative concepts of violence continued to be restated in the very scope of the two Protocols: I applied to international, and II to non-international, armed conflicts. Moreover, armed conflict was itself understood as a distinct concept of violence, and had to meet certain threshold conditions, although these were not legally defined. Even though the protections were now more fully developed than previously in the case of the non-international in Protocol II, they still did not equate to those in Protocol I, but remained comparatively 'much fewer and far less restrictive' (Roberts and Guelff 2000: 482). It was also the case that the applicability of Protocol II continued to depend on the violence meeting the test of an 'armed conflict', leaving its lesser forms beyond the pale. In these various ways, relative degrees of vulnerability (by category) continued to depend crucially on the respective concepts of political violence in which they were located. The utility of this distinction between international and non-international armed conflict is now widely challenged by international lawyers (Cullen 2010: 1). The reason for their critique is precisely that it results in unequal application of law, and may in this way be positively harmful.

As shown, the 1949 Geneva Conventions are demonstrably organized around those distinct concepts and categories, and any treatment due is determined strictly by the concept of the violence (international or non-international) and the category into which the individual falls (civilian or combatant). It is, it has been noted, 'the shift from one category to the other that raises questions' (Van Engeland 2011: 101). However, what must also be stressed is the extent of the liability that accompanied each status. Combatants were assuredly accorded certain positive entitlements (treatment when sick and wounded, POW status), and enjoyed immunity from prosecution under what had traditionally been regarded as 'combatant's privilege' (Solis 2010: 42). These protections must, however, be placed in the context of the additional liability that their social status conferred on them. In effect, to be a combatant 'means that one is a legitimate target for attack' (Van Engeland 2011: 38), and, in this sense, the 'liability to be killed' is indeed categorically established. The effect of this is, of course, that the mass slaughter of combatants, as during World War I, does not by itself constitute any violation of the laws of war (Roberts and Guelff 2000: 29). While international society's laws of war provide succour to some, at one level, they do so by rendering others (namely combatants) acceptably vulnerable, in a way that non-combatants are not.

If the practice of war now routinely subverts that specific rationale in many ways, it can fairly be said that international society's principles no longer enjoy complete coherence. The 1949 Geneva Conventions have been described as 'an institutional bridge between the laws of war and emerging human rights norms' (Cardenas 2010: 13), and some have seen their recent discomfiture as resulting from their attempt to straddle the two stools as these move steadily further apart (Van Engeland 2011: xiv, 162). What contributes to this widening gap is that human rights law resists differentiating between human beings, whereas fundamental to the laws of war, in terms of the present argument, has been precisely its development of 'distinct categories' of people (Roberts 2008: 239). This is the source of the resulting tension between the two approaches.

Thus understood, the development of warfare in the twentieth century and beyond (guerrilla/unconventional warfare, aerial bombardment, nuclear weapons) has presented a major challenge to international society's dominant concept, and recent examples of terrorist violence have simply compounded an already existing tendency: alternative forms of vulnerability have been deployed explicitly to challenge the privileged position of the one that had hitherto prevailed. Although states can be regarded as the principal losers by this development, they have been, as will be demonstrated shortly, surprisingly complicit in helping to bring it about. In the manner of their so doing, they have contributed to the trend towards subversion of their own allocation of social vulnerability. It is to these multiple challenges that we can now turn.

CONTESTING THE CATEGORIES OF THE VULNERABLE

Some of these challenges have been long term, and reflect profound, if gradual, transformations in basic conceptions of statehood, and in the citizen's relationship to the state. Many of these developments sat increasingly uncomfortably with the existing war convention, which rested on a simple and straightforward dichotomy: each individual 'must be either a soldier or a civilian' (Walzer 1977: 179). Historical trends, in any case, were making that separation progressively harder to maintain. According to historian Michael Howard, during the course of the nineteenth century, 'every economic, intellectual, and political development in Europe eroded the distinction between "society" and the "state"' (Howard 1979b: 9–10). Where then, in turn, did this leave the existing distribution of vulnerability, insofar as it rested squarely upon the tenability of that distinction?

The forms of political violence that did most to destabilize the prevailing war convention were the following: guerrilla/unconventional/irregular warfare; strategic bombardment and its intellectual derivative, the diplomacy of nuclear violence; and finally other forms of terrorism. Each of these draws upon alternative concepts of violence, and they all possess striking family resemblances that challenge the pre-existing distributions of the vulnerable. As such, they represent a threat to the interests of international society collectively, since its definition of the vulnerable entrenched what was most compatible with the preferences of its state members. Hedley Bull had fully appreciated the scale of the challenge presented by these alternative concepts of violence:

> In the post-1945 period international society has had a certain success in confining interstate war within limits consistent with the survival of the states system . . . But as this has happened, war waged by political units other than states has expanded in scope. Civil factions have emerged as violent world actors, challenging the monopoly of international violence which sovereign states have long claimed for themselves, and escaping the restraints and rules by which sovereign states are bound . . . International society will not be able to afford to allow these new forms of war to lie permanently beyond the compass of its rules. (Bull 1977: 199)

Thus conceived, the existing concepts and categories of the vulnerable have found themselves encroached upon from various directions. From one direction comes the pressure to retain the state monopoly on violence, along with the specific categories of discrimination that flow naturally from it. At the same time, the members of international society have made their own contribution to unsettling their own preferred categories, as will be shown shortly. There are also the pressures from challengers who seek overtly to overturn these traditional concepts. The outcome is that categories of the vulnerable have become highly unstable, insofar as the distinction between war and other forms of violence has begun to break down (Bobbitt 2008: 153). These trends have been aggravated by the seeming erosion of distinct public and private spheres in relation to the use of force. As private activities in the field have expanded, these have posed new questions for state control and limitation (Duffield 2001; Coady 2008: 223; Pattison 2008; Walzer 2008; McEvoy 2011: 126). On various fronts, this has forced re-examination of the categories of the vulnerable deemed relevant to the use of force in the twenty-first century. What has characterized these changes is their combined tendency to push for an essential 'substitutability' in the targets of violence (Armborst 2010: 425). While the category of the vulnerable seemingly remains in place, it has become increasingly indeterminate, not just in practice but also in theory. The underlying reason is that it now lacks any convincing normative concept to sustain it.

These challenges have not appeared suddenly on the scene. In medieval and early modern warfare, sieges had already put civilian populations directly in harm's way, usually by exposing them to starvation and disease. In more recent forms of warfare, similar practices persisted with the siege of major cities, as famously in the case of Leningrad in World War II. More generally, the establishment of blockades from the eighteenth to the twentieth centuries exposed millions of civilians to deprivation, even when it did not place them directly in the line of fire. In these many instances, military necessity has been the mother of all sorts of inventions that had already placed the war convention at risk. Inequality between belligerents was also, in a more fundamental sense, to challenge the limits of the invulnerability of enemy civilians.

These challenges to traditional discriminations were exacerbated in radical fashion by the 'area bombing' during World War II, and by the onset of the nuclear age. Here, paradoxically, the major development was not simply encroachment on the category of the invulnerable for reasons of military necessity (as one might have expected), but more subversively an attempted wholesale inversion of the traditional rationale for protecting civilians. Moreover, international society took a leading part in legitimating these new conceptions, even if their consequences were eventually to be turned back against it. In the course of the 1960s, these notions were captured in what became familiarly known as the posture of mutual assured destruction. Alternatively viewed, from the point of view of the present discussion, this doctrine can be more appropriately described as one of mutual assured vulnerability. Moreover, this logic came to be sanctified in arms control doctrine and agreements (Clark 1988: 99–100), and thereby achieved some status as a norm in international society.

This issue had been crystallized in the context of two strategic choices that presented themselves, given the technological developments of the 1960s. The first was the nature of the targets to be attacked, a choice framed as either counter-force (against missiles) or counter-value (against cities). The second concerned the wisdom of introducing active defences against nuclear attack, and if these were to be deployed, a similar choice was on offer about the targets they should be used to protect. The core argument against deploying an anti-ballistic missile (ABM) system, as finally embodied in the Strategic Arms Limitation Treaty (SALT) 1's ABM Treaty of 1972, was precisely that defence of cities could upset the deterrence relationship on which a stable nuclear posture between the two superpowers depended. It is noteworthy that, to insure against this outcome, the term coined by US officials at the time to describe this strategic requirement was none other than 'assured vulnerability' (Brennan 1989: 246). In other words, vulnerability was to be a conscious creation of policy, rather than any bare fact of nuclear life. What this explicitly recommended was that vulnerability should be guaranteed as part of the nuclear war convention, rather than as part of the natural order of things. To achieve this, international society should place its weight behind a proscription of active defensive measures that might otherwise protect centres of population. While it seems likely that, in the event, the decisive objection to deployment of ABMs was that these systems would be largely ineffective, and always likely to be overwhelmed by offensive forces in any case, there was at least some explicit endorsement of the principle that rendering population centres invulnerable was inherently a bad thing (Treverton 1989: 200–2). That case had been strongly advocated in the mid-1960s, on the following rationale: 'where offensive weapons are invulnerable to attack while cities are extremely vulnerable a curious and unprecedented stability is maintained' (Ruina and Gell-Mann 1989: 263). Vulnerability was, in that way, to be maintained as a necessary condition of the diplomacy of violence; it assured cities (and civilians) remained vulnerable as hostages, and thereby kept in play 'the bargaining power of an undischarged capacity for violence' (Schelling 1989: 229).

In historical terms, this was an unconventional piece of logic (Clark 1982: 33). If the logic of nuclear deterrence insisted that 'killing weapons is bad, killing people is good' (Treverton 1989: 200), then there was a need to rethink the contours of vulnerability in a radically new way, and to redistribute it accordingly. This may not have mattered much as long as deterrence continued to work, and provided this nuclear war convention was not called upon in practice. However, we should not allow amnesia to block our recollection of this hugely significant development.

The example it set is especially pertinent when we turn our attention to the subject of the terroristic uses of political violence. The best way to discern the impact that international society has had on the distribution of vulnerability is to approach it via the ongoing encounter between war and other concepts of political violence, of which terrorism has been one distinctive subset. As soon as we do so, we discover that there has been throughout both a practical and a theoretical dialogue between war and terrorism. So much is this so that, in its beginnings, it has been insisted that 'terrorism in the strict sense . . . emerged only . . . after it had become a feature of conventional war' (Walzer 1977: 198). As a result, ethically speaking, 'the questions raised by war and by terrorism are identical' (Nathanson 2010: 50).

The hallmark of terrorism as a type of political violence lies not in its distinctive motivations, nor in who undertakes it, but rather in its deliberate choice of a strategy predicated on the indeterminateness of the vulnerable. Essential to its very purpose is the requirement for the 'substitutability' of its victims (Armborst 2010: 424). 'Randomness', in Walzer's choice of terminology, 'is the crucial feature of terrorist activity' (Walzer 1977: 197). This places it at the polar opposite of any concept of war governed by a convention structured around the permissibility and prohibition accorded to various categories of targets: the indeterminateness of its victims, in the one, is thus opposed starkly against their precise stipulation, in the other. In this way, what terrorism attacks is the very principle of discrimination *in any form*. Instead, the vulnerable as a universal category is to take the place of the vulnerable as a specified category.

How has this challenge been mounted? It has been executed through a revisiting of the categories of state/society, and the associated categories of guilt/innocence. These are now subject to attempted reinterpretation such that they can no longer restrict the scope of violence in traditional ways (Armborst 2010: 415). The further along the spectrum of political violence towards randomness that the action moves, the more it obliterates any meaningful distinctions of this kind. While it is these categories that have been unsettled, the underlying challenge has been to the fundamental concepts of violence that underwrite them.

This process of destabilization can be further illustrated with reference to recent developments in counterterrorism, and here again international society has contributed, through its own actions, to the precariousness of its own concepts and categories. What kind of 'war' was being fought against global terrorism, and what did this signify about the equality, or otherwise, of those parties engaged in it? The problem manifested itself specifically with respect to which body of law was applicable, as emerged sharply in the aftermath of the 9/11 attacks on the United States. On the face of it, it was difficult to apply IHL to this case, but this left a legal void for dealing with those suspected of involvement in the planning or execution of the attacks. One instance of this legal instability was the insertion of a third category, namely that of 'unlawful combatant', expanding on the precedent that had been set by the US Supreme Court in 1942 in the Quirin case (Van Engeland 2011: 120). When Al-Qaeda and Taliban prisoners were classed as 'unlawful enemy combatants' (Luban 2003), this seemingly placed them beyond the reach of IHL, since the latter operated on the basis of the accepted distinction between soldier and civilian: a 'combatant' regarded as 'unlawful' blurred that prevailing understanding, and created a 'legal limbo' as a result (McKeown 2009: 13). 'With domestic law irrelevant and international law inapplicable', it has been observed, 'the war on terrorism was thus to be conducted within what we have termed here a No-Law Zone' (Blum and Heymann 2010: xiii; see Evangelista 2008). Here was a gap into which the socially vulnerable could fall.

This general point about the rules depending on the concept is graphically made in the proceedings in the case of *Hamdan v. Rumsfeld*, taken to the US Supreme Court. At stake was whether or not the law of international armed conflict applied in the war in Afghanistan, and how it applied in the particular case of this Yemeni national, apprehended in Afghanistan and suspected of being an Al-Qaeda member. The important point for this discussion was that the US authorities made the argument that there were two simultaneous conflicts in Afghanistan, one against the Taliban, and one separately against Al-Qaeda. While acknowledging that the Geneva Conventions applied in full to the former, they maintained that they did not—not even Common

Article 3—apply to the latter. Their contrary suggestion was that the Common Article related only to internal armed conflict, but 'since the conflict with Al-Qaeda was transnational in nature, it was neither inter-state nor internal'. In effect, the US position was that there was a 'gap in the application of the Conventions—that there were some armed conflicts to which no part of the Conventions could apply' (Cerone 2006).

What had compounded this uncertainty was the US administration's own predilection for describing the ensuing military campaign as a *war* on terrorism, thereby inadvertently reinstating by the back door the assumed applicability of the war convention that had already been summarily evicted through the front. It also flew in the face of common state practice of denying a state of war to be operative against private groups employing force, and hence was a departure from the dominant tendency to reject the applicability of IHL to those cases (Heinze 2011: 1086). Normally, terrorists were treated as subject to domestic criminal law. Instead, a new hybrid was put in place that gave the United States 'the powers of a nation at war', while at the same time 'denying those captured . . . the basic protections provided for under the Geneva Conventions' (Mansell and Openshaw 2010: 27).

Nonetheless, US administration staff lawyers did consider the language of war appropriate in this instance, apparently on the grounds that '[n]ecessity creates war, not a zeitgeist called "law"', even though this remarkable legal pragmatism, in turn, duly required 'adapting the rules of war to provide a new framework to address the new enemies of the twenty-first century' (Yoo 2006: 9, 17). The adoption of this idiosyncratic language post-2001 ensured that in its aftermath war and terrorism would continue to be intertwined in complex—and often highly confusing—ways. At the very least, this unsettling of categories has had knock-on effects on IHL: 'because the US invoked the language, methods, and institution of war as the primary vehicle to advance US counter-terrorist operations', it has been pointedly suggested, 'it has *ipso facto* implicated the laws of war' (Heinze 2011: 1069–70). Dealing with these situations does create urgent dilemmas, particularly for liberal states: can they defend liberal causes by illiberal means (Dunne 2009: 113)? Specifically, controversial issues revolved around the resort to illegal means, such as torture, in the name of counterterrorism (Foot 2004: 78; Gross 2010: ch. 6). In consequence, the ensuing judicial process has assigned a quasi-legal personality to private terrorist groups, wholly contrary to the intentions of the state practitioners who acted against any such outcome. If the latter aimed to 'empower' states in their operations against those groups, their efforts turned out to be surprisingly counterproductive (Heinze 2011: 1093). If the dominant conceptual paradigm is now unsettled, these events certainly contributed to that outcome.

The subject of humanitarian intervention also illustrates some of these destabilizing developments. If the resort to force has always had major implications for human rights, then this is doubly so when the objective of the use of that force is explicitly to promote or protect the human rights of others (Walzer 2004: 16–17; Johnson 2006; Heinze 2009; Gross 2010: ch. 9). Inescapably, this creates severe dilemmas about the nature and extent of the force that can be used, and asks troubling questions about whose rights can reasonably be placed at risk to protect the rights of others (Altman and Wellman 2008: 237). Paradoxically, the more 'discretionary' the conflict is seen to be, the greater the risk that combatants' lives will be placed ahead of those of civilians caught in the line of fire. In short, in edging towards a doctrine that allows it to use force to protect certain categories of the vulnerable (as it sees them), international society is at the same time compelled to develop a doctrine as to who can reasonably be made vulnerable in the effort to achieve this objective. In making any trade-off of this kind, it is palpably engaged in the vulnerability business (Walzer 2004: 137; Roberts 2008: 251; Shue 2011: 137; Whetham 2011b: 21–2).

What prompts the resort to violence in these cases is the need to protect the rights of those who are threatened by a regime, or by conditions of civil strife within a state, as for example in Libya in 2011. In such cases, the use of force is explicitly authorized to protect the civilian population in the state. What does this mean in practice for the combatants charged with military responsibility for enforcing the action, and for other civilians that may become caught up in their forceful interventions? The history of recent humanitarian actions demonstrates a strong proclivity to minimize the threat to the intervening forces by resorting, as far as possible, to air rather than ground operations, as was demonstrated in Kosovo in 1999 (Walzer 2004: 101; Hartle 2008: 176; Kashnikov 2008: 232) and once again in Libya in 2011. 'Thus, the adoption of a zero-casualty strategy by NATO in the Kosovo intervention', we are told, 'led to bombardment from very high altitudes as a result of which 500 civilian Serbs died and no NATO military were killed' (Asad 2010: 13). The laws of armed conflict had evolved, as we have already seen, under very great pressure to tolerate 'collateral damage', in order to fill the 'unbridgeable gap between the norm of noncombatant immunity and the reality of civilian vulnerability' (Asad 2010: 13). There can be many compelling political considerations lying behind the choice of air power as the preferred instrument of force, but a pervasive one in this context is the wish to minimize casualties on the part of the intervening forces (Shue 2011). Confining military operations to the air is evidently one way of achieving this goal. Unfortunately, air strikes tend to lead to the heightened risk of mistaken attacks on civilian populations, and hence of accidental deaths. At this point, the distinction between 'not intending' and 'intending not' to kill civilians becomes ethically extremely moot (Kamm 2004: 655). The paradox is that the resort to violence to protect the rights of some people frequently entails greater exposure on the part of others.

In short, by themselves subverting the accepted distinctions on which a state practice of the vulnerable had traditionally rested, states may have enhanced their powers of discretion in the short term, but only at the significant cost of damaging their own preferred legal regime in the longer term. In further destabilizing the preferred concept of the vulnerable, international society has contributed to the erosion of its own authority to enforce it.

CONCEPTS OF EQUALITY AND CATEGORIES OF INEQUALITY

So what is now at stake? The objective here is not to contribute directly to the ethics of violence but to demonstrate instead how two interrelated develop-ments have shaped the ethical issues that now must be addressed, for the sake of effective future regulation in this area. They are, first, the disturbance of that concept of violence that was predicated on the equality of belligerents. In the cases of humanitarian intervention and terrorism, for example, the condition of equality is believed no longer to hold, either because the target regime in question has forfeited its own legitimacy by its human rights failures, or because the agents of terrorism never possessed proper authority in the first place. This lack of equality is the pervasive characteristic of many instances of contemporary 'asymmetrical' conflicts. Secondly, and in no small measure as a direct consequence of the state practice recorded above, there has been the destabilization of the associated categories of combatant and civilian: these categories acquired their purchase as part of that hitherto prevailing concept, and they are now left exposed by the assorted challenges to it.

The various erosions of belief in the equality of belligerents have entailed a commensurate set of challenges to the claimed inequality between combatants and non-combatants. In general, these issues surrounding the regulation of violence have been portrayed as requiring practical or pragmatic adjustments, but at base they are inherently conceptual and normative. The laws of war had depended on a notion of the 'moral equality of soldiers', such that their standing in the law was equal, regardless of whether they fought on the just or unjust side. For this reason, there had to be a radical separation between the *ad bellum* and the *in bello* components of just war in order for the law to be applied effectively (Rodin and Shue 2008b: 15; McEvoy 2011: 123). As long as the soldier complied with the law in respect to the means of war, he or she would face no legal redress with respect to its ends.

As a matter of moral theory, if not yet of legal theory, this doctrine is now experiencing some fundamental questioning, based on attempts logically to reconnect the twin components of just war theory, such that ideas of sym-metry are no longer considered fully tenable (McMahan 2008, 2010; Rodin 2008: 45). According to these arguments, 'only the just warriors are entitled to kill enemy soldiers', and conversely, 'unjust warriors have no moral license to kill at all' (Coady 2008: 19). Just soldiers should be regarded as analogous with police officers using legal force, and any claimed moral equivalence with the law breaker is then deemed patently absurd (Rodin and Shue 2008b: 4). Legally, of course, the issue that is opened up by this line of attack is precisely whether a soldier can, as a result, 'be held responsible for fighting in a war that is illegal or unjust' (Rodin and Shue 2008b: 1), even if the fighting is otherwise in accordance with the laws of war.

This 'moral equality of soldiers' has been thought to derive essentially from their relationship of mutual vulnerability, insofar as all combatants—and they alone—are equally assigned a social liability to be killed. There have, of course, been recent technological developments that have further unsettled that assumption. The use of drones to kill specific targets illustrates this asymmetry rather sharply. 'You can't kill', Walzer has insisted, 'unless you are prepared to die' (Walzer 2004: 101). The drone pilot is safely extracted from that relationship, to an even greater degree than an aircrew instructed to fly above a certain height.

This moral asymmetry compounds the problems that have already become manifest as a result of other military and legal forms of asymmetry. In some versions, asymmetry is regarded as largely a reference to large-scale disparities in the military resources and technology of the belligerents, a condition that itself has been thought inhospitable to the maintenance of the laws of war, in part because of the lack of the possibility of reciprocity which it entails (Gross 2010: 33–4). In other versions, the concern has been about the differential legal capacity to adhere to and enforce the laws of war, such that a multiplicity of irregular and non-state actors can be regarded as radically unequal in the legal sense, with similarly adverse consequences for respect for IHL (Roberts 2008: 241; Steele and Heinze 2009). All of these types of asymmetry potentially put pressure on the implementation of the legal rules of war.

Once these moves are made, however, simultaneously those subsidiary categories are destabilized that had made sense only within that overall concept. If the equality of combatants is no longer to be regarded as self-evident, then it follows also that the assumed 'inequality' between combatants and non-combatants may be similarly open to challenge. The reason for this is the logical connection between the arguments that have been advanced in support of both positions. We need to consider each of these in turn to understand the problems that now result from the instability that has been introduced into the system as a whole.

The attempt to differentiate war from other uses of armed force has been made on a variety of grounds. Most frequent has been the explicit association made between war and the 'public' exercise of violence, as set against an assortment of 'private' usages that are to be considered, to varying degrees, criminal acts (Bobbitt 2008: 140)—although evidently criminal acts can also take place *within* war, as the development of IHL's notion of 'war crimes' has demonstrated. For most of the time, international society has acted vigorously to assert the connection between the public and the state (regarded as the legitimate agent in war), and thereby to delegitimize the activities of all other agents, presenting them as engaged in 'lesser' forms of violence. It does so through its denial of the possibility that such other acts of violence can ever enjoy proper authority for their undertaking. Common definitions of terrorism typically juxtapose two separate elements: *'violence against civilians perpetrated by non-state groups for political purposes'* (Duner 2007: 7–8, emphasis in original). These implicitly combine what might be termed violations of the *ius ad terrorem* (the lack of proper authority on the part of non-state groups) and of the *ius in terrore* (directed against civilians). But which of these two elements creates the greater offence? If we adapt the traditional dichotomy of just war principles, it is very much a moot point whether the routine condemnation of acts of political terror derives from the particular method of violence that is employed (indiscriminate, and hence an infringement of *in terrore*) (Coady 2004; Coady 2007: 137–8), or whether at base it mostly concerns this issue of legitimate authority (lacking proper authority, and hence contrary to *ad terrorem*) (McPherson 2007: 524; Steele and Heinze 2009; Steinhoff 2007: chs 1 and 5; Couto 2010). 'Perhaps it is this failure to be a legitimate agent', queries the latter position, 'that makes the use of terror . . . into the act of only a terrorist' (Kamm 2004: 652; see Finlay 2010: 288; Nathanson 2010: 122).

This framing has been used as a powerful source of control by international society and has been directly responsible for defining the categories of the vulnerable in particular ways. 'The development of the modern concept of war as organised violence among sovereign states', as Hedley Bull was to suggest, 'was the outcome of a process of limitation or confinement of violence' (Bull 1977: 185). This underpinning logic has been explained at length elsewhere:

> The rationale for restricting the conferral of the right to wage war to public, sovereign authorities is the following. Wars are normally fought in defence of communal, state interests, such as sovereignty and territorial integrity. Whether or not such interests are under threat, and thus warrant resorting to war, is a matter for public judgement . . . This in turn dictates against private wars, and in favour of vesting the authority to wage war in the prince. (Fabre 2008: 968)

Once this association was made, other resorts to violence inevitably came to be seen—implicitly or explicitly—as challenges to the state's putative monopoly: they symbolize 'reactions to' and 'rejections of' the state's claims (Wight 2009: 101). This is commonly acknowledged in assertions that terrorism is 'the *ultima ratio* of resistance to state power', insofar as it is intended directly to challenge its monopoly on force (Armborst 2010: 417). That is to say that this doctrine sought to limit or confine violence by prohibiting private agents from recourse to it. Any such historical process was, of course, profoundly political.

The dominant binary employed in this has been that between the public and the private uses of force (Coppieters 2008: 55; Johnson 2011: 90). Indeed, so pervasive did this way of thinking become that it 'structures virtually the entire tradition of western political thought and practice' (Owens 2008: 979). Owens has, in fact, rebutted the validity of this dichotomy as a convincing basis for distinguishing between war and other forms of violence, insisting that war is inherently political, rather than necessarily public (Owens 2008: 989). The more important conclusion for this argument, however, is that international society has, for much of its history, been able successfully to impose that distinction in its own terms. In her own conclusion, Owens acknowledges what is in fact the central claim of this chapter: 'Some forms of violence are *made* public and others are *made* private through historically varying ways of organizing and justifying force', and through 'political struggle and definition' (Owens 2008: 990, emphasis added). This is assuredly so, and fully captures the argument that international society has been a potent agent in this process, persistently pressing for acceptance of one particular form of violence, to the exclusion of all others.

Why this matters so much is that this concept of war—centred on states as the only *legitimate agents*—was predicated on assumptions about the equality of the warring parties. It also brought with it an associated package of attitudes towards its proper targets: it had a second effect by establishing an inextricable link between the nature of war and the scope of its *legitimate targets*. This connection had been early established in Gentili's concise rendering: 'war is a contention of arms', he suggested, and in consequence 'there can be no war with unarmed men' (quoted in Clark 1988: 262). At stake in debates about appropriate social *status* ever since have then been two competing perspectives: the first narrowly stresses the bearing of arms; the second emphasizes instead the role of the individual as part of the state, or in relation to national society more generally. How these arguments have played out has, in turn, had decisive significance for the proclaimed category of the vulnerable, and for the stability of the category of civilians.

In the first instance, there has been the straightforward suggestion that those vulnerable in war are, prima facie, combatants in the act of bearing arms, as they have a liability to be killed (since they are themselves trying to inflict harm): all others retain their human rights, including the right to life, although this cannot always be safeguarded in practice. Accordingly, discrimination must centre on categories of civilians and non-combatants, as contrasted with soldiers or combatants.

This pushes the discussion towards the second perspective, namely the status of the individual with respect to state and society. Is there any distinction to be made between the latter two? According to Rousseau this lies at the very heart of the concept of war, with obvious implications for the manner of its conduct. The distinction on which he insisted is between the soldier and the citizen: the former alone represents the justifiably vulnerable individual, and the latter is to be considered off limits (Clark 1982: 82). His argument developed along the following lines:

> If war is between states, and the state is separable in theory as well as in practice from society, it can be argued that this conception of war leads directly to a principle of discrimination in the conduct of war since the targets of war are, presumably, the rival *states* but by no means the entire populations of the belligerents. (Clark 1988: 18)

However, the real-life situation overall is much more complex than this would suggest. The paradox, as already noted, is that in any purely statistical sense the risk of being killed has actually moved decisively in favour of civilians, as a matter of fact, whatever international society may have prescribed, in terms of its allocated social liability. Unhappily, the tide of battle has recently flowed in the opposite direction from its ideal theory, and civilians are now often 'preferentially targeted' (Johnson 2011: 31). According to various estimates, civilians amounted to somewhere between 50 and 80 per cent of all deaths and casualties in war during the twentieth century as a whole (Van Engeland 2011: xii; Bobbitt 2008: 12; Coady 2008: 121). So how can it be claimed that international society distributes vulnerability, when the impacts of violence are so contrary to its own normative strictures? Is this simply evidence of how violence now conforms to the general characteristics of risk society (Rasmussen 2006)?

There are three short answers. First, we should not expect, in any event, that adherence to any of its laws of war will correspond exactly to its prescriptive codes. This is true of international law generally, and the compliance gap is particularly wide where violence is concerned (Slim 2007: 295). Secondly, as already demonstrated, international society has acted in manifold ways that have placed further pressure on its own categorical scheme: it has countenanced the vulnerability of civilians in its regimes of nuclear deterrence, subverted distinctions between war and terrorism, and placed civilians at risk in its multilateral military operations intended to protect them.

Thirdly, in imposing its various regulations, international society has always adopted a permissive approach that has allowed degrees of latitude in favour of the exercise of violence. The qualifying phrase in Lieber's code ('as much as the exigencies of war will admit') was noted above. Similarly, the Geneva Conventions also introduced occasional safeguards, such as for occupying powers, so that any required measures were not 'prejudicial to the security of such State' (Geneva Convention IV, Art. 4, Roberts and Guelff 2000: 303). Generally, implicit permissions of this kind ensure that IHL 'does not prohibit collateral damage as such' (Van Engeland 2011: 50): it requires 'proportional' military action only, deemed not to be 'excessive'. International society has invested much in its categories of the vulnerable, but its overall concept of violence has throughout been sufficiently liberal with regard to 'military necessity' as to ensure a degree of subversion of them in practice. In the same way, it has been said of just war theory that collateral damage is its 'Achilles' heel' (Nathanson 2010: 95). To this extent, the problem is not now regarded as being about discrimination as such, but instead about what constitutes appropriate justification of the collateral damage that actually takes place (Coady 2008: 121). Indeed, by condoning the shift to aerial bombardment as a way of circumventing the attrition warfare of World War I, international society may have incidentally encouraged the transference of risks away from soldiers and towards civilians (Coady 2008: 181). It is this that opens the door to charges of double standards when states condemn terrorists for killing innocent civilians. Even those, like Walzer, who seek to strengthen the principle of non-combatant immunity, have been accused of actually eroding it through allowing an appeal to 'supreme emergency' as one permissible reason to override it (Nathanson 2010: 91–2; Primoratz 2011).

In sum, there has been an integral relationship between concepts of violence and the operational categories of the vulnerable. Intrinsic to international society's dominant conception of the former was an assumption of the equality of the parties to the conflict, each invested with legitimate authority to undertake it, and with the legal capacity to hold the prosecution of it to agreed codes of practice. It was no accident that this concept required not just any form of discrimination in targets, but precisely a discrimination that highlighted the central role of the state in the production and guarantee of security. By concentrating on combatants, and seeking to exclude civilians, states reinforced the conception that war was their business alone, and soldiers were to be viewed as its agents. It was on this basis, ever since Vattel's arguments of the eighteenth century, that the laws of war had been sustained. This view held that combatants were 'mere instruments of their states', and this supported 'the principle of belligerent equality' (McKeogh 2007: 75). Indirectly, this understanding further bolstered the contract whereby the state provided security to its citizens.

There has been a widespread view that the unravelling of the war convention has been the result primarily of the technologies of modern warfare, and the resultant practical difficulties of sustaining any distinctions between combatants and non-combatants on the battlefield. There are now too many 'ambiguities' in the prevailing categories (Slim 2007: 188–204) for them to regulate war effectively. Contemporary wars cannot be fought at all, it is routinely asserted, without placing civilians in harm's way. There are, of course, elements of truth in all such interpretations, but they do not go far enough in shedding light on these developments. The more fundamental transformation, of which the subversion of discrimination is a symptom, is to be found in the erosion of the overarching concept of violence that informed that distinction in the first place. The recent expressions of political violence no longer readily conform to established assumptions about the equality of belligerents (Gross 2010: 33–4), and in this increasingly inhospitable environment the principle of civilian immunity has been losing more of its already tenuous handhold on the always slippery edifice of violence.

CONCLUSION

Of the many ways in which international society has imposed its own concept of the vulnerable, few have had such important consequences as its actions in the field of political violence. This is so for two reasons. Firstly, and most obviously, action in this area has been palpably a matter of life and death, given its potentially deadly subject matter. Secondly, however, international society has been compelled to act strenuously in this area precisely because it is a matter that strikes at the very essence of its state members: from the perspective of the state, it has few institutional interests more important to its own self-identity than its need to monopolize the resort to political violence, not least if it is to be able to maintain its own contract with its citizens (even if many states have chosen not to do so).

It has sought this objective through its promotion of war as the only acceptable concept of political violence. War is the preserve of public author-ities, and it carries with it an implied prohibition on all other resorts to violence by private agents. This has been a powerful instrument in its own right. However, in addition, international society has expressed through this particu-lar conception of violence its own system of regulation, through its preferred categories. In particular, this has led to crucial discriminations in the conduct of war—nowhere more so than in its stipulation of its justifiable targets.

What it has demonstrably sought to conventionalize is the identity of those people who, in Walzer's words, are liable to be killed. In any naturalistic condition we could scarcely begin to describe particular peoples as bearing such a liability, at least not to any special or unusual degree. This is where political art has taken over from nature. The focus of international society's endeavours has been upon not the technical calculation of the risk to which people are exposed in war—international society does not serve as some kind of global actuary—but instead upon the differential status of people engaged in, and exposed to, different forms of violence. As soon as it has made the argument in this way—status matters—it has been inevitably drawn into a moral dialogue about what kind of status makes plausible sense for the purposes of exercising and regulating violence. Even if international society is not the author of just war theory, that theory has replicated many of its own normative assumptions, and has been widely regarded as little more than international society's handmaiden as a result. To the extent that the two are so closely intertwined, international society is therefore exposed to the same critique that, 'with its concepts of "proportionality" and the "double effect", just war theory fatally undermines its own normative integrity by creating rules which harm rather than protect the innocent' (Burke 2004: 351). Meanwhile, other would-be exponents of political violence have been driven to make their own challenges to these dominant frameworks. The more international society has tried to insist on the conceptual distinction between war and terror—instantiated in the categories of combatant and civilian—the more its own historical practices have served only to erode any fully convincing separation between the two. In its own response to terrorism, it has made its own contribution to the further unsettling of any sharp division between war and terrorism as concepts of violence. By making its own determinations on these matters, as it routinely does, international society underlines its own role in the social production of vulnerability.

On key aspects of the regulation of political violence, international society currently advances no consistent or convincing position. However, the lack of a coherent moral voice of its own does not by any means imply that they should be treated as technical or legal problems only, without the need to engage with their ethical dimensions. To do so is simply to ensure failure, because there can be no satisfactory resolution that evades the fundamentally moral nature of these problems. Diverse actors bring their own differing moral priorities into the picture, and it is at this level that it needs to be addressed. International society's erstwhile insistence on its members' monopoly of the legitimate use of force, and its consequential attempts to develop a system of regulation that made sense within such a concept no longer seem to meet the needs of the situation in which we now find ourselves. In order to challenge that prevailing framework, other actors have sought to erode the capacity of the state to protect its own citizens, and thereby to undermine international society's ability to impose its own code of violence. In today's world, 'uncivil wars ransack the legal monopoly of armed force long claimed by states' (Keane 1996: 141). In response, international society's lack of any coherent concept of the vulnerable—in no small measure a reflection of its own selective encroachment on the innocent—is, to that extent, part of the contemporary problem, rather than any part of its solution: the challenge, both in theory and practice, to its own preferred categories of combatant and civilian is but a symptom of this even deeper malaise.

3

Climate Change and the Vulnerable

When Christiana Figueres, the Executive Secretary of the UN's Framework Convention on Climate Change (UNFCCC), addressed the opening of the Conference of the Parties (COP) 17 at Durban on 6 December 2011, she made this passionate plea to the assembled international delegates: 'The vulnerable need solutions from you' (UNFCCC 2011). But just who are the vulnerable with respect to climate change, and what kind of solutions was international society being called upon to deliver? Were they to be rescued from their existing vulnerability (deemed to apply universally, and inherent in objective conditions) or, more fundamentally, was international society being called upon to liberate them from one prevailing concept of climate change in which their vulnerability had been largely assigned? In its Human Development Report 2011, the United Nations Development Programme (UNDP) presented its own accumulated evidence that 'environmental degradation hurts poor and vulnerable groups more than others' (UNDP 2011: 12). Is it the task of international society to protect those vulnerable as it finds them, or instead to deal with the vulnerable as it has helped to make them? The following case demonstrates how this appeal to the vulnerable as the grounds for international action can be understood only in the context of an important underlying concept of climate change, and its associated categories, of which international society has been the principal author. In consequence, there can be no long-term solution to the problems of climate change until the implications of this argument are faced.

This chapter proceeds in the following stages: how notions of vulnerability have become so prominent in this context; historically, how a *particular set* of ideas have become established in the climate regime; how the international negotiations on climate are essentially about contested versions of vulnerability and its distribution; and how, in consequence, deep-seated ethical issues inform these debates and the politics surrounding them. The reason this has such widespread ramifications is that climate change is integral to all the other policy cases discussed in this book. Climate change has pronounced effects on the forms, level, and distribution of economic activities, and is a major determinant of relative access to food and water. It will quite possibly be a source of future violent conflict. It can shape decisively global patterns of health, and poses critical challenges for human movement. For all these reasons, the distribution of vulnerability takes us to the very heart of this issue: any and all future international climate regimes will necessarily have major impacts on that distribution, and reveal how international society is a very powerful agent in this process. While climate change is commonly presented as the classic demonstration of *universal* vulnerability, it is instead its *partial* allocations that have been so striking.

There is by now a widespread consensus that the problem of climate change is unusually intractable, and may just possibly defy any internationally agreed solution. Partly this is due to its sheer complexity (Karlsson et al. 2011: 93). As a result, it is adjudged that the 'basic conditions' for any agreement are 'largely absent', and that it is, accordingly, 'hard to think of an international problem which lends itself less to a coherent, credible, and sufficiently robust and comprehensive general agreement' (Helm 2009a: 18–19). However, the issue is doubly troublesome because even the *absence* of any solution has decisive impacts on the distribution of vulnerability.

Essentially, what makes the problem so complex are the deep ethical issues lying at its core. These derive from competing perceptions of the unfair distribution of vulnerability: moreover, the actions and non-actions of international society are perceived to be complicit in bringing this distribution into being. It is for this reason that moral issues must be recognized as fundamental (Baskin 2009). They are not just supplementary moral glosses that we, as observers, inject by way of commentary, but central to the essence of the issue, as seen by the participants themselves. That this is so has been widely acknowledged (Paterson 2001: 119). 'The issue of reconciling social justice with environmental protection', we are told, 'has surfaced at every major international meeting since the first environment and development conference at Stockholm in 1972' (Roberts and Parks 2007: 2). The Intergovernmental Panel on Climate Change (IPCC), in its own series of periodic assessments, has explicitly pointed out that matters of equity are integral to any effort to address climate change (Page 2006: 7). Moreover, those issues of equity are closely interwoven with 'differential vulnerability' (Richardson, Steffen, and Liverman 2011: 242).

The clearest expression of these issues of equity and justice is revealed in that social distribution of vulnerability towards which international society has made its own substantial contribution. Indeed, it has been suggested that the failure to date of international negotiations to make any substantial headway in slowing global emissions can be explained in this way: 'This "triple inequality" of responsibility, vulnerability, and mitigation . . . offers a powerful and parsimonious explanation for the negotiation positions adopted by rich and poor nations' (Roberts and Parks 2007: 7). This is a compelling analysis. However, what is just as important to stress is that inequality in vulnerability is not simply a cause of negotiating failure, and as such one reason for the lack of

progress in reaching solutions. This would imply that (pre-existing) vulnerability is to be viewed only as an *input* into the negotiations. Just as importantly, however, differential vulnerability must be seen as an *output* of the
negotiations, and it is at this point that issues of equity exercise their most
potent influence. Vulnerability does not just impede successful negotiation:
stalled negotiation results in its own version of vulnerability, and in this way
the vicious circle is complete.

In terms of the international politics of climate change, it is crucial then to
understand the vulnerable not as wholly predetermined, simply awaiting our
identification as a category of people facing specific harmful conditions. The
vulnerable are much more indeterminate, and need to be approached instead as
associated with a particular concept, and emerging from the social conflict that
surrounds it: in this way, the precise identity of the vulnerable is a site of
continuous moral contestation, out of which some specific categories and
conditions of the vulnerable do contingently emerge. It is the overall concept
through which climate change is understood that gives rise to its particular
categories and conditions, rather than the other way round. This complexity, in
turn, is compounded by the fact that there are two separate, but interacting,
layers of the social operating within the sphere of climate change: the 'causal' and
the 'adaptive'. The first is that, with respect to anthropogenic climate change, its
contributory causes have been socially produced, with marked unevenness in the
resulting distribution of causal responsibility. Secondly, the relative capacity to
respond or adapt to its impacts is likewise socially configured, and this is a potent
set of factors in determining the distribution of actual risk.

THE VULNERABLE AND CONCEPTS OF CLIMATE
CHANGE

Key to addressing these issues is the nature of vulnerability in this context, and
there has been much attention devoted to this topic, and many attempts made to
develop specific indices by which vulnerability might be scientifically measured
(Füssel 2010: 601; Soares, Gagnon, and Doherty 2012). Indeed, the UNFCCC
has itself promoted such vulnerability assessments as part of its proposed
mechanisms for distributing international funding for adaptation. However, it
remains widely accepted that, as used in these assessments, the 'natural' science
is more highly developed than is the 'social'. In one major review, the US
National Research Council readily admitted that 'our understanding of the
impacts of climate changes on human well-being and vulnerabilities is much
less developed than our understanding of the natural climate system' (quoted
in Moser 2010: 466). Just as there are social constraints on the capacity of

individuals to adapt (and hence to reduce their sensitivity to climate change), so international society shapes this capacity of individual states. Accordingly, international society needs to be considered as a social system of opportunities and constraints: how it affects the capacity to respond to change generates its own distinctive pattern of vulnerability. It does so not only in terms of the policies that it elects to implement, but also with regard to the policies that it *fails* to adopt. Even more basically, it exercises its influence through its underlying conception of the problem, including how it conceives of the issue of vulnerability. This embodies its own social choices about what is to be made possible, or not, and produces a contingent configuration of vulnerabilities as a result. All of this reminds us of the extent to which the problems of climate change are embedded in much deeper social conditions, including its many 'existing inequities', and, in consequence, draws our attention to the 'underlying and often inequitable factors that contribute to vulnerability' (O'Brien, St Clair, and Kristoffersen 2010b: 8).

It is certainly the case that, on current trends and without successful efforts at mitigation, everyone is potentially exposed in the longer run to the negative impacts of climate change. However, that general risk is further mediated through the interventions of international society, both in terms of what it agrees to implement as policy, and just as importantly in terms of what it elects not to do by declining to take action. In practice, *universal* exposure is replaced by *selective* exposure, as international frameworks impact outcomes among those many priorities and competing versions of vulnerability that clamour for attention. The developed states certainly consider themselves to be exposed to the material consequences of changing climate. At the same time, they argue that they face other kinds of vulnerability as well, arising from international demands. Foremost among these is their perceived exposure to loss of comparative economic competitiveness—to the extent that developed countries take on non-reciprocal obligations to reduce emissions—thereby placing developing economies at a competitive advantage. This has demonstrably been the core objection raised by Congress—as in the Byrd-Hagel Resolution of 1997—and successive US administrations against the proclaimed 'unfairness' of the Kyoto approach. Moreover, those developed countries feel vulnerable to the financial demands emanating from the developing world that seeks assistance towards, and remedial compensation for, the mitigation and adaptation that they will also be compelled to undertake. On their side, in contrast, the developing countries feel even more exposed to the physical impacts of climate change, given their minimal adaptive capacity. However, they consider themselves additionally vulnerable to the risks of underdevelopment, to the extent that tackling climate might further impede their poverty-reduction strategies. There is no single conception of vulnerability associated with climate change, and international norms and frameworks impose their own mediated account of which of these contested variants should be prioritized and set in place. Accordingly, international society's interventions help to shape a distinctively social distribution of vulnerabilities, rather than one produced by nature alone.

What do the concepts of risk and vulnerability mean in the context of climate change, and who is exposed to its negative impacts? This section demonstrates how generic ideas of vulnerability have come to be applied in this policy sphere. This is a preliminary to showing how these notions have been expressed through the climate negotiations, and what specific effects result from this process. It reinforces the central point that there is an important difference between basic exposure to the physical impacts of climate change and the additional sensitivity created, over and above, by the entire social and political framing within which it occurs.

Ideas about vulnerability have become central to the analysis of climate change, and to conflicting assessments about what needs to be done to tackle it effectively. It is because climate change manifests itself through physical effects, but is at the same time deeply embedded in social practices, that it is politically so challenging. This theme is fully captured in the standard discourse about climate vulnerability, as set out in IPCC assessments, which presents it as a compound of three factors. It is typically summarized in the following version:

> Who is vulnerable to the changes and their impacts? . . . All of us are vulnerable to climate change, though to varying degrees . . .
>
> The propensity of people or systems to be harmed by stresses, referred to as vulnerability, is determined by their exposures to stresses, their sensitivity to the exposures, and their capacities to resist . . . The impacts will depend in part on the nature, rate and severity of the changes in climate. They will also depend to an important degree on social, economic, governance and other forces that determine who and what are exposed to climate stresses, their sensitivities to stresses, and their capacities. (AIACC 2007: 7)

We can see in this quotation the direct influence of the analysis previously set out in the IPCC reports, with its definition of the tripartite elements of vulnerability: exposure, sensitivity, and adaptive capacity (IPCC 2007; Polsky and Eakin 2011: 206). In the case of climate change, each of these three dimensions is heavily influenced by social structures and dynamics, as is the resultant overall distribution of vulnerability. On these crucial matters, the planet 'cannot speak for itself' (Hajer and Versteeg 2011: 82), and the actual pattern of vulnerability is in large measure what society, including international society, chooses to make of it.

That this is so is generally accepted, and is especially acknowledged with reference to how vulnerability tracks other social dimensions, particularly the distribution of wealth and poverty. 'Internationally, the disadvantaged are much more vulnerable to the negative impacts of climate change, both because these are expected to occur more often and more severely in areas of the world where they live . . . and because they have poorer support mechanisms with which to cope' (Gardiner 2011b: 311). Vulnerability thus is a compound of the 'natural' or physical world, acting along with the social, and it has been claimed that an 'integrated view', combining both these dimensions, is now the 'current paradigm' (Soares, Gagnon, and Doherty 2012: 10). If risk of harm is determined by such things as temperature and precipitation patterns, on the one hand, vulnerability is shaped also, on the other, 'by the fact that resources and wealth are distributed unevenly' (Olmas 2001: 3). These distributions are deeply embedded in the practices of international society. Accordingly, 'differential social outcomes associated with climate stress may have as much (or more) to do with historical inequities and disparities in the social and institutional context of human activity than with differential exposure to climate shocks' (Polsky and Eakin 2011: 207). These variable outcomes are, of course, found also in social structures within individual national societies. It is for this reason that climate change vulnerability displays a pronounced gender dimension, for example, with women suffering disproportionate exposure in some societies (Roy and Venema 2002; UNDP 2011).

Accordingly, we can trace in climate change that more general shift in understandings of vulnerability, away from any kind of 'natural' model, and towards one in which a *social vulnerability* assessment has become predomin-ant (Roberts and Parks 2007: 107). If risk connotes two distinct dimensions—magnitude of impact and the probability of its occurrence (Schneider 2007: 781)—then with regard to climate change both are affected by social inputs. The former certainly cannot be assessed without consideration of the affected population's resources and capacities to take adaptive or precautionary action. Crucially, then, 'the level of vulnerability is determined by the adverse conse-quences that remain after the process of adaptation has taken place' (quoted in Olmas 2001: 4).

Such a framing brings the capacity to adapt to the centre of our understand-ing of vulnerability. What it also makes clear is that sensitivity is in large measure a social variable, as in the case of the social 'sensitivity' of different socio-economic groups to the impacts of Hurricane Katrina. However, what such a social perspective does, in turn, is to generate complex international problems in distinguishing between those financial transfers required specif-ically to assist adaptation in the face of climate change, as opposed to the aid needed to promote economic development more generally (Baer 2011: 331): in this case, any discussion of climate vulnerability morphs readily into a much wider analysis of the conditions of underdevelopment and strategies for its rectification (Polsky and Eakin 2011: 210). This connection was readily acknowledged by President Obama when addressing the United Nations in 2009. He stressed the need to put the 'poorest and most vulnerable' on the path to sustainable growth because 'they do not have the same resources to combat climate change', but are 'already living with the unfolding effects of a warming planet' (*New York Times*, 23 September 2009). However, this was a partial acknowledgement at best: in 'objectifying' that condition of vulnerability, he did not address its full underlying nature.

In short, any fully comprehensive assessment of social vulnerability must include allocations socially made at the international level, and this is the perspective that this study brings to the forefront. How, and with what effects, has climate change vulnerability as a physical variable been translated into a social practice of the vulnerable in international society?

THE CLIMATE REGIME AND THE MAKING OF THE VULNERABLE

The international management of climate change has been explicitly subject to multilateral negotiation for well over twenty years. As a result, this process has imposed its own 'construction' on the nature of the problem and how best to deal with it (Depledge and Yamin 2009). At the very least, this reminds us of the important double jeopardy involved in climate change: exposure to the impacts of climate, along with exposure to the impacts of decisions of others about the collective response to this risk. International society already does much to shape the problem and the response by construing it as an *international* issue, to be addressed by states as unitary actors, thereby concealing internal variations in responsibility (profligate lifestyles of some sections of the population in developing countries, and high levels of exposure of some sectors of the population in developed countries) (Shearer 2012: 62). For some, it is precisely this international format of the negotiations that has already distorted key issues of climate justice (Harris 2010, 2011: 640–1).

Not only is climate change to be understood as an international problem, but it is to be tackled within specific, and restricted, parameters. Because climate change is understood in a particular way, as will be shown, there are inbuilt limits as to what may be done to mitigate it. As a result of this prevailing concept of climate change, international society works within its own chosen binaries and categories. The principal ones have been the developed versus developing states, and the major emitters of greenhouse gases (GHGs) as against the minor emitters. These categories have, in turn, done powerful work in configuring the limits of the response to the problem, and hence have created additional degrees of socially imposed risk.

In which specific ways has international society shaped our understanding of climate change, and how has this contributed to the resulting distribution of vulnerability? The major body under which climate change has been addressed internationally since 1992 has been the UNFCCC, and it has been suggested that the Rio Declaration of that year can be regarded as a 'universally accepted constitutional text' (Falkner 2012: 513) for governance of this issue. It is highly revealing to begin with the Framework Convention's own stated goal at the time: 'The ultimate objective of this Convention . . . is to achieve stabilization of greenhouse gas concentrations in the atmosphere at a level that would prevent dangerous anthropogenic interference in the climate system' (UNFCCC 1992). What this formulation conspicuously did not address was at which specific level this interference would become 'dangerous', and—very much to the present point—to whom. In the way in which it has subsequently, and in incremental fashion, offered some answers to those questions, international society has already had a profound impact on actual and potential distributions of vulnerability: not only is climate change anthropogenic, but so also are some of the resultant vulnerabilities to it.

The UNFCCC, for all its many necessary qualifications and equivocations, articulated a very clear concept of the climate change problem, and of the bounds within which it was to be tackled. This governing concept already determined how the vulnerable were to be understood, and what inevitable allocations would result from it. The core logic was set out in the many glosses included in its Preamble. These included the following noteworthy understandings. Climate change was presented as a 'common concern of mankind', and as such it called for 'the widest possible cooperation by all countries and their participation in an effective and appropriate international response'. At the same time, there were limits to what could be asked of the Parties, since 'States have . . . the sovereign right to exploit their own resources pursuant to their own environmental and developmental policies', and accordingly the Convention must respect 'the principle of sovereignty of States in international cooperation to address climate change'. While international society was acceding to new environmental responsibilities, it did so very much within the bounds of prevailing norms about sovereignty (Falkner 2012: 516). Even more so, the Convention limited its own purview by affirming overriding economic goals and values. In this respect, the Convention insisted that prevention of dangerous climate change must be consistent with its overall objective 'to enable economic development to proceed in a sustainable manner' (Article 2), that according to this basic purpose 'economic development is essential for adopting measures to address climate change' (Articles 3, 4), that 'various actions to address climate change can be justified economically in their own right' (Preamble), and that 'responses to climate change should be coordinated with social and economic development in an integrated manner with a view to avoiding adverse impacts on the latter' (Preamble). Moreover, mitigation action should be such as to sustain an 'open international economic system that would lead to sustainable economic growth and development in all Parties' (Articles 3, 5).

In short, this was not a charter for prevention of climate change at all costs. Instead, it was an agreement to approach climate change, understood as conceptually integrated with a commitment to economic growth, and in the context of a particular international economic system. It represented no 'neutral' response to the problem, but was an exposition of a concept of climate change, embedded in a powerful set of economic and political assumptions. In order to achieve these wider goals and commitments, the Convention had already approached climate change as a problem that, *in principle*, must be addressed by a number of trade-offs that would selectively impact the vulnerability of certain categories of people.

In all the routine statements emanating from the UNFCCC process, the stress throughout has been on the responsibilities of some states (see Bukovansky et al. 2012: Ch. 4), as a counterpoint to the vulnerabilities of others. For the most part, if not exclusively so, these two themes—responsibility and vulnerability—have been mapped onto the two broad groupings of developed and developing states, and this has become the standout feature of the climate negotiations to date. The principal way in which international society has intervened is thus by imposing on the nature of the problem this dichotomy between two categories of states—the developed and those still developing: responsibilities and obligations have been allocated primarily on the basis of respective membership of either of these two groups (Depledge and Yamin 2009: 445). Since the COP in Bali in 2007, this has been yet further institutionalized in the establishment of two separate tracks of negotiations, each with distinct memberships, one held under the Kyoto Protocol, and the other generally under the UNFCCC (Dimitrov 2010: 799–800; Vihma, Mulugetta, and Karlsson-Vinkhuyzen 2011: 324). Integral to the entire international management of climate has, therefore, been its assignment of asymmetrical entitlements and obligations, as allocated between those two distinct categories: anything that could not readily be accommodated within that framework has, as a result, been precluded by default. It is in this respect that the imprint of international society is most clearly visible.

This binary approach has taken place within the multilateral forum of the UNFCCC, although this format had already become a notable source of controversy from the very outset. Major developed countries, especially the United States, had initially pushed for climate change to be discussed within a technical committee of the United Nations Environment Programme (UNEP) and the World Meteorological Organization (WMO). It was the developing countries that resisted any arrangement of this kind, and insisted instead on a wide political negotiation within the UN framework (Okereke 2010: 45–6). The reason for this preference was evidently to ensure that deep-seated political problems were not pushed aside in favour of seemingly more convenient technocratic solutions. Moreover, this sensibility on the part of the developing countries betrayed one overriding concern: that their greatest vulnerability was to decisions of the more powerful. This concern has been abiding, and was again expressed at the COP15 in Copenhagen in 2009, and particularly in response to the ad hoc grouping that emerged between the BASIC countries (Brazil, South Africa, India, and China) and the United States.

In turn, the key vulnerability felt by many of those states has been about their potential loss of political voice. Indeed, if anything, what the past few years have revealed is the widening fissures between different groups of developing states, each with slightly different interests in the outcome of the negotiations. This can be illustrated at several levels. Until recently, what had unified the G77 was its insistence that the developed countries must act first on mitigation, before there could be any consideration of international commitments on the part of developing states. Accordingly, countries like Egypt protested at the holding of climate change discussions in the UN Security Council, criticizing it as an attempt to promote 'shared responsibilities' (Vihma, Mulugetta, and Karlsson-Vinkhuyzen 2011: 321), contrary to the UNFCCC principle of differentiated responsibility (Dimitrov 2010: 804). This unity is no longer so steadfast, with several developing states now voicing the need for contributions from the major developing emitters as well (Vihma, Mulugetta, and Karlsson-Vinkhuyzen 2011: 330–1). Elsewhere, there has been resistance to the claims of current oil exporters to be eligible for adaptation funding, on grounds of their purported 'vulnerability' to shifts in energy demand. Saudi Arabia, for instance, has promoted its concern for those who are 'victims to policy mitigating climate change' (quoted in Vihma, Mulugetta, and Karlsson-Vinkhuyzen 2011: 328). Most other least-developed countries (LDCs) have been largely unsympathetic to those suggestions.

If the division into the categories of developed and developing states has been the principal 'firewall' to date, it has recently been challenged, and is in effect being replaced, by one between major emitters and the rest. The reasoning underlying this transition has been simply that only by capturing all the major emitters within a single legal framework (but not necessarily with the same obligations under it) can there be any effective solution to the problem. This was the argument, for example, that Britain's then Secretary of State for Energy and Climate Change, Chris Huhne, set out in a speech to the Grantham Institute on 24 November 2011: 'We need to move to a system that reflects the genuine diversity of responsibility and capacity, rather than a binary one which says you are "developed" if you happened to be in the OECD in 1992' (UK Parliament 2012). The important point for the present argument is that, *whichever* specific categories international society elects to work with (be it developed, or big emitters), this generic modus operandi necessarily has serious consequences for the resultant distribution of vulnerability.

This issue continues to manifest itself in resistance to proposals for delegating the negotiations to any other 'minilateral' group of major emitters (Eckersley 2012b), as a possible supplement, or substitute, to acting through the UNFCCC. Some informed observers have insisted that major progress does now indeed require resort to these more select forums, with the role of the

UNFCCC becoming to 'verify and legitimise actions and decisions' taken elsewhere (Smith School 2011: 19). This alternative approach has been viewed as necessary for progress, given the manifest reluctance of the two biggest emitters, China and the United States, to submit to any internationally imposed targets for emissions. The perennial concern about all such proposals has been that any forum of this kind, if confined exclusively to major emitters, would disempower 'the main victims of climate change: the small island states, LDCs, and other poorer developing countries' (Depledge and Yamin 2009: 451).

We can trace the depiction of vulnerability that emerges from this structuring in the history of the multilateral negotiations, through the various landmark conventions and COPs, from Rio in 1992 to Durban in 2011. Of particular relevance here was the sixth principle of the Rio Declaration. This affirmed that the 'special situation and needs of developing countries, particularly the least developed and those most environmentally vulnerable, shall be given special priority' (quoted in Harris 2010: 67). While this did not specify the level at which GHG concentration becomes dangerous, it certainly began to structure understanding of exposure to the impacts of climate change in one specific way. In particular, it focused attention on the special needs of the 'environmentally vulnerable', and of the 'least developed'. Whether the former were to be considered vulnerable because of the latter condition, or for separate reasons, is again not made fully clear. However, at the very least, a strong association was immediately established between climate change vulnerability and the level of economic development. Moreover, according to Article 3 of the Framework Convention, full consideration had to be given to the 'specific needs and special circumstances of developing country Parties, especially those that are particularly vulnerable to the adverse effects of climate change' (UNFCCC 1992: Articles 3, 2). With regard to the Kyoto Protocol in 1997, its Clean Development Mechanism employed the very same formulation to ensure funds were directed to those countries in particular 'to meet the costs of adaptation' (UNFCCC 1998: 12). Again, what is not clarified is what it is that makes some states 'particularly vulnerable' to climate impacts. By implication, this is simply an existential condition that happens to befall some (to varying degrees).

The subsequent Bali roadmap reiterated similar themes, but with some yet further refinement. It confirmed the requirement for enhanced adaptation actions 'to enable climate-resilient development and reduce vulnerability *of all Parties*', while at the same time drawing attention to the 'urgent and immediate needs of developing countries that are particularly vulnerable to the adverse effects of climate change, especially the least-developed countries and small island developing states' (UNFCCC 2007: 4, emphasis added). In this version, climate vulnerability was indeed deemed to be universal, while over and above there remained pressing claims for special consideration from particular groups of states. Similar formulations have been reiterated since, including at COP16 in Cancún in December 2010 (UNFCCC 2010: 4).

We can now track the evolution of this de facto distribution of vulnerability in those disputes that have marked the negotiations to date. Fundamentally, regardless of the specific language actually deployed, these have been about the different ways in which vulnerability should be allocated, and the implications for vulnerability of adopting, or not adopting, specific courses of action. In the categories that it has deployed, international society has had a marked impact on those outcomes.

THE CLASH OF VULNERABILITIES

There are two separate types of concern about what might be emerging internationally in response to climate change. The first is that there is insufficient political agreement about how vulnerabilities are to be distributed to allow for sufficiently purposeful concerted action, at least on required timetables. The second—in the event of the former—is that if some arrangement is emerging without any underlying consensus, it simply reflects the preferences of the most powerful. To the extent that it does, it will perpetuate one possible allocation of vulnerability. Any such outcome reproduces those very conditions that were the subject of Carr's attack on the dominant peacemakers at Versailles: a climate regime is emerging by default, but it is imposed by the strongest, and lacks acceptance by the rest, because it is held to lack any foundations in justice. What this highlights is some general characteristics of the social practice of the vulnerable in all areas, given an imperfect international consensus on values and taken together with marked disparities in material power.

The structuring of the entire issue around the two groups of developed and developing states has generated a heated contestation about vulnerability. Both sides in the negotiation have advanced their own preferred conception, each pressing for its own version and for adoption of the various priorities associated with it. The result has been a dispute configured around the developed and developing countries, with vulnerability at its core.

This clash has been yet further intensified by the shifting balance of climatic power: this is towards the relatively greater contribution of GHG emissions now made by fast-developing countries. There has as yet been no radical transformation in historic nor in per capita terms, but the trend is marked with respect to the relative shares of aggregate global emissions per annum. It is widely accepted that China overtook the USA as the largest single emitter in 2007. China accounts for approximately 24 per cent of annual global emissions, and some projections place China's future share at 37 per cent by 2030 (Garnaut, Jutzo, and Howes 2008: 180). India has now emerged as the third largest emitter. Over the next quarter century, the developing countries combined will be the source of 75 per cent of the growth in global emissions (Stern and Antholis 2007/8: 183). It is this trajectory that has underpinned the crucial role played by the BASIC states over the last few years (Xinran 2011). Overall, this has contributed to the vulnerability felt in the developed world that they are no longer capable of solving the problem on their own. To some developed countries this has become the primary reason to question those differentiated obligations under the Kyoto Protocol, as if the slate of historical responsibility can now be wiped clean. To developing countries this trend in emissions is only fair, as it symbolizes the developmental catch-up that is their due: what is now placed at risk is their opportunity to pursue it. In any case, aggregate national emissions omit to tell the quite different story about per capita emissions, where countries like China and India fall much further down the league tables: on some reckonings, they appear in places 78 and 139 respectively (Xinran 2011: 299).

Just how strident the conflict between their respective positions was to become can be fully illustrated by the periodic accusations made by African spokesmen that developed countries' emissions are tantamount to an 'act of aggression', or to 'low intensity biological or chemical warfare' against the developing world (quoted in Brown, Hammill, and McLeman 2007: 1142). Even more stridently, the spokesperson for Sudan criticized the Copenhagen Accord as 'murderous', and requiring a 'suicide pact' on the part of African states, before going on to make his infamous allusions to the Holocaust (Dimitrov 2010: 811). However melodramatic the rhetoric, what that language conveys is one powerful sense of vulnerability, equating the case of climate with other resorts to political violence. What is so interesting about these metaphors is the emotional appeal they make to the assumed innocence of the victims.

This binary opposition has conspicuously shaped the politics of climate change over the past two decades and has been the single most important obstacle to any progress. This has already had real-life impacts on particular members of international society. While the UNFCCC encouraged parties to prevent 'dangerous' increases in temperature, it left unresolved for a lengthy period the precise level of increase that was considered dangerous. The resolution of this issue, in effect by a non-decision, provides one clear illustration of how international society contributes to the distribution of vulnerability. Insofar as an international consensus has only latterly developed around the declared need to prevent any more than a two-degree increase in temperature (increasingly formalized at Copenhagen in 2009 and Cancún in 2010), those at risk to increases occurring *below* this level have already, in effect, been rendered more vulnerable as a result of those decisions, and the failure to reach them sooner. It is no surprise, then, that at Copenhagen in 2009 the group of small island states (AOSIS) pressed very hard for a target of 1.5 degrees instead 'because of their extreme vulnerability to sea-level rise' (Steffen 2011: 24; see Christoff 2010: 641). As the delegate from Grenada made poignantly clear at the COP, 'as small island states going under water . . . we stand to lose the most if nothing happens here' (quoted in Dimitrov 2010: 805).

In refusing to adopt any more ambitious target (even if not finally closing the door on it, as it is subject to review in 2015), international society has de facto entrenched the vulnerability of those left more exposed as a result. The effect of its choice not to pursue a more demanding goal has been an actual increase in the level of risk posed to some of its members. In this way, their 'sensitivity' is as much down to international decisions as it is directly to sea-level rise. Since they are, in the words of the President of the Maldives, the 'canaries in the coalmine' (Benwell 2011; McAdam 2012: 118), the principal vulnerability experienced by AOSIS countries is to international society's *target*. It also results from international society's imposed *timetable*, as we shall see. If an international agreement is not to take effect until 2020, as envisaged under the Durban Platform, then that will generate its own impacts, as the Head of UNEP, Achim Steiner, has protested: 'Those countries that are currently talking about deferring an agreement [to come into force] in 2020 are essentially saying we are taking you from high risk to very high risk . . . This is a choice—a political choice' (*The Guardian*, 23 November 2011). Demonstrably, if so, this is international society's choice.

The medium through which these competing conceptions of vulnerability have been pressed has been the general principle in the UNFCCC of 'common but differentiated responsibilities' (CBDR). On the one hand, this represents an area of broad agreement, given its inclusion in the original climate convention, and captures the partial consensus that has underpinned the climate regime: it would be wholly misleading to think of the regime evolving as a norm-free zone. On the other, there has remained throughout substantial differences in interpretation as to its actual meaning (Bukovansky et al. 2012: ch. 4; Steffek 2006). The developed countries have mostly understood it to refer only to the greater financial and technological capabilities that they possess, whereas the developing countries have viewed these differentiated responsibilities 'from the optic of culpability' with respect to historical responsibility (Okereke 2010: 51). The language of the UNFCCC has tended to fall somewhere in the middle of these two positions. Its statement of principle in Article 3 went no further than to affirm the aspiration that the 'developed country Parties should take the lead' (UNFCCC 1992), whereas in other statements, such as at the 2010 COP16 in Cancún, there has been a fuller admission that this leadership requirement results from 'historical responsibility', insofar as 'the largest share of historical global emissions of greenhouse gases originated in developed countries' (UNFCCC 2010: 8).

It is this issue of CBDR that maps out the morally most highly contested terrain, and lies at the centre of the social practice of the vulnerable in this area. From the perspective of the least-developed countries, the onus lies squarely on the developed world to take the lead in reducing emissions and to transfer funding to assist others to adapt, without in any way sacrificing the former's developmental aspirations. At the heart of the complex politics of climate change has been this guiding idea that, whatever mitigation strategies are adopted, they must not be at the cost of the 'right to development' (Kartha 2011: 505). This view has been most strenuously pressed by those states that fall into the category of 'least responsible, weakest capacity and most vulnerable' (Christoff and Eckersley 2011: 439). For most of the period of negotiations up to Kyoto and beyond, the principle of CBDR has been accepted by the developed states, but without necessarily sharing the same reason for its adoption (Steffek 2006: 124–5). In more recent years, some developed states, including particularly the United States, have openly challenged the continuing validity of this principle on the grounds that there must now be more symmetrical (if not identical) obligations on the part of both categories if meaningful reductions in emissions are to be achieved. The EU too now endorses this approach, and has helped to prepare the diplomatic ground for an alternative to this existing 'binary' or 'firewall', through the participation in the Cartagena Dialogue since Copenhagen of several EU states (Eckersley 2012a: 20–1). While this debate has been conducted mostly through the language of emissions targets and possible future funding transfers, what has more fundamentally been at stake is how the risks of exposure to climate change are actually to be distributed: whose account of vulnerability is international society to endorse, or which compromise between competing accounts is now politically and ethically most sustainable?

What captures the wider ramifications of this debate has been the insistence throughout by the developing world that mitigation must not come at the price of its own development. Just as the principle of CBDR papered over some of the deep cracks about how climate change should be tackled, so the notion of sustainable development has been deployed to square the circle of continuing development, even in the context of deep emissions reductions (Helm 2009b: 227): both principles have, as a result, become inseparable intellectual stablemates (Depledge and Yamin 2009: 435; Harris 2010: 66), each insisting that collective goals can be achieved, without either group having to sacrifice its principal objectives. As Chinese premier Wen insisted at Copenhagen, 'action on climate change must be taken within the framework of sustainable development and should in no way compromise the efforts of developing countries to get rid of poverty' (quoted in Christoff 2010: 646). In short, the pretence has been that there exists a basic harmony of interests in which all goals are achievable without any heightened vulnerability on anyone's part. The practice, in fact, has been that the resulting partial or non-action on the part of international society has already aggravated the vulnerability of some to a far greater extent than that of the others. International society has intensified this skewed distribution in what it has so far decided not to undertake by way of a response.

Social distributions potentially increase the exposure to climate change of already physically at-risk states in a number of ways. For instance, the problems are more severe in Africa because its economies are so closely tied to agriculture, and hence more sensitive to climatic variation (Collier, Conway, and Venables 2009: 125). The greatest exposure is to changes in precipitation and impacts on agriculture, flooding, new challenges in health, and sea-level rise (particularly in the Nile delta) (Collier, Conway, and Venables 2009: 127–30). Some of these impacts will no doubt result in movements of people, forced to flee these adverse conditions, and accordingly the problems of climate change vulnerability will overlap considerably with the problems of human movement. Just as migrants are often the most vulnerable category of people in any event, they become doubly so when exposed additionally to the risks of climate change (Kälin 2009; Hanna 2011). Similarly exposed is the group of indigenous peoples, often intimately dependent on the resources provided by existing patterns of climate (Ford and Pearce 2012; Shearer 2012). Their lifestyles are now rendered acutely vulnerable. Accordingly, the Convention on Biological Diversity attested that 'indigenous and local communities are among the first to face the direct adverse consequences of climate change, due to their dependence upon and close relationship with the environment and its resources' (UNEP 2007, quoted in Figueroa 2011: 232). Here is a category of people that has always been rendered vulnerable by the legal impositions of an alien international society, and that is now further exposed by international society's timid response to the management of climate change.

This ongoing clash over vulnerabilities has been exacerbated by the fact that remedial efforts to date appear very modest, to say the least. The UNFCCC, enjoying almost universal membership, came into force in 1994, but without entailing any specific commitments. These were subsequently negotiated over the three succeeding COPs, culminating in Kyoto in 1997. The commitment undertaken by the Kyoto Protocol Annex 1 countries was for average reductions (with 1990 as the base year) of some 5 per cent by the end of the first commitment period in 2012. Within these, the EU had a target of 8 per cent, USA 7 per cent, and Japan 6 per cent. The United States never ratified the treaty. Moreover, as is well known, the treaty established no specified reduction targets for developing countries, in accordance with the UNFCCC principle of CBDR. As a result, even if fully successful in its own terms, Kyoto would deliver very little towards necessary reduction targets.

Much the same can be said of the Copenhagen Accord. Although the majority of states had signed up to it, their combined commitments appeared likely to place global temperatures on a trajectory headed for at least a three-degree increase, with 'significant risks for human society' (Backstrand 2011: 675; Smith School 2011: 14). The stated target of restricting temperature rise to within two degrees, on its own, was regarded as largely unconvincing given, as

an Oxfam International spokesman commented in 2009, that it was accompanied by 'no attempt to turn down the heat any time soon' (quoted in Nanda
2011b: 2). Commitments under the Accord were calculated to deliver at most
some 12–19 per cent reduction in emissions by 2020, against the widely
acknowledged IPCC requirement of a 40 per cent reduction (Christoff 2010:
641–2), thereby leaving a very large gap between the pledges and what the
science said was actually needed. Even more to the point, such an outcome
would guarantee a particular distribution of vulnerability in which those societies already at risk would find their exposure significantly heightened. At the
same time, their vulnerability to a deteriorating climate is already intensifying
those juxtaposed claims to vulnerability issuing from the affluent North, given
the prospect of further migrations from the South (Doyle and Chaturvedi 2011:
288). In this way, the vulnerability of the South, substantially heightened by
international society's own actions, is itself being inverted and presented as a
counterclaim about the increased risk now presented by the South. In these
incoherent ways has the clash of vulnerabilities played out in the negotiations.

WHO ARE THE VULNERABLE?

There are many prominent sources of division remaining amongst the negotiating parties (Christoff 2010: 638). The first is obviously the scale of cuts still
to be agreed after 2012. The IPCC's current requirement is for reductions of
25–40 per cent by 2020, at which point emissions need to peak, and thereafter
begin to fall back in absolute terms. Such deep cuts, US climate envoy Todd
Stern had insisted early on, were 'not on the cards' (*The Guardian*, 24 June
2009). Instead, targets subsequently notified under the Copenhagen Accord
were largely at levels that had been previously announced: 17 per cent reduction from 2005 levels by the USA, 20 per cent from 1990 levels by 2020 by the
EU, 25 per cent from 1990 levels by Japan, and 5–25 per cent from 2000 levels
by Australia (McKibben, Morris, and Wilcoxen 2010: 6).

Secondly, there is the deep-seated issue of whether and how developing
countries are expected to contribute. Copenhagen had broadly endorsed a
bottom-up 'pledge-and-review', rather than a top-down international target,
style of agreement (Christoff 2010: 653; Smith School 2011: 12). Key targets
notified under the Copenhagen Accord have been a cut in emissions *intensity*
of 40–45 per cent from 2005 levels by China, and 20–25 per cent by India; cuts
from Business as Usual (BAU) of 34 per cent for South Africa, and 36–39 per
cent for Brazil (McKibben, Morris, and Wilcoxen 2010: 6). For historical
reasons, the developing world is profoundly sceptical of the likelihood of
satisfactory financial transfers becoming available to support their efforts,
and there are solid grounds for this scepticism (Smith School 2011: 14).

It remains unclear just how far the COP17 at Durban in December 2011 has moved this process along. It inaugurated what is known as the Durban Platform on Enhanced Action. Critically, this makes no mention of previous formulae about CBDR. If Copenhagen signalled a de facto breach in the firewall between developed and developing countries—a breach regarded by some commentators as a highly positive development (Smith School 2011: 13)—then Durban appeared to indicate a *de jure* ratification of its abandonment. It was widely publicized as heralding a future legal treaty that would embrace all the major emitters, including the developed and developing. Unlike Kyoto, this would place all the major emitters on an equal legal footing, and embrace them within a single framework. This was widely regarded as a major breakthrough. It is to be agreed by 2015, and implemented by 2020. The relatively long gap before implementation was understood to have been a necessary concession to get the key BASIC countries, China and India, as well as the United States, on board. However, there is sufficient ambiguity in the actual wording of the Durban Platform to leave considerable doubt as to what exactly is intended, let alone what will finally eventuate. Its key passage was as follows:

> *Decides* that the Ad Hoc Working Group on the Durban Platform for Enhanced Action should complete its work as early as possible but no later than 2015 in order to adopt this protocol, another legal instrument or an *agreed outcome with legal force* at the twenty-first session of the Conference of the Parties and for it to come into effect and be implemented from 2020. (UNFCCC 2011, Article 4: 2, emphasis added)

This wording left broad latitude about the precise form of any future arrangement; nor is it absolutely clear that the 'legal' aspect will apply specifically to emission reduction rather than to other parts of its climate programme. Equally, there remained considerable scepticism about the credibility of the further steps taken in regard to the Green Climate Fund and the existing commitment to support it by contributions to the tune of $100 billion per year, given the generally straitened international financial environment. While the Kyoto Protocol was to be extended for a further commitment period for the EU, this did nothing to capture the very largest national emissions; some countries were unprepared to undertake a second commitment period (such as Russia and Japan); and there were further withdrawals from the Protocol, as in the case of Canada.

All these complex problems become, in turn, seriously compounded when issues of fairness and justice are taken into consideration. Some of the specific issues that continue to bedevil the negotiations are viewed as problems of justice, relating to the *substance* of climate change solutions, and others as relating to the *process* of arriving at these solutions.

There are a number of issues that fall under the first heading, as matters of *substance*. For illustrative purposes, three will be briefly considered: the kind of targets for reduction that would be considered fair, and whether these need to be on a per capita basis; the difficulties of national accounting of emissions, given the problem of 'outsourcing'; and the relative balance between adaptation and mitigation.

To reiterate, no global deal is likely to emerge that is not widely considered to be fair (Füssel 2010: 597; Young 2011: 627). But which criteria of fairness are relevant to this assessment? Thus far, national targets in agreements such as the Kyoto Protocol and the Copenhagen Accord are precisely that: aggregate reduction targets for the country as a whole. Such an approach is widely criticized because it does not take into account population size, and hence gives a measure of emissions that disregards their per capita distribution. It also ignores the wide disparities in contributions to emissions within a national population. This is the basis of the case that Harris makes, that a purely interstate deal flouts basic principles of justice because it does not take into account these marked internal discrepancies (Harris 2010). As an alternative, many have advocated an approach to climate mitigation that stresses instead per capita measurements, and possibly movement towards adoption of an equal per capita emissions allowance. Proponents of such an approach emphasize its virtues of simplicity and practicality, and above all its appeal to fairness (Garnaut 2008: 202). This last aspect is clearly crucial, but is politically toxic in developed countries, as any fair allocation per head based on historic usage would inevitably require swift, and draconian, cuts in developed country allowances. It is this requirement for fairness that makes it so terribly problematic, and fairness rests on moral judgements, not simply technical assessments. How those ideas of fairness are, in turn, put into practice has major implications for the resulting patterns of vulnerability.

A second substantive problem is that of leakage in the form of what is usually described as the outsourcing of national emissions. Are national emissions to be calculated simply on the basis of where goods are produced, or in terms of the final destination where they are consumed? Where does responsibility for emissions finally rest, with the producer or the consumer (Helm 2009a: 21)? This more nuanced question challenges any simple statistical portrayal of the reductions of emissions in the developed world and a commensurate increase in that of the developing states. Instead, some of that shift is attributable to the export of 'dirty' industries to China and elsewhere, with no sacrifice of consumption levels in the developed world where the goods produced finally end up (Christoff and Eckersley 2011: 432). What this points to is yet another market failure with respect to climate change. While the distribution of production facilities globally may follow a race to the bottom in terms of costs, there is no overall market logic that seeks to locate those facilities in places where the energy intensities are lowest. If anything, the opposite seems to pertain (Pan, Phillips, and Chen 2009: 159).

Thirdly, there is the vexed package of issues revolving around the relative pursuit of mitigation and adaptation strategies. Virtually all responses to climate change require both mitigation and adaptation, but there are potentially also difficult trade-offs to be made, and these choices have differential impacts on a variety of populations. Some enjoy a greater capability to pursue the latter, and there is then always the risk that the strong will 'substitute the local public good of adaptation for the global public good of mitigation' (Barrett 2009: 76). Others, meanwhile, have a greater stake in the active pursuit of mitigation instead. The balance that is finally struck between these two approaches can have 'potentially negative consequences for the vulnerable', and this exposes its stark 'moral dimension' (Adger, Brown, and Waters 2011: 699). In short, of the many ways in which international society distributes vulnerability, a key instrument is the choices it may be led to make about the balance of effort between these respective objectives.

Similar ethical concerns inform the *process* of responding to climate change. Of all the vulnerabilities to which the smaller developing countries feel exposed, none is more significant than the sense of vulnerability to decisions dictated by those who have a different set of climate priorities. Hence the insistence of these countries on an inclusive negotiating forum. However, the downside of this commitment to a broadly based regime has been the very slow pace of the negotiations, and a set of targets for reduction of emissions that falls well short of what is required to achieve the goal of stabilizing any increase in mean temperature to within two degrees Celsius. This was well illustrated in the original Framework Convention: to ensure its inclusiveness, it had to sacrifice any specific commitments or reduction targets (Okereke 2010: 47). In that sense, the main problem to emerge has been the seeming contradiction between the politically most acceptable and legitimate format of negotiations and the likely effectiveness of outcome that this process is capable of delivering: the principal deficit in climate governance has been one of performance (Helm 2009a: 10; Harris 2011: 640). This outcome has already had direct consequences for the vulnerability of some states and peoples.

Accordingly, what has emerged is a wider issue of whether the negotiations belong solely within the UN framework, or whether these might be supplemented within some alternative forum. The problem with Kyoto, for instance, was that while it left out too many states that seriously mattered, it also included too many that simply did not (Busby 2009: 89). On the other side, it has been noted, supporters of any alternative 'exclusive minilateralism appear ready to sacrifice procedural justice at the altar of an efficient and best-practical outcome that ensures the buy-in of the major emitters' (Eckersley 2012b: 25). For that reason, there have been numerous proposals in recent years for the adoption of some alternative forum for climate change, instead of through the universalism of the UNFCCC. Whatever the shortcomings of the UNFCCC COPs, their great virtue, so it is claimed, is their 'unique status as inclusive venues' (Dobriansky and Turekian 2009/10: 22–3).

Another facet of this concern manifested itself in the actual negotiating dynamic at Copenhagen, with regard to the small caucus of states that managed finally to push through the face-saving Accord. Accordingly, the Copenhagen COP has been criticized for weak outcomes, but just as much for procedural shortcomings, in that it infringed the universal open multilateralism that is supposed to be the hallmark of the UNFCCC approach. Its major failing, in this respect, was that its process was seen to be undemocratic (Dimitrov 2010: 810; Vihma, Mulugetta, and Karlsson-Vinkhuyzen 2011: 326), even if this was largely attributable to failings of the presidency. Within the G77, there were specific complaints about the lack of transparency, including on the part of the BASIC group (Xinran 2011: 307). As a result, there have been suggestions that this has resulted in a 'legitimacy crisis for international climate diplomacy' (Backstrand 2011: 669). To the extent that this might be so, this has actual consequences for resulting vulnerabilities: a stalemate in international society's response does not, regrettably, put climate change on hold while it is sorted out. If we cannot negotiate with nature, neither should we expect it to show sympathy for the sluggish tempo of international deliberations. Of all the current ways in which international society distributes vulnerability, none is more significant than its protracted delay in taking serious action.

This is the key to understanding the essence of the problem. While it is tempting to succumb to the metaphor that 'we're all in the same boat', this logic needs to be rejected (Hajer and Versteeg 2011: 88). The salient dilemma is precisely the differential range of risk and exposure to which climate change gives rise, and the variable and contingent distribution of vulnerabilities that result. This latter feature is now commonly recognized. For example, even if Africa is the most vulnerable continent, the degree of risk even within that continent ranges widely (IPCC 2007: 65; Collier, Conway, and Venables 2009). More generally, the problematic feature of climate change inheres exactly in this 'inequality in the distribution of risk' (Barnett, Matthew, and O'Brien 2010; J. Barnett 2011: 272), and the corresponding challenge is to find an 'equitable sharing of risks and costs' (Gough and Meadowcroft 2011: 494; see also Dryzek, Norgaard, and Schlosberg 2011b: 9). The search for equity, however, brings out the moral complexity of the issue. All this is compounded by the fact that 'the wealthy people who seem to be least vulnerable to climate change are those who are the most responsible for the problem' (J. Barnett 2011: 272). This dimension injects a yet further ethical twist into the very heart of the policy debate.

To the extent that climate change is induced by human activities, there can in any case be no wholly natural distribution of vulnerability to its impacts. For that reason, what climate change demonstrates is 'the way in which certain *natural* phenomena are conceptualized within *institutional* practices' (Hajer and Versteeg 2011: 83). If we accept this, then quite literally it is true that 'climate change is as much a social problem as an environmental problem'

(J. Barnett 2011: 271): as such, it is a major problem for international society in particular.

CONCLUSION

Vulnerability is a key concept in understanding the consequences of climate change. However, vulnerability is not some condition that is already out there, simply awaiting our detection and measurement. Vulnerability is in many ways a projection of the social structures that create climate change in the first place, and also of the distribution of capabilities that differentially empower or disempower segments of society in responding to it. Social attributes, as much as physical processes, are a fundamental part of this spatial map of vulnerability. One highly pertinent social structure has been international society, and it has been deeply implicated in the distribution of climate vulnerability.

Nowhere is this more clearly so than in the way it has imposed its own rigid structure on the issue. For the most part, and since the UNFCCC, this has created a polarized debate between the developed and developing worlds, each with its own set of differentiated responsibilities. More recently, this has been supplemented with a new division into large and small emitters. The very language of the convention seems to recognize the fundamentally moral character of the problem it seeks to address. However, this has been largely superficial, and the seemingly moral division of labour between the two sets of claimants has, in fact, provided a recipe for political inaction. Unfortunately, the outcome of this stalemate has not been neutral for the distribution of vulnerability. On the contrary, the failure to act has entrenched existing disparities, and significantly aggravated them in some cases: while the political response may have been frozen, the physical manifestations of the problem have not, and these continue to accelerate apace. This is an outcome that international society, by its non-action, seems prepared to tolerate. It has done so to the extent that it has not developed a politics capable of dealing with the deep-seated ethical issues that it confronts. Its non-decisions to date are a measure of this failure.

The moral problem at the heart of climate change results from its two interrelated asymmetries: one of power on the one hand, and one between vulnerability and responsibility on the other. The former intensifies the latter in a morally vicious circle. The result is that, while the vulnerable are exposed to the forces of nature, their vulnerability is even more a consequence of their exposure to the decisions of powerful others over which they have little control. The great moral challenge at the heart of climate change politics goes beyond its own anthropogenic causal story: it demands, in addition, awareness of its own anthropogenic distribution of vulnerability to those very physical forces that it has itself helped to unleash.

4

Human Movement and the Vulnerable

Why should we consider the vulnerable in the context of human movement? There are two good reasons. First, when on the move, people face a combination of risky conditions, heightened by a degree of socially produced vulnerability to those hazards (McAdam 2012: 4, fn. 15). Secondly, it has been pointed out that the best starting place for consideration of this particular topic is exactly with the notion of vulnerability, since that is a term 'already widely used and operationalized in the international policy community serving refugees, displaced persons, and other individuals in need of assistance' (Suhike 2003: 105–6). If this is a subject already routinely approached through the language of vulnerability, and in which ideas of social vulnerability are prominent, it presents the possibility of a highly effective third case study.

Moreover, in no other field is this distribution of vulnerability so integral to the very normative structure of international society. While seemingly deployed just as empirical signifiers, its operative concepts and categories also have deeply normative consequences (Haddad 2008: 25). International society straightforwardly distributes vulnerability, since the way it implements its own categories is often 'a matter of life and death' (Haddad 2008: 45). For example, the specific category of refugees can be understood only 'with the very workings of international society', and, in effect, 'without an international states system there would be no refugees' (Haddad 2008: 4). We therefore need to be highly attuned to the normative underpinnings of the vulnerabilities that arise in the context of human movement.

At the same time, we must be cognizant of the fact that 'the main characteristic of the international politics of migration is power asymmetry' (Betts 2011c: 315). In its approach to human movement, international society has displayed elements of considerable consensus, both with respect to the need to regulate that movement while also leaving key decisions about admission to the individual states. In that 'anarchic' setting, significant hierarchies do come into play, with the result that powerful states have influenced the agendas about human emigration in the past, just as they now set the agenda with respect to immigration. Once again, vulnerability effectively brings together the twin issues of power and morality, and it does so through those profound inequalities that pervade management of this issue.

This topic is additionally revealing because of its very intimate connections to our other cases of violence, climate, and health. All of these have potentially close associations with human movement. The broad question that this poses is: if international society does have a Responsibility to Protect, how widely should that responsibility now be cast, and can the responsibility be assigned in one area without simultaneous consideration of other related areas of similar need (Davies and Glanville 2010b: 2)? In the case of human movement, however, international society has if anything actively encouraged a fragmented approach, preferring to treat separately those who may otherwise be experiencing very similar conditions: its focus has been upon the distinct triggers for movement (political persecution, for instance, rather than climate insecurity), to the neglect of the difficulties experienced in common once it is undertaken, and regardless of motivation.

Issues of human movement are, in any event, inextricably bound up with the development of international society, and profoundly affected by its deeply embedded norms. It is hard to think of any other dimension of human life where the highly selective impact of those norms on individuals is so clearly demonstrated. This is so because international society views that human movement through its own distinctive conceptual lens. Even more to the point, it is the way in which international society has approached and defined human movement that has become the proximate source of many of the problems confronting the peoples engaged in it. Moreover, we gain a clear insight into the powerful impact of the categories used by international society to manage this issue: it is through these that it proactively distributes the risks to which individuals become exposed. In many areas, such as the internally displaced, or human movements induced by climate, analysts have accordingly identified a plethora of protection and normative 'gaps' in prevailing arrangements (Martin 2010: 30; McAdam 2012: 1).

These have led to calls for coordination across issue areas so that 'responses are cross-cutting, complementary, and holistic' (McAdam 2012: 270), rather than disaggregated as is currently the case. These 'gaps' represent the socially allocated degrees of vulnerability that are to be found in this area. In response, a number of intergovernmental organizations have been created, committed generally to the 'management' of migration as a whole. Unhappily, rather than ensuring 'greater coherence', these have if anything added to institutional proliferation and fragmentation. There are reasons to doubt that this will be resolved any time soon, as this very fragmentation appears to be considered 'functional' by states, precisely because it maximizes their own selectivity in deciding 'what issues they wish to address in which institutional context' (Geiger and Pécoud 2010b: 4–5).

These gaps occur both *within* the area of human movement, and *between* it and other issues. For example, international society operates inconsistently and selectively, when its regimes for movement and global health are placed side by side. In tandem, both seek increasingly to protect those vulnerable to the spread of epidemics arising from the movement of other peoples, by keeping 'in quarantine' those most likely to transmit disease (and hence by policing their movement). At the same time, the global health regime is further distorted by selectively allowing the free movement from developing countries of trained health professionals to staff developed-country health facilities. In short, the precise balance between regulation and laissez-faire in the movement of people seems calibrated, in both directions, to best suit the needs of those already enjoying the greatest advantages. The vulnerabilities of some are catered for by the creation of deeper configurations of vulnerability elsewhere, and in this respect international society's institutions for the management of human movement and health appear jointly complicit in producing outcomes that are unstable, in measure to their perceived injustice.

There are many anomalies and gaps both within and amongst the various categories employed by international society to structure this field (Haddad 2008: 26–7, 79). Above all, international society's responsibility for outcomes can be traced back to its 'toleration' of state practice in regulating this area. To an exceptional degree, compared to other issues, there has been 'astonishingly little pressure' (Hurrell 2011: 94) to hold state activities to any international account. This non-action, as much as its acts of commission, has contributed to specific patterns of human vulnerability as a result. However, this does not mean that the situation is one of laissez-faire overall. International society does little to instil a norm requiring a right of entry, but what it does do is inculcate a norm preventing restrictions on the right of exit (Betts and Cerna 2011: 63). This creates a very wide gap into which the vulnerable are prone to fall, while at the same time actively encouraging a huge drain on skilled manpower resources from developing countries. As a result, the very poorest refugees tend largely to get stuck in the South, while the best trained professionals make their way to a much more welcoming North (Betts 2011b: 26). As in so many other areas, it is this highly asymmetric impact of international society's interventions that is so highly revealing—and so deeply problematic.

MOVEMENT AND THE VULNERABLE

Human migration has taken place in response to a multitude of adverse conditions, and has generated its own vulnerabilities for others in turn. Traditionally, migration has acted as an economic safety valve, as in the migrations from Scotland and Ireland in the wake of clearance and famine. It has also served as the principal escape route for the politically most vulnerable (for political, religious, cultural, or ethnic reasons). These movements have, however, taken place against a shifting international normative background that has been variably permissive or restrictive towards them. The international political order of the states system has both stimulated, and greatly complicated, 'natural' movements of any kind, as regulations have sought ever more to control the whole process. Refugees are demonstrably the product of the particular international context in which they were invented as a category. While refugees are initially at risk to the original conditions that create their reasons for flight, there then follows a double jeopardy in their subsequent vulnerability to the decisions of powerful others about whether and where to admit them for protection.

At a superficial level, international society's regulation of human movement simply tracks the play of international politics, and reflects the prevailing interests of key players at specific moments in time. The international politics of human movement are infused with striking paradoxes that demonstrate the contingent way in which vulnerability comes to be distributed. A clear illustration is provided by the case of Libya, and how its role with respect to human movement was to change so dramatically within a relatively few years. During 2011, Libyan civilians became subject to international protection as the Gadaffi regime was brought to an end. The activities of the dying regime and the associated fighting between it and other factions prompted the flight of thousands of Libyans, who sought sanctuary elsewhere, both internally and externally. In its intervention, international society acted to protect Libyans no longer adequately protected by their own political community, and its own military action prompted many others, in turn, to flee. At this point, the underlying conditions generating human movement within and from Libya were the prime object of international concern.

This is in sharp contrast to the situation prevailing a few years earlier in 2004–5. At that time, European economic sanctions against Libya were lifted 'in exchange for a Libyan promise to help staunch a growing flow of North African migrants and asylum seekers across the Mediterranean and on to European soil' (Greenhill 2010: 1). Under arrangements at the time, Libyan authorities intercepted migrant boats and returned them to Libya, 'which had no asylum law or procedures and is not bound by the 1951 Refugee Convention' (Grant 2011b: 54). During this period, the Libyan authorities were being invited to play a key role in the restriction of human movement. In short, international society eventually acted to protect Libyan citizens from their own regime, but had hitherto been just as content to entrust that same regime as the custodian of vulnerable migrants from other parts of Africa. The inconsistency, not to say hypocrisy, is striking indeed.

A more general example of this interplay with international politics is to be found in the inversion of the perception of vulnerability that has been associated with the policies of Europe and North America in recent years. If some of the recent wave of human migration has been encouraged by environmental stresses associated with climate change, those states—as we have already seen—

that bear greatest causal responsibility for creating these effects are those now most resistant to accepting the human consequences of that condition. Instead, attention has been 'flipped' away from the 'most vulnerable communities affected by climate change impacts', and instead towards the 'security of developed states that may receive climate migrants' (McAdam 2011: 174).

These may be regarded as little more than the usual vagaries of international politics. It is therefore relatively uncontroversial to demonstrate, as in these examples, that the 'causes, consequences, and responses to refugees are all closely intertwined with world politics' (Betts and Loescher 2011b: 1). The shaping of human movement, in this way, is deeply embedded in the narrative of international politics.

However, the argument of this chapter runs much more deeply: it is that the very nature of the issue of human movement has been configured in particular ways because of the fundamental norms of international society (Haddad 2008: 65). It is the existence of international society that lends a very specific meaning to human movement, and this meaning is the source of its allocation of vulnerability. To the extent that there is a 'problem' with human movement, it exists *only* because of the impact of international society. Issues deriving from international human movement *are* simply a transcription of the essentials of contemporary international society itself. In this chapter, the task is to clarify how the vulnerability of various categories of people has been the direct outcome of the normative structures that international society has itself put in place.

So, as regards human movement, who is vulnerable, and in what does their vulnerability consist? To answer these questions, we need to restate the general approach taken to that concept. Standard answers are normally a variation on the core idea that the refugee is a 'fitting analogue of the hurt and vulnerable stranger', and refugees have become vulnerable 'because they lacked the protection of a political community' (Gibney 2004: 232). We will explore that central claim in due course. However, what this immediately suggests is that the vulnerability presents itself in two dimensions. The first refers to the physical risks that are inherent in any human movement. The second emphasizes instead the specific risks bound up with a form of movement that takes someone beyond the jurisdiction of any political community, and thus exposes that person to the lack of protection inherent in that particular condition. Accordingly, the significant border that is crossed here is conceptual as much as physical. The resultant 'lack of protection' is a direct consequence of the social significance of that movement, and this is what makes it so central to the argument that follows. Human movement becomes especially problematic because it takes people into a dangerous space—the international—where their relationship with a protective political community is placed in question.

In the specific field of human migration, the problem has been that migrants find themselves 'caught between international principles of universality and exclusionary rules of state sovereignty and national law' (Grant 2011a: 25). In this sense, physical risks are compounded by a vulnerability that reflects its 'sociopolitical causality'. In particular, vulnerability is claimed to be a product of a 'double structure':

> The external side of vulnerability . . . involves exposure to environmental stress and is predominantly structural in nature . . . The internal side . . . involves the capacity to cope with insecurity and encompasses factors that enable and constrain human agency. (Brklacich, Chazan, and Bohle 2010: 38–9)

Both structural and agential dimensions are accordingly in play, and our interest lies in how each is conditioned by international society: it affects both the causal circumstances inducing flight in the first place, as well as the availability of resources to adapt to them. With respect to the latter, we shall see that its provision in this regard is highly selective, and very much a matter of state 'categorical' discretion.

Accordingly, although human migration is a constant of history and, as such, is a vast topic, this chapter will focus on issues that illustrate three of its dimensions: human movement involving the crossing of international borders; human movement resulting in internal displacement; and those specific forms of movement that fall under the auspices of the refugee regime. These are selected because they demonstrate the prominent role played by the norms of international society. Each of these dimensions is, in effect, regulated by its own operative category, as imposed by international society. The review will begin by placing the overall argument in its historical context.

HISTORY, HUMAN MOVEMENT, AND THE MAKING OF THE VULNERABLE

On the face of it, human movement currently takes place on a much greater scale than at any previous point in history. In the last quarter of the twentieth century, numbers of international migrants swelled from an already high figure of 82 million to some 200 million by 2005, representing 3 per cent of all humanity (Betts 2011b: 1). So what is the problem? Obviously, high points in levels of *forced* migration or displacement have been closely associated with international events, such as World Wars I and II and the end of the Cold War (Panayi 2011: 3). However, there is a yet more revealing story to be told about international society's historical role, and much of this is implicated in asymmetrical power. While the increased legalization of migration over the past century is interesting in general, particularly so is the fact that the 'migration laws that "matter" are those of prosperous Western states' (Dauvergne 2008: 173).

While it is demonstrably the case that human movement has been a permanent feature of human history, the issue has taken on its contemporary form only since the early years of the twentieth century. This can be shown specifically with reference to the refugee. While people have sought refuge in other lands since time immemorial, the modern concept of the refugee was a specific legal construction of the post-World War I era. For it to become necessary, and indeed to make any sense at all, required in addition the concomitant higher levels of *regulation* of human movement that became evident during this same period: 'the modern refugee was born', it has been said, as a result of the disappearance of the nineteenth-century havens (Adelman and Barkan 2011: 29).

Accordingly, while it is the general argument of this study that the vulnerable are defined in terms of the norms of international society, in this particular case we can go further and insist that there has been a considerable *legalization* of vulnerability in this regard, at least as much as in the case of political violence, and considerably more than in the cases of climate and health. This is simply the other side of the coin of the pervasive legalization of the whole process of human movement. The paradox, then, is that the more widespread has been the assertion of claims to free movement, the much stricter have been the actual constraints on the exercise of any such legal right (Juss 2006: 5). If, hitherto, free movement was largely the default setting of international society de facto, after 1919 this came to be replaced instead by a default position restricting movement *de jure*, beyond clearly defined exceptions (Newman 2003: 3–4; Zimmermann 2011: 6).

It is in this context that the particular forms of vulnerability associated with an absence of legal protection have arisen. For instance, it has been suggested that, as an extension of the progressive legalization of migration during the twentieth century, we are now reaching a point best described as the 'illegalization' of migration (Dauvergne 2008: 2). More specifically, one category—and numerically a greatly increasing one—is now that of 'irregular migrants'. These have been estimated recently to amount to some 40 million, or a fifth of all migrants (Düvell 2011: 78). Typically, this category has been described as a 'product of specific political–economic conditions and a legal, political, and social construct of the late twentieth century' (Düvell 2011: 81). There is, to this extent, nothing 'natural' about the hazards faced by 'irregular' migrants, and for there to be any such category at all required in the first place the establishment of a recognized category of 'regular' migrants, to which they were deemed to represent the illegal exceptions. The degrees of protection and non-protection accorded by international society have, to this extent, been a direct function of the expansion of the process of legal control over human movement as a whole, as a new concept governing that movement came to prevail. The subsidiary allocations of vulnerability have since been made by application of international society's own system of categories.

This may seem a curious claim to make, and we must make clear the particular terms in which it is made. In contrast to many other areas of human life, it is generally fair to say—as many have pointed out—that the subject of human movement is much less than most subject to *multilateral* international control. Decisions about admissions of persons are deemed too close to the sovereign prerogatives of states for there to have been any effective pooling of decision-making powers in this area. Hence, relatively speaking, human movement is much less subject to formalized and institutionalized international governance: within this broad area, that pertaining to refugees is the most formal of all, and for this reason stands out as something of an exception (Betts 2011b). That said, it would be mistaken to conclude that international society is innocent of the degree of control that has been set in place. Much of the governance that applies derives from other aspects of international law, such as human rights, rather than relating directly to matters of migration. A brief review of international society's development of its own tutelage of human movement will serve to make this point.

The general framing observation is that, currently, laws pertaining to human movement follow from the complex intersection that took place after 1945 of the push for universal human rights law, set against the continuing concern of states not to accept any 'blank cheque' as far as their responsibilities either to protect or to admit were concerned. Symbolically, as we will see, what best captures this contested area is the emerging gulf between a right of 'exit', now widely accepted, as against any automatic right of 'entry', still almost universally resisted. For many people, the most telling vulnerability they encounter is a construct of the increasingly congested non-space between these two legal domains.

The great symbol of the regulation of state borders from the early part of the twentieth century was the systematic, rather than ad hoc, introduction of passports (Salter 2003). This is, of course, an inherently ambivalent document, intentionally designed both to facilitate and impede movement, representing as it does the 'tension between the desire for free movement and the desire for security and homogeneity' (Salter 2003: 158–9). While the passport contributed to the decline of 'refuges' for those compelled to flee—and international society was visibly complicit in diffusing this norm of restriction during the post-1919 period—on the other hand, international society was itself instrumental in encouraging the movement of populations in pursuit of that very same ideal of 'security and homogeneity'. While the introduction of the passport obstructed the movement of many, the post-war peace settlements, as they pertained to the collapsing Russian, Ottoman, and Austro-Hungarian empires, endorsed the practice of taking active measures to tidy up the messy residue of self-determination: the settlements explicitly sanctioned '*legalized forced population transfers*', and international agencies of the period 'endorsed and sponsored ethnic separation' (Adelman and Barkan 2011: 38,

46; Panayi and Virdee 2011b: viii–ix). The forced movement that international society was subsequently to outlaw had been aided and abetted by its own agreements.

If the ostensible purpose of the passport was to 'structure legitimate and illegitimate international movement' (Salter 2003: 2), its more deep-seated consequence was to institutionalize a practice of legitimate vulnerability for certain categories of those on the move. While this widespread closing of doors was the culmination of the nationalist ideas and doctrines of the late nineteenth century, the tendency was given further impetus by what I have previously referred to as the general 'fragmentation' unleashed in the post-1919 period, in reaction to the comparatively 'open' internationalism of the preceding generation (Clark 1997).

The first great initiative of the League of Nations in this regard was to deal with the flow of refugees from revolutionary Russia by introducing the Nansen passport system, later extended to cover Armenian refugees as well. It was not until 1926 that the first definition of a refugee was essayed, and this centred upon that class of persons who 'no longer enjoyed the protection' of their previous government, without having acquired any replacement. This reproduced the logic of the national-state system of the time, insofar as refugees 'posed a "problem" precisely because the link between themselves and their national home was lacking' (Zimmermann 2011: 9). In the absence of international society, there could be no such category of people at all, and to this extent the problem of refugees was essentially what states had made of it.

By 1933, the Convention of that year had provided the first legal statement of the *non-refoulement* principle that was to become such a central feature of the subsequent 1951 Refugee Convention. In terms of its Article 3, the State parties undertook in 1933 not to 'remove or keep from its territory' those authorized to reside there. This did represent a significant departure in state practice, albeit somewhat tempered by the qualifying provision 'unless the said measures are dictated by reasons of national security or public order' (Zimmermann 2011: 18), thereby retaining the same state safeguards that were to appear in the Geneva Conventions with respect to violence, and the UNFCCC with respect to climate. Also, the ambit of the Convention covered existing refugees only, and was therefore limited in not applying to the emerging exodus from Nazi Germany. Already the two opposing counter-pressures that have since become such a perennial feature of the international refugee regime—specific protections combined with loose responsibilities—had become highly visible.

World War II instigated the next great crisis of human movement, and was followed by new legal and institutional initiatives. Two observations are immediately relevant. First, the temper from 1945 was heavily infused by new doctrines of universal human rights, all of which had much implicitly to say about the entitlements of people, whether on the move or not. Secondly, however, legal historians of the post-war United Nations High Commissioner for Refugees (UNHCR) and the 1951 Refugee Convention are at pains to remind us that the emerging regime was much more strongly influenced by existing interwar practice and precedents than directly shaped by the new human rights thinking. In short, state practice of dealing with refugees already preceded its attachment to human rights norms, and this has been important in its subsequent evolution, leading to serious questions being asked about the precise relationship between the two. For instance, the references in the 1951 Convention to protection were understood very much in traditional terms of 'diplomatic and consular protection', rather than as any requirement for application of human rights codes (Goodwin-Gill and McAdam 2007: 10; Zimmermann 2011: 67). Once again, contradictory tendencies were on display. As the new regime was devised in the late 1940s, this coincided with actual policies of 'ethnic and national homogenization' (Adelman and Barkan 2011: 58), such as characterized the partition in the Indian subcontinent. However, the priorities, first of the United Nations Relief and Rehabilitation Administration (UNRRA), and then of the office of the UNHCR, remained for the moment very much inside Europe.

Nonetheless, there was an opposite side to the coin, so much so that the 1951 Refugee Convention has been described as 'the first steps in the creation of well-defined and binding human rights in international law for an especially vulnerable group of persons, namely refugees' (Zimmermann 2011: 232). At the same time, the precise motivations underlying the 1951 Convention appear to have been primarily 'statist' in conception. Its drafting was shaped by some accidents of the Cold War, such as the non-participation of Soviet and Polish representatives, even if it has been denied that the Convention overall was unduly coloured by Cold War considerations (Zimmermann 2011: 54, 67). One of its principal objectives was to distribute equally the burdens of responsibility for refugees, as was amply revealed in the Preamble's expressed concern that 'the grant of asylum may place unduly heavy burdens on certain countries' (UNHCR 1978: 11). The Preamble also emphasized the need to deal with refugees 'to prevent this problem from becoming a cause of tension between States' (UNHCR 1978: 11). To this extent, it approached refugees as a potential problem for international society, rather than just as a problem for the people who found themselves in that situation. The Convention's Articles 9 and 33 also included specific safeguards on grounds of 'national security' (UNHCR 1978: 15, 22).

It defined the refugee in the very specific, and limited, context of the time. By placing its emphasis on victims of 'persecution', the Convention deliberately excluded the impact of natural and environmental events, on the grounds voiced by the Israeli delegate at the time that it could not be envisaged that 'fires, floods, earthquakes and volcanic eruptions ... differentiated between their victims on the grounds of race, religion or political opinion' (Zimmermann 2011: 61). The work of the UNHCR was, in any case, to be very much bound by the interests and concerns of its key donor states (Loescher and Milner 2011: 201). Retrospectively, it has been suggested, a convenient myth about the Cold War origins of the Convention has been invented in order to apply a more restrictive understanding of the refugee definition, and thereby exclude the new waves of immigration from the global South (Zimmermann 2011: 68).

In the meantime, however, the geographical restriction to Europe had been removed by the 1967 Protocol to the Convention (Loescher and Milner 2011: 191). This was in recognition of the shifting geographical focus of the refugee problem beyond Europe. Other international instruments of the period also adopted a broader conception of the vulnerability to which refugees had been exposed. Symptomatically, the then Organization of African Unity's own refugee convention of 1969 added to the 1951 understanding an additional clause referring to 'external aggression, occupation, foreign domination, or events seriously disturbing public order' (Zimmermann 2011: 317). Refugees could, in this way, result from international, and not exclusively domestic, sources of political action.

Statist interests again drove the refugee and asylum agendas at the end of the Cold War. This was particularly so as the spectre of large movements of refugees returned to Europe, associated with the latest version of the practice of ethnic cleansing. Asylum additionally fell victim to the security priorities established in the wake of the 9/11 attacks, and ensured that whatever responsibilities were owed to those fleeing from danger would be just as much tempered by the potential implications that any admissions of persons might have for the new post-9/11 conceptions of national security.

INTERNATIONAL SOCIETY AND THE CONSTITUTION OF THE VULNERABLE

That outline history traces some of the obvious ways in which, historically, international politics have interacted with the regulation of human movement. However, the more fundamental claim of this chapter goes further: it is not simply how international society shapes certain regulatory concerns but how it actually constitutes the nature of the issue in the first place. The core of this argument can be set out at this stage. It will demonstrate that the particular allocations of vulnerability—to be mapped in the subsequent section—follow directly from the prevailing concepts and categories applied by international society. In the case of its practices, such as those concerning refugees, international society has determined exactly who is 'in' and who is 'out', with immense consequences for the exposure of various categories of people (Haddad 2008: 26–7). In its various determinations about who is a refugee (as opposed to an economic migrant), who is an 'irregular' migrant, and who is a displaced person (but not a refugee), international society holds the fate of millions in its grasp.

The case also illustrates the paradox at the heart of this study, namely that international society displays unity and diversity at the same time. While international society speaks with many voices on the subject of human movement, even those who dissent from some of its collective agreements nonetheless largely frame their positions in relation to those very instruments. This is best demonstrated with reference to Southeast Asia, where many states are signatories neither to the Refugee Convention nor to its Protocol. Despite this, they vindicate their stance by appeal to 'non-genuine' refugees, as distinct from 'genuine' ones in terms of the Convention, thereby confirming the importance of international society's own categories. To this extent, they do not wholly reject international instruments, but actually 'legitimate their position *within the framework of international refugee law*' (Davies 2008: 19).

Why should we single out international society as a distinctive source of these problems? One answer is that the endemic inequalities of international society provide massive incentives for human movement (Carens 1992: 34–5). Even so, Hurrell is surely correct when he points out that there would be many other causes of human movement, even in the absence of the 'particular pathologies' of the international system (Hurrell 2011: 92). Indeed, rather than play an exclusively negative role with regard to human movement, it can just as convincingly be asserted that international society has made a significant, and highly positive, contribution. 'The ability to flee is an important value secured by the plurality of independent states', Hendrickson insists, 'and has always formed one of its most compelling justifications' (Hendrickson 1992: 217). Far from being an obstacle to human refuge, it is the very structure of international society that creates this possibility in the first place. There is undoubted force to that claim. Nonetheless, while it is certainly the case that the story of human movement goes far beyond the impacts of international society, there remains a sense in which international society is fundamentally implicated in the distribution of particular vulnerabilities—a number of these exist only because of the nature of international society.

This is true in both general and specific senses. Most generally, the refugee is an 'integral part' of the international system of states (Betts and Loescher 2011b: 15; Gammeltoft-Hansen 2011: 12). This is so because sovereignty 'represents the constitutive norm of the international system and creates the concept of exclusive political community, on which the very concept of international migration is premised' (Betts 2011b: 15). In the absence of international society, there would assuredly still be forms of human movement, but these would not possess the same significance that is attached to any movement that takes the person beyond, or between, political communities.

This is where the primary source of vulnerability is located for those who cross borders, or, in some opposite cases, for those who fail to do so. To this extent, its most pervasive impacts are implicit rather than explicit, insofar as there 'is no formal migration regime', as such, at the international level (Betts 2011b: 8). In its absence, however, basic norms like self-determination create other subsidiary categories—'refugees, minorities, stateless peoples, unwanted aliens, and displaced populations'—that actively determine the spectrum of applied vulnerability on the ground (Hurrell 2011: 90).

The specific sense results from those particular regulatory arrangements that do apply to human movement. We have already noted the deep significance of the introduction of universal passports. From its earliest beginnings in the Nansen system, this 'is one of the primary ways that this abnormality–normality, refugee–citizen matrix was constructed' (Salter 2003: 84). On this basis, IR has been criticized for regarding the refugee as an 'exception', rather than as an 'exemplar', of modern interstate politics (Owens 2011: 133–4). If the refugee is defined by international society, he or she illustrates also some of its most fundamental characteristics.

There is yet another specific feature of the evolution of the migration regime that makes essentially the same point. It stresses an intrinsic quality of international society itself, rather than some deficiency in the policy pursued by particular members of it. In a recently published piece by Hedley Bull (although written in the early 1980s), he makes the pertinent point: 'The right of persons to exit from their own country . . . is asserted by liberal doctrine . . . The right of entry into countries, by contrast, is universally denied as a legal right, even (indeed especially) by the Western democracies' (Bull 2011: xii). What this highlights is a fundamental asymmetry in the practices of international society with respect to movement: the right to exit is not matched by any right of entry (Noll 2003: 277). It is this that generates the protection deficit. What marks the refugee out for special attention is, then, 'not geographical movement *per se*', but a gap in the system of political protection that can be filled only by the intervention of another state, or by international society generally (Betts and Loescher 2011b: 6). This highlights the ethical problem because it points to a 'contradiction' within liberal doctrine itself:

> Civil society requires us to respect other people's basic rights no matter where they happen to be, whereas the society of democratic and democratizing states allows us to put the interest of our own people above the rights protected by civil society . . . *Had the state system not existed*, they would have been free to move into this portion of global civil society'. (Frost 2003a: 124–5, emphasis added)

This ethical problem is an existential one, and derives from those asymmetrical relationships that are fundamental to the practice of international society: even when a system of values is widely shared, its implementation can be deformed by those with the capacity to resist the full force of its implications. When this happens, it places a further strain on the acceptability of existing hierarchies, not least because of the ethical deficits that are so prominently on display.

How does this take us any closer to an appreciation of the vulnerabilities associated with human movement? Once again, we are led to acknowledge the distinction between the risks inherent in human movement itself, as contrasted with the vulnerabilities that result from the application of the particular conceptions and categories of international society. In a 'state of nature', there would be universal hazards associated with movement (lack of resources and protection from family or tribe, the clash with other populations, and the uncertainties of provision of food, water, and shelter). These persist under the vulnerability imposed by international society, but to them is added a further layer of social vulnerability: the variable provision or withholding of degrees of protection, depending on the category devised by international society to which the individual happens to be assigned. Just as the distinction is made between the hazards presented by the 'physical environment of New Orleans' in the face of Hurricane Katrina, as against the socio-demographic 'vulnerability of specific groups' (Basolo 2010: 106–7), so in the case of human movement broadly it is international society that determines the distribution of vulnerability to those various social categories it has created. Theorists of vulnerability detail a range of factors that shape exposure, but also stress the importance of the ability to respond to it. This includes control of and access to assets; institutional factors; distribution of rights and resources; and ecological and geographical conditions (Brklacich, Chazan, and Bohle 2010: 42). If so, the first three of these sets of factors is largely in the gift of international society, and the fourth is at least partially a consequence of its activities in other areas. Hence, international society allocates degrees of exposure as well as distributing those assets, degrees of institutional access, and rights that are fundamental to any capacity to adapt and respond to them. In those ways, there can be no meaningful discussion of those vulnerable in the act of moving without first locating them in the deep normative structures of international society.

MOVEMENT AND THE CATEGORIZATION OF THE VULNERABLE

The preceding section makes the case in broad theoretical terms. It can now be restated with reference to the specific activities that have characterized the practice of human movement. It is hard to imagine any sphere of human life where the impact of definitions—of inclusions and exclusions—is of such import. In the case of human movement, vulnerability is in large measure a matter of definition, or at least of how these definitions are implemented and executed in practice. The point has been strongly made by Haddad in her claim that 'the refugee "problem" is, first and foremost, one of categorization, of making distinctions' (quoted in Juss 2006: 198). This section will demonstrate the issue of vulnerability with regard to several categories of human movement, and the vital distinctions between them: refugees and the quest for asylum, environmental refugees, irregular migrants, and internally displaced persons. Each faces its own forms of vulnerability (and occasionally of protection) as a result of the way it has been viewed by international society. How states implement their understanding of these categories matters so much because it determines access 'to human rights, human development, and security' (Betts 2011b: 9). The most dangerous places have been described as 'migratory fault lines', understood as physical locations (Grant 2011b: 49). However, it is important to stress the extent to which these fault lines are conceptual as much as geographical.

There is thus a double-edged aspect to this discussion. On the one side, we can—as many do—ask questions about the effectiveness with which international society's regimes protect the interests of the vulnerable migrant. But on the other side, we are compelled to note the extent to which that vulnerability results from the very practices that international society itself has set in place. It has been commonplace to criticize the fragmentary nature of the protection systems afforded to those exposed to danger by movement (Grant 2011a: 47). Different treaties and regimes apply in different contexts, 'making protection for the most vulnerable more, not less, difficult' (Grant 2011a: 47). But it is hard to see this as wholly haphazard, and merely the product of an unfortunate contingency. Discrete regimes have been designed for a variety of purposes, not least of which has been a general intent on the part of states to maximize their own discretion in these matters. The flip side of that coin is then the 'discretionary' nature of the resulting rights enjoyed by many migrants, so much so that the pointed question has been asked: 'Are human rights for migrants?' (Dembour and Kelly 2011b: 5).

Each of the separate categories provides a slightly different answer to that question: the difference captures the degree of vulnerability to which each is exposed. We can begin with the refugee regime, and how it has been practised in recent times. Refugees, it has been suggested, 'are prima facie evidence of human rights violations and vulnerability' (Betts and Loescher 2011b: 1). They may be vulnerable to the loss of rights that they have already suffered, but they become doubly so because they are then exposed to the decisions of others about their ensuing fate. As already noted, of all the international regimes covering human movement, this one is the most formal. It might then be thought that the refugee is the category whose rights are most secure. However, that is not necessarily the case. There are several general observations that must be made about this category. First, it is itself an 'exclusive' category, and many find themselves outside the confines of its protection and the 'privileges' accorded by it. Secondly, there are characteristics of its recent implementation that, to say the least, have made it increasingly difficult for people to secure the benefits of this status. Thirdly, as a result, there is a striking maldistribution in the sharing of the refugee burden, and seemingly no good fit between the location of the refugees and those with the resources best placed to assist them. Some 90 per cent of the world's refugees find themselves hosted by the poorest states (Loescher 2003: 33), reflecting what has been aptly described as 'the structural capacity of the rich to set the terms of global burden-sharing on refugee protection' (Hurrell 2011: 95).

At first glance, refugees do represent a relatively privileged category of migrants (Phuong 2004: 18). International society, we are told, 'has prioritized the human rights protection needs of refugees over other migrants' (Loescher and Milner 2011: 190). However, in its original formulation, refugee status applied only to those outside their country of origin, and subject to acts of individual persecution of specific types (Goodwin-Gill and McAdam 2007: 37). In recent decades, most people fleeing their homes have not been covered by this strict conception (van Selm 2003: 66). Importantly, we must empha-size, in assigning a substitute state as protector, in cases where the original host state is unable or unwilling to act itself, the regime is 'not only protecting the individual but also protecting the integrity of the states system' (van Selm 2003: 88–9). Its arrangements overall reflect what has been described as the 'classical trinity of nation–state–territory with its ideas of citizenship and rights' (Owens 2011: 137). To be protected, an individual must be assigned to one state, or failing that to a substitute. There can be no protection without such assignment. Just as states have sought to award themselves the monopoly on the legitimate resort to violence, so they monopolize also the legitimate provision of human protection, even if international society exercises its good offices in facilitating that process.

So the first challenge for the would-be refugee to overcome is to achieve that assignment of responsibility. This has become an even greater challenge in recent years as the majority of potential rich host states have placed further obstacles in the path of securing such protection: people in flight are now subject to a range of practices that leave refugees vulnerable to decisions about which category is to apply (Phuong 2004: 4). They have 'systematically eroded the principle and practice of asylum' over the past two decades (Loescher and Milner 2011: 197). Especially noteworthy has been the near universality of making admissions decisions *beyond* state borders, as part of the general strategy of 'containment' (Hurwitz 2009: 2–3). It is those 'non-arrival prac-tices' that have done much to undermine the spirit of the 1951 Convention (Gibney 2006: 143; Kneebone 2009b: 8; Grant 2011a: 31). This has been made possible by state actions 'to prevent those individuals from arriving on their doorsteps' (Adelman and Barkan 2011: 65). One obvious instance has been Australia's 'Pacific Solution', and particularly its legal redefinition of its own 'migration zone', thereby restricting applicability of the Convention (Inder 2010: 231).

The intent of the Refugee Convention is thus eroded, either by attempts to relabel people as other than refugees (Goodwin-Gill and McAdam 2007: 50), or by forestalling them from reaching national territory in the first place. How should we understand such manoeuvres? There is one positive gloss that has been placed upon them. In a back-handed way, it has been suggested that the lengths to which states go not to breach directly the letter of the law is testimony to their deep respect for it: it confirms that 'norms do still matter' in this area (Gammeltoft-Hansen 2011: 243). Even if this is admitted, it must be counterbalanced by the further realization that this makes the situation of the would-be refugee even more precarious, as there can be no guarantee that the category will be recognized and acted upon. With regard to the law, 'large gaps are deliberately exploited to realise sovereign power and prerogatives' (Gammeltoft-Hansen 2011: 243).

As such, refugee law amounts to, as is widely conceded, 'an incomplete legal regime of protection' (Goodwin-Gill and McAdam 2007: 1). Arguably, this has been inherent in it from the outset. In setting up UNHCR, states opted for a narrow definition 'to limit their responsibilities' (M. Barnett 2011: 119). What the drafting history of the 1951 Convention so amply reveals is that original tension between conceptions of universality and the wish to retain sovereign prerogative in this sensitive area (Gammeltoft-Hansen 2011: 53). This continues to the present day, resulting in what has been described as a 'kind of schizophrenia' in response to the issue: on the one hand, 'great importance is attached to the principle of asylum', but on the other, 'enormous efforts are made to ensure that refugees . . . never reach the territory of the state where they could receive protection' (Gibney 2004: 2). If there is an ethical issue about human movement, this surely lies at its heart.

Refugees are thus the category to which international society has extended its most formal and prioritized protection. They have been officially classified as a category of the vulnerable, and a system to safeguard them is in place. At the same time, actual refugee practice has aggravated the vulnerability that attaches to the whole process of securing that status. This is as a result of two principal factors. The first is the generally fragmented legal nature of the regime itself. 'Refugee protection is not guaranteed in a global homogenous juridical space', it is lamented, 'but materialises as a patchwork of commitments' (Gammeltoft-Hansen 2011: 24). This results in a large number of potential gaps and cracks through which the hapless can readily fall. The other reason is the deep-seated tension between the various norms in play, and the clash between universality and particularity to which these inevitably give rise. This is symbolized, for example, by the refugee regime's ambivalent relationship to human rights law. This leads one observer to note that refugee protection is either fundamentally about human rights, or else it is a wholly separate matter: human rights are something that everyone can claim, whereas 'refugee status is most explicitly *not* available to everyone' (Dauvergne 2008: 61–2).

Despite all these uncertainties, the practices of international society render refugees slightly less vulnerable than some other categories of human migrants. This general point about categories is amply made with respect to the contested language of 'environmental refugees': to be forced to flee for environmental reasons as a *refugee* would be a marginally better condition than fleeing without that status, but this category is currently unavailable. The terminology of 'environmental refugees' first emerged in the 1970s. However, the standard Convention definition of a refugee precludes any such under-standing, since 'it does not accurately reflect in legal terms those who move' (McAdam 2011: 157–8). For the same reason, the term 'climate change refugee' is considered to be 'legally and conceptually flawed' (McAdam 2012: 39). Hence, international society allocates greater vulnerability to environmental migrants than to overtly political ones, albeit that those environmental conditions can be just as directly related to state actions and policies as are other types of overt political persecution (Burson 2010: 7). If the term has enjoyed widespread currency of late, the critics suggest that this is for political reasons, to create a further pretext for denial of entry (Juss 2006: 173).

The spectre of the likelihood of any future large-scale migration induced by climate change and other environmental pressures has contributed to a widespread sense of the need to expand the original definition of the refugee (Betts and Loescher 2011b: 10). At the 'soft' edges of the refugee regime there is abundant evidence of evolution in this direction. For example, in 2009, the African Union adopted the Kampala Convention, which requires its members to 'take measures to protect and assist persons who have been internally displaced due to natural or human-made disasters, including climate change' (quoted in McAdam 2011: 162). For the time being, however, there remains no effective governance of climate-induced movement, nor any internation-ally agreed definition of an environmental migrant, refugee, or displaced person (McAdam 2011: 153–5; Vlassopoulos 2010: 19–21; McAdam 2012). Yet, for practical purposes of allocating vulnerability and protection, these differentiations matter crucially. At the moment, the lack of any discrimin-ation in this regard leaves all those who move for environmental reasons equally vulnerable, rather than equally protected (Burson 2010: 6; Martin 2010: 17–18). While in some cases the problem is one of 'compartmental-ization', in others it results precisely from the *lack* of any appropriate com-partment within which it can be addressed in policy terms (McAdam 2012: 249). In short, the downside of the specification of some categories of the vulnerable is the consequence that international institutions are incapable of acting to protect those who are not appropriately labelled.

Another category that is clearly more vulnerable than the refugee is that of the 'irregular' migrant: this is 'increasingly recognised as a distinct category with specific vulnerabilities and protection needs' (Grant 2011a: 29). As such, it exists only as a construct of international society, and reflects the recent widespread diffusion of a norm within it. The more that international society has acted to 'legalize' migration, the greater the gaps into which the vulnerable can fall, and the greater the obstacles to their achieving any kind of redress. 'Each extension of the law regulating migration', it has been pointedly observed, 'increases illegal migration through defining increasingly larger categories as being outside the law' (Dauvergne 2008: 15; Dembour and Kelly 2011b: 8). Here again we encounter the tyranny of categories. If the refugee has often been considered the anomaly that does not fit into international society, the irregular migrant is doubly so because that person stands in violation of the positive laws governing human movement. In terms of the analogy employed in the Introduction, these are the people who seemingly choose to drive in the wrong direction on the motorway: their risk is augmented because they do something 'wrong'. In strict legal terms, this should not be the case, as the illegal migrant continues to enjoy rights in the country of entry 'regardless of their legal status'. However, in practice this is rarely so—'whatever the legal theory', life for the irregular migrant brings with it all the additional hazards of being an 'outlaw' (Grant 2011b: 57), and the 'illegal' tends to find securing legal redress 'almost insurmountable' (Dauvergne 2008: 19). The additional hazards to which people are exposed by their status include the entire gamut of possible forms of exploitation, including by others such as traffickers and organizers of enforced labour. This brings out the wholly contradictory nature of their 'illegality', since they are in fact the victims (at multiple levels), and their label as illegal 'will hardly stick' (Dauvergne 2008: 69; Martin and Calloway 2011: 226). These migrants are especially vulnerable not because of their natural condition, but precisely because they fall outside the law, and their condition is aggravated by that very fact: international society is implicated not just by what it does, but also by what it fails to do. This development is not accidental, but has to be understood as part of the more general 'crackdown' on migration by Western states in particular (Dauvergne 2008: 19), acting within the discretion that existing regimes avowedly permit them to exercise. In this case, there seems little prospect of their condition being 'regularized' by international law, as such, and so analysts concerned about the scale and nature of the problem tend to advocate instead the development of 'soft law' to try to accommodate their needs (Betts 2010).

Finally, there is the category of 'internally displaced person' (IDP) which includes those who, in many respects, might be deemed to be 'even more vulnerable than refugees' (Koser 2007: 72; Koser 2011: 212), in no small part because they do not form, strictly speaking, any legal category at all (Phuong 2004: 236). If the plight of the refugee is conditional on the act of crossing a national border, then it can just as tellingly be said that the plight of the IDP arises directly from failure to do so, as only then would he or she potentially become the legal responsibility of an international regime (Koser 2007: 72): interstate borders, in this way, double up as the problem and the solution at the very same time. IDPs have become an increasingly large category: 1.2 million in 1982, 14 million in 1986, 20 million in 1995, and some 26 million more recently (Koser 2011: 216). Moreover, women and children compose some 75–80 per cent of this category (Newman 2003: 25). They are, for the most part, concentrated in the least-developed countries (Bagshaw 2005: 123). At first glance, this would appear to have nothing at all to do with international society, since the IDP remains within the jurisdiction of the original state, and continues to be entitled to protection from it: this is a matter for domestic, not international, law (Goodwin-Gill and McAdam 2007: 33). The priority of domestic responsibility is reflected likewise in institutional arrangements, whereby the international community serves only as a supplementary safety net, while 'national authorities' have the primary duty (Koser 2011: 214), just as is generally the case with emerging notions of the Responsibility to Protect.

However, matters are not entirely so straightforward. The construction of a category of the 'internally' displaced has developed largely as a marker to differentiate that person from the refugee who has, in fact, crossed a national border: absent the international, the internal has no meaning on its own (Phuong 2004: 13). In this way, the legal reach of international society has been utterly pervasive, and this is why, as a category, they fall into a '*protection gap*' (Kleine-Ahlbrandt 2004: 6). For this reason, those who are internally displaced have no automatic recourse to the entitlements of the refugee regime—even if, as a pragmatic development, international agencies have come to treat them as 'objects of concern', and try to bring some assistance to them where they are, even though they have not crossed national borders (Adelman and Barkan 2011: 64; M. Barnett 2011: 121). They have been covered not by the refugee regime proper, but by further 'soft' developments, such as through the Guiding Principles on Internal Displacement (Bagshaw 2005: 15–16; Betts 2011b: 16–17). They become '*functional* responsibilities' of international bodies, but strictly not 'legal obligations of States' (Goodwin-Gill and McAdam 2007: 47). In these sundry ways, and by the various distinctions that it draws, international society serves to distribute degrees of vulnerability to those humans moving on the ground. At the same time, it generates a set of problems that are endemic in international society, and that are inescapably ethical in nature. There can be no resolution of them without facing their full ethical force.

CONCLUSION

It might be argued that, in some cases, vulnerability is an incidental and accidental by-product of the activities of international society, something that it unwittingly creates in pursuit of other goals. No such plea in mitigation can be entered in the case of human movement. While there would be reasons for humans to move, and problems encountered by their doing so, within any global institutional structure, the particular vulnerabilities that arise in crossing borders (or staying within them) derive directly from the very essence of international society: the significance of this movement, and the vulnerabilities attached to it, are unaccountable in its absence. People on the move might otherwise be vulnerable, but certainly not in these particular ways. Moreover, the forms of movement of which it is permissive, as well as those that it explicitly restricts, are a reflection of its own choices. At base, these put in place pervasive normative structures that have a pronounced effect on the chances, and quality, of life for many millions of people.

Conceptually, the entire domain of human movement has, over the past century, come to be governed internationally by the presumption that it is an activity that must be legally controlled, and often restricted. Operationally, that concept is implemented through systematic categorization. International society allocates vulnerability by definition. While it may be true that many migrants are already exposed to hazard, in the sense that they may be marginalized people with modest access to resources, what makes them specifically vulnerable is the collective decisions of international society about the content and application of its own categories. While refugees enjoy very imperfect protection at the hands of international society because it is incomplete, they arguably face better conditions than some other categories, allowing only that their claims are secured. Others, such as irregular migrants, can find themselves precariously outside the law altogether: and indeed, in the face of the restrictive application of the asylum process, people from the former category may end up dropping down into the latter, by default, and in the absence of any other choice. If international society has privileged the need for international protection of the refugee, this is paradoxically because the existence of the refugee actually reinforces international society's basic norms; in contrast, most other forms of human movement come up against its predilection for state autonomy on matters of entry.

To seek to address the above problems by appealing for a radical reconstruction of international society is to attempt to wish the problems away, since such a transformation is unlikely any time soon. The urgency of the situation faced by millions on the ground therefore makes compelling sense of Chris Brown's injunction that we abandon the quest for a generally applicable moral theory, and instead pragmatically do what we can to address the specific difficulties of discernible groups of people (C. Brown 2011). The worry about this approach, however, must surely be that it will simply aggravate the highly selective basis on which the issue is already substantially approached. As long as that is the case, particular state interests are likely always to trump more general considerations, and the discretion thereby accorded will strengthen the hands of those who are already strong.

If it is at once accepted that any application of sovereignty must entail profound implications for human movement, then it may still be conceded that this should never be done in a way that aggravates the vulnerability of some sections of humankind. To tolerate this imposition of vulnerability is to condone the infliction of harm on others, and there can never be any stable and tolerated system of regulation of human movement if this is one of its most visible effects. This is the ethical core of the problem that international society is now required to face.

If a complete transformation of international society is not soon to be expected, a minimal starting point at least, as suggested at the outset of this chapter, is to begin from the notion of vulnerability, and acknowledgement of how international society's decisions already have an impact on the way it is generated and distributed. A necessary first step is to reach some awareness of the extent to which international society itself is the source of many of the problems: only then can it start to work towards any solution. This may be as much as can reasonably be expected in an area of public life that sits so uncomfortably close to the symbolic heart of international society—namely its doctrine of sovereignty. Routine predictions of the impending demise of sovereignty must appear especially disingenuous to those people whose movement brings them hard up against its very harsh reality.

The hazards to which people are exposed through movement are greatly compounded by the vulnerability that is created by socially determined concepts and categories. International society attaches very specific meanings to human movement in accordance with its normative principles of sovereignty and self-determination: at the heart of its concept of movement is the deep symbolic meaning involved in crossing borders, and the loss of protection that is otherwise entailed by such movement. At the same time as international society has promoted the legalization of that movement, it has encouraged international attempts to deal with it through the proliferation of its own relevant categories: the category into which people then fall has immense consequences for the degree of protection that they might subsequently be afforded. In this sense, the case of human movement demonstrates the vagaries of the application of its system of categories, which creates significant gaps in degrees of protection between them. Those lacking any defined category of protection at all find themselves thereby twice cursed. Moreover, the tyranny of these categories has the further unwanted side effect that it is even more difficult to address issues of human movement in any holistic way, since international society has already worked so hard to parcel them out into its respective institutional fiefdoms. On top of the hazards to which people are already exposed by movement, international society has added this extra layer of socially generated vulnerability.

5

Global Health and the Vulnerable

In the words of Margaret Chan, Director-General of the World Health Organization (WHO), 'vulnerability is universal' (WHO 2007: vi). With regard to human health this is palpably true, and might appear as only the most patent confirmation of the frailty of the human condition. In the face of disease, vulnerability is seemingly the most natural and universal of conditions. Otherwise regarded, however, this claim profoundly misconstrues the distribution of health outcomes on the ground. While vulnerability is indeed hypothetically universal, in practice it is highly differentiated and selective. Moreover, this outcome is far from contingent. Once again, international society will be shown to mediate between people and the hazards to which they are otherwise exposed, and thereby to make its own distinctive contribution to the configuration of vulnerability to ill health.

Accordingly, this chapter addresses a number of issues in order to answer the fundamental question: why should a study of the vulnerable in international society be concerned with the case of global health, and what specific meaning does vulnerability have in this particular context? The chapter proceeds in the following stages. It first establishes how, historically and currently, international society has worked within its own preferred concepts of global health. These have entailed, in turn, attempts to manage health within distinct categories of disease that reflect its main priorities. The chapter then illustrates how this has contributed to the making of the vulnerable in matters of health. In what sense has this issue been the responsibility of international society, and how are we to connect an *international* society with a set of *global* outcomes and processes? What emerges starkly from this case is how patterns of health map onto other social categories that are substantially reinforced by the workings of international society, further entrenching deep-seated inequalities, and producing a marked disparity between the discourse of vulnerability and actual exposure to the risks of ill health.

Once again, we must highlight the profound interconnections between this particular case and those discussed in previous chapters. It scarcely needs stating that if international society has placed its distinctive imprint on political violence, climate change, and human movement, then it has already had major indirect impacts on human health by its actions in these adjacent areas. Nobody would dispute that wars and other forms of violence take an immense toll on human health, both on the battlefield and beyond. Climate change has the potential to encourage new patterns and distributions of disease (Baer and Singer 2009: ch. 6), for example, as in the case of malaria (Saker et al. 2004: 21). Human movement of any kind is a known vector of disease transmission, most infamously in the European incursion into the Americas and elsewhere, and the 'fatal impact' on indigenous societies that resulted. Conversely, attempts to tackle the transmission of disease can result in restrictions on human movement, such as through historical practices of quarantine.

However, important as these causal connections are, the point of the following analysis is to go beyond them. Once again, its remit is not just to establish that international society's management of those issues has had indirect consequences for global health. Rather, the deeper claim is that international society directly configures the vulnerable in global health by the way it approaches the problem: its own normative structure has had inevitable consequences for the distribution of human health, and not merely as a set of contingent outcomes of its everyday activities elsewhere (McInnes and Lee 2012). This is the reason also that the issue of global health has to be considered inherently normative. Its highly complex, and often insidious, politics betray the enormity of this moral challenge.

In this regard, the very terminology of 'global health' conceals an important ambiguity. Are we to understand by it what is actually happening on the ground, measured in terms of the health outcomes experienced by people across the world? Alternatively, do we mean by it those arrangements, processes, and objectives in terms of which global health is *conceived*? This set of assumptions, often unspoken, provides the foundation on which policy, and the architecture of health governance, is subsequently constructed. This chapter is principally concerned with the latter, but the force of its argument derives from the extent to which this, in turn, has a direct impact on the former. Accordingly, its central claim is that actual health outcomes have been a reflection of the myriad values and preferences already embedded in the way that management of global health has been approached by international society. Moreover, this has the effect of amplifying those many other inequities which already characterize the human condition. Accordingly, global health is as much a function of social distributions of power as it is of any natural threats to human health, and international society has been a key broker of outcomes in this regard.

One way of beginning to tease out these issues is by reflection upon the highly contrasting judgements that are routinely made about global health. Some commentators have claimed that '[g]lobal health is in a crisis' and that, as a result, the 'international community . . . has now begun to respond'

(Cooper, Kirton, and Schrecker 2007b: 3). What this implies is that any crisis of global health exists independently, and international society is called upon to respond to a set of conditions that objectively already exists. At the same time, these same writers acknowledge that the UN World Summit in New York in September 2005 'failed to include health in its outcome document as one of the values to which the organisation was devoted as a priority' (Cooper, Kirton, and Schrecker 2007b: 4). What this seeming neglect demonstrates is that international society is itself deeply implicated in any crisis of global health, and can scarcely wash its hands of it. From this side, the dominant assessment has been one of 'failure' (Kay and Williams 2009b: 2).

On the other side of the ledger, of course, there are appreciations of the many positive achievements in this field. There is widespread acknowledgement of the major scientific accomplishments in countering disease. There is a corresponding recognition of the vastly greater resources now made available for the global health effort, drawing on large private foundations in addition to other public sources. Above all, in terms of health outputs, there is justifiable emphasis on such things as increased life expectancy and decreased mortality, including among infants, reflected in the swelling of global population past the seven billion mark. This evidence of improvement is undeniable. The qualification, as in so many other things, lies in the distribution of these benefits, and particularly in their highly unequal spread. The nature and cause of this distribution will be considered below. It is this that is the source of the moral problem that international society must address if a more substantive and sustainable progress is to be achieved.

In what follows, the argument is set out that international society has legitimated a highly unequal distribution of health vulnerability, and that if there is now a crisis of global health, it is in no small measure one of its own making: it is a crisis of vulnerability for which it has been largely responsible. Equally, if that crisis is to be overcome, it can be only as a result of facing up to the normative problem that lies at its heart. In order to understand this crisis, we must begin with an overview of its historical development.

HISTORY AND THE INTERNATIONAL MANAGEMENT OF HEALTH

History is replete with examples of the impact of international relations on global health: wars, conflicts, colonial expansion and contraction, and so on, have all taken their toll on human health. However, those events are not the main focus of this short review. What is important is the way in which international society has conceived its own approach to managing health, and the policies it has adopted in that pursuit. Fundamental to this section is an attempt to explain when and how international society has been brought to recognize that there is a global health problem 'out there', and why it should properly be the business of international society to deal with it.

One of the most momentous impacts, as noted earlier, was the transmission of new diseases into the Americas and elsewhere as a result of European discovery and conquest. However, we must in this case distinguish between the scale of the impact on the ground, and any perception on the part of international society that there was a problem that it might be called upon to address, given its priority concerns, and the very limited state of medical knowledge. In the wake of the encounter with the New World, the introduction of new diseases led to estimated deaths of between 50 and 90 per cent of the indigenous population, and the spread of smallpox to Australia killed in the region of one-third of the Aboriginal population (Lee 2003: 41–2). In this regard, Rushton is surely correct to maintain that 'protection of the domestic population and economy from the effects of infectious disease goes to the very heart of what a state is for' (Rushton 2009: 63). The corollary of this was that those unfortunate not to enjoy the protection of a state, recognized as such, were immediately rendered vulnerable not just *to* the ravages of disease, but *by* their inherent exclusion from whatever protection international society might otherwise have been able to afford them: exposure to disease was a result not just of physical transmission, but of social location in relation to international society, and of proximity to its centres of relevant power.

This had already been amply demonstrated in the centuries-long history of the international practices of imposing a cordon sanitaire or quarantine. The former sought to check human movement by physical barriers and punishments for crossing them, including by death. The latter held people and goods in designated places for specific periods (Goodman 1952: 29–31). The quarantine system of Venice was widely emulated elsewhere and had become virtually universal by the mid-nineteenth century (Goodman 1952: 31). However, this universality concealed differential interests underlying calls for and against its use. Those Mediterranean states most directly exposed to the threat of disease from the Asiatic trade had a greater interest in quarantine as a form of protection. Those that stood to profit from the trade, but were less immediately exposed, were just as mindful of the commercial dislocation that such quarantines were apt to entail (Harrison 2009: 12). It was hardly surprising then that when international society first actively sought to intervene in the management of international health, via the international sanitary conferences from the mid-nineteenth century, it was stimulated to do so by an asymmetrical interest and purpose. Above all, it was driven by 'the desire to protect civilized Europe from exotic diseases and pathogens that emanated from the uncivilized non-European societies' (Aginam 2004: 299–300), and all the early instruments had a very specific focus on preventing the spread of disease from

Asia and the Middle East (Fidler 2005: 331–2). Insofar as full membership of international society was then underpinned by the criterion of 'civilization' in its Eurocentric version (Clark 2005; Gong 1984), that society acted instrumentally to safeguard the interests of its core members. What was privileged was their sense of vulnerability; what could be readily discounted was any actual vulnerability suffered by those excluded from membership, and who had been already exposed to heightened risk, without any recourse in international law.

Unsurprisingly, the conferences after 1851 were largely focused on preventing the importation into Europe of cholera, and until 1851 those international gatherings were exclusively European affairs (Harrison 2009: 22). They were as much preoccupied with the damage that uncoordinated regulation was doing to commerce (Goodman 1952: 36; Fidler 2005: 329) as with any improvement in health as such, as many of the existing quarantines had been notoriously ineffective in controlling the spread of infection (Zacher and Keefe 2008: 33). For example, the Preamble to the 1892 Convention explained its rationale as acting to protect public health against cholera 'without uselessly distracting commercial transactions and passenger traffic' (quoted in Youde 2010: 152). The former should not thus be pursued to the point where it would entail damage to the latter. All international society's attempts since to regulate health have been shaped, and limited, by this need to find a compromise among a number of conflicting state goals, primarily where health is in tension with trade and security (Rushton 2009: 65).

What was just as striking about these expressed international concerns was their betrayal of a potential interventionist temptation. Quarantines epitomized the desire to contain external threats at the border, in much the same way that passports would prevent threatening movements of peoples, and the issuing of health certificates demonstrated a common intent underlying both practices, negotiating as they did between safeguarding health and regulating the movement of people and goods. The problem that had come increasingly to be realized was that, at least on its own, any such system of control was 'generally useless' (Goodman 1952: 34), and was limited in effectiveness, not least because of the very rudimentary medical scientific knowledge that underpinned it. Far better to tackle the root of the problem at source, and this encouraged a heightened ambition for intervention: it was best to prevent diseases within the affected state, rather than to await their arrival at the border and then have to deal with them there (Zacher and Keefe 2008: 36; Fidler 2009a).

Just as after the end of the Cold War there were to be calls to stem the 'infection' of human movement at source, so in the area of global health there have been parallel moves to address the problem of disease *in situ*. While this can be presented as evidence of an increasingly cosmopolitan humanitarian concern, and an attempt to live up to the declared goal of equal health for all, it can just as readily be viewed as a form of non-altruistic instrumentalism: in security terms, it amounts to a kind of roll-back, going beyond the containment of a threat at national borders, to its eradication in the territory beyond. What matters so much in distinguishing between the two approaches is that the former addresses the vulnerability of the recipient, whereas the priority of the latter is largely reduction of the vulnerability of the donor.

The high level of instrumentalism in state practice during the first half of the twentieth century is further exemplified in the relative non-observance of the International Health Regulations (IHR) during this period, and in the reasons for their neglect. As against any altruistic interpretation that the great breakthroughs in western medical techniques during the century led to 'trickle down' benefits elsewhere, the opposite conclusion has been reached that it was exactly this medical success on the part of the developed countries that contributed directly to a drop-off in interest in the health problems of others, because they were now considered even less of a threat to their own societies. The international regulations so painstakingly set in place could now be safely ignored because any problems associated with infectious diseases could be dealt with just as efficaciously by medical intervention at home. 'Developed countries lost interest in the IHR', we are told, 'because they found that they could prevent and control outbreaks on their own in their territories. They did not need to rely on international rules' (Zacher 2007: 16; see also Fidler 2005: 335). Nonetheless, these instruments remained the only legal treaty governing global health for most of the twentieth century, and the legal silences on so many other topics speak eloquently of the priorities that underpinned them.

What particular concept of global health do we find enunciated in the foundational documents of the WHO? In its practice to date, that body has been criticized by some for applying an unduly narrow 'absence of disease' framework (Youde 2010: 168). Of course, at the declaratory level, this had been explicitly disavowed in its own Constitution. That document had affirmed health positively instead, and defined it as a 'state of complete physical, mental and social well-being and not merely the absence of disease or infirmity' (WHO 1946: 100). Within this framing, however, a number of competing principles had also jostled for attention: parts of the Constitution stressed health as a matter of individual rights, whereas others stressed instead its social functions and collective benefits. On the former, the Preamble affirmed that the 'enjoyment of the highest attainable standard of health is one of the fundamental rights of every human being' (WHO 1946: 100). However, the social value of health was frequently stressed also. The opening session of the conference held to establish the WHO, on 19 June 1946, was sharply reminded of President Roosevelt's statement in 1939 that health is a 'public concern', not least because ill health is a cause of 'economic loss and dependency' (WHO 1946: 32). In the Chair's closing address to the conference, on 22 July, the delegates were warned that 'low standards of health laid a burden upon prosperity and trade, imposing an economic handicap on every nation' (WHO 1946: 94). The Constitution's Preamble was to attest also that health was 'fundamental to the attainment of peace and security' (WHO 1946: 100). In these various ways, human-, society-, and state-centred concepts of health all sought some kind of amicable coexistence in that foundational document.

There was, equally, a strong emphasis on the collective responsibility enjoyed by each and every state towards international society, given new conditions that heightened mutual exposure to risk, and we can see here the reiteration of the abiding concern with communicable disease as the highest international social priority. This theme was specifically highlighted by the rapporteur of the Technical Committee before the conference on 20 June 1946. He suggested that air transport 'would now largely nullify protective barriers against disease', and since no state could now count 'on its own arrangements alone', attention must be devoted to 'satisfactory controls in other countries as well' (WHO 1946: 33). This chain of reasoning was given prominence in the Constitution's declared concern that 'unequal development in different countries in the promotion of health and control of disease, especially communicable disease, is a common danger' (WHO 1946: 100): in short, those with the highest public health standards must be considered vulnerable to those with the lowest.

This elaborate post-World War II regime for global health, with the WHO at its summit, soon disappointed the early hopes inspired by its proclamation of a human rights-based commitment to the universalization of health care. The WHO itself increasingly turned its own back on such a conception, and chose instead to chart its course through less troubled political waters. In doing so, it reflected the contemporary faith that the problems of global health could best be addressed by the application of new medical techniques (by those who had the good fortune to have access to them), rather than risk becoming mired in the greater complexities surrounding the social dimensions of disease and its spread. Accordingly, it has been observed of the WHO in the early 1950s that by '[t]urning its attention to purely technical enterprises, which it approached through a medical lens, WHO sought a vertical, disease-specific approach to international public health' (Meier 2010: 172). Its subsequent attempts to reconnect with the original 1948 conception through its 1970s initiative of 'health for all', as incorporated in the 1978 Declaration of Alma-Ata, was largely unsuccessful in the longer term, given its previous ambivalence on the issue (Thomas and Weber 2009; Meier 2010: 177–8). Even if the 'right to health' was a 'revolutionary concept', it failed to be matched by 'equally revolutionary results on the ground' (Fidler 2005: 388).

Moreover, it was only again during the 1990s that serious international momentum was restored to revision of the IHR (Zacher and Keefe 2008: 66–7), and the reasons for this latest development are just as revealing of the purposes behind it (Kickbusch 2009: 399). Reinvigoration of interest in restoring the effectiveness of the IHR emerged in the 1990s, and was further encouraged in the early 2000s. The SARS outbreak in 2003 was decisive in this regard (Fidler 2005: 356; Kamrad-Scott 2010: 83; Katz and Muldoon 2012: 81).

This process of revision was accompanied by a more intense politicization of the whole field of global health (Zacher and Keefe 2008: 129–30), and reflected also the WHO's own organizational challenges and imperatives (Brown, Cueto, and Fee 2011: 76). This period mirrored the revival of concerns about the re-emergence of infectious disease, particularly in the cases of HIV/AIDS and subsequently SARS and avian flu. These compounded new anxieties about national security and the threat to health from new forms of bioterrorism.

In conjunction, these sundry factors drove greater interest in creating an effective, and enlarged, system of notification. At the same time, the new internet technologies had raised the prospect of more comprehensive and reliable reporting of incidents, given that national governments could no longer fully control those sources of information. The revised IHR of 2005 incorporated this new reality (Fidler 2005: 346), and this new reporting norm had been actively promoted by WHO officials (Kamrad-Scott 2010: 73). This betokened a formal shift from a concept of international health to one of global health. The paradox underlying this transition has been referred to as one in which 'states would be better protected from microbial traffic by ending the state's monopoly on disease surveillance' (Fidler 2009b: 220). Why, if the state has been so determined to preserve its monopoly over the use of violence, and over the control of human movement, was it to react quite differently in the case of health? Before addressing the notion of vulnerability directly, we must first consider the full significance for the wider argument of this purported transition to 'global' health.

GLOBAL HEALTH IN INTERNATIONAL SOCIETY

A diverse range of international impacts on health are widely accepted and discussed in the literature (McInnes and Lee 2012). In recent years, they have fallen into three broad categories, each of which stresses important connections between health and other international conditions. The most pervasive has been the intimate interrelationship posited between health and globalization, insofar as it has been the latter that has put the global into the former, but in which health also provides one important illustration of the process of globalization itself. This shift is mirrored in the simultaneous transition to a concern with global health governance. Secondly, there is the growing literature on the impact of global health on the various aspects of the global economy, not least its instruments of trade, production, distribution, finance, and investment. All impinge directly on health outcomes. Finally, there has been a pronounced recent trend towards exploring the connections between health and international security. Once again, this relationship is deemed to work in both directions, with health becoming increasingly securitized, while at the same time various dimensions of international security are shaped by concerns about global health (McInnes and Lee 2006).

The puzzle in this section, accordingly, is to reconcile these disparate claims by making sense of the role of *international* society in the field of *global* health. On the face of it, the assertion that health now responds to a global dynamic appears to undermine any suggestion of the role played by international society in distributing exposure to its risks. Surely an image of global health displaces any view of health as governed by the normative frameworks of international society, since *international* society does not possess effective *global* reach or competence?

The move from a concept of international public health to one of global health has been pronounced over the past two to three decades: globalization is regarded as a primary causal factor in the contemporary condition of global health, while at the same time global health vindicates the concept of global-ization by providing a convincing demonstration of the shift to an increasingly 'borderless' world. For instance, it has been suggested that 'the growing sense of vulnerability to . . . infectious diseases is not simply linked to the emergence of new diseases . . . ; it is . . . also associated with the recognition that states are less able to secure their borders against them' (T. Brown 2011: 321). This again shifts the focus from the seemingly physical sources of risk, and towards the more porous condition of international society. The common factor is the increased level of all types of movements across national borders, and this draws our attention to 'the problems produced by, and vulnerabilities associ-ated with, such enhanced mobilities' (T. Brown 2011: 320).

Many of these changed conditions are not the result merely of autonomous processes of globalization, impacting on international society from the outside, but reflect the choices that international society itself has promoted to foster open borders on other issues (Clark 1999). However, it is not just people and communicable diseases that can travel, but also the risks associated with certain lifestyles, hitherto found preponderantly in developed countries. As a WHO report concluded in 2003, 'modern dietary patterns and physical activity patterns are risk behaviours that travel across countries and are transferable from one population to another like an infectious disease, affecting disease patterns globally' (quoted in T. Brown 2011: 322). So while there may be fears in the developed North of contagious diseases emanating from the poor South, just as insidious is the reverse contagion whereby emulation of Northern lifestyles can lead to 'infection' in the South. This diffusion is actively promoted by various characteristics of the global economy.

As we have seen in the previous chapter, the allocation of vulnerability in terms of human movement has been principally wrought by systematic definition and categorization, all of which reflect the deep-seated international social structure in which they are embedded: degrees of vulnerability and protection reflect how human movement maps onto borders, and the social geographies of political community associated with them. Its core interest was in the movement of the vulnerable themselves, and how their vulnerability was heightened or lessened as a result of the operation of those categories. In the case of global health, it is the movement of other things as well (pathogens, lifestyles, global investment, food production, and the like) that contributes to the social geography of health. International society's regulations for dealing with health are, accordingly, 'concerned primarily with pathogens crossing borders' (Rushton 2009: 71).

However, just as jobs or GHG emissions can be outsourced to other countries and locations, so disease and ill health can be 'outsourced' as well, generating a similarly intense politics of 'protection'. To this extent, there are interesting parallels between the Refugee Convention and the IHR with regard to international society's underlying social purposes. In the case of the latter, the main objective has been the 'protection of the nation-state from exogenous disease threats' (Rushton 2009: 71), while in the case of the former it has been to guard against similar threats from human movement. However, in the age of globalization jobs can be readily moved to people, rather than vice versa, and likewise diseases can be moved to people rather than moving people into situations of exposure to disease. For that reason, there is now a great variety of different ways in which vulnerability can potentially be distributed.

This view of the relationship between globalization and health is widely and deeply entrenched, and there are multiple facets to it: the 'de-territorialization' of disease and of the conditions that encourage it (Labonté et al. 2011b vol. I: xxvi; Lee 2003: 213); its location in the pervasive global economy (Kay and Williams 2009b); the transnationalization of the actors and stakeholders involved; the cultural transmission of lifestyles, with health implications (Hawkes 2011: 275), and so on. In combination, these shape the general view that 'health risks and opportunities are becoming globalised' (Saker et al. 2004; Collin, Lee, and Bissell 2009: 377). With respect to one example specifically, namely cholera, it is claimed that globalization 'has shaped the pattern of the disease, the vulnerability of certain populations, and the ability of public health systems to respond effectively' (Lee and Dodgson 2011: 125). For all these reasons, the intimate association between globalization and health vulnerability is a pervasive theme of recent analysis (Chen and Narasimhan 2003: 10–11; Lee 2003: 112).

There is also some acknowledgement that this linkage may have been intentionally encouraged (Fidler 2011: 347–8), and this suggestion alone must immediately give us some pause. At the very least, it would be rash to assume that any such transition marks the end of the impact of international society on global health processes. In the same way that globalization in general cannot be wholly dissociated from the activities of those leading states that have promoted and encouraged it (Clark 1997, 1999), neither can developments in global health be understood in isolation from state activities, even if they do not wholly control that process. In Rushton's salutary reminder, even in a global age, 'states and IOs create and legitimise the international rules, norms, principles and procedures which constitute the global governance of health' (Rushton 2009: 63).

There are multiple ways in which international society remains a potent force. The WHO has actively encouraged new international law in some areas, most notably the Framework Convention on Tobacco Control (FCTC) (Bernard 2012; Elbe 2010: 140). This outcome was by no means an exclusively state-centric one (Collin, Lee, and Bissell 2009: 383). Nonetheless, the overall effectiveness of the law remains similarly circumscribed by state attitudes towards it, as for instance in the failure to date of the USA to ratify it (Elbe 2010: 142). In this way, it must again be stressed, international society does not speak with one single voice on issues, for instance in the case of smoking. While WHO officials have assisted the Australian government in its campaign for the introduction of plain packaging for cigarettes, and in dealing with the subsequent legal cases brought by the tobacco companies, at the same time this initiative has been subject to challenge from trade law through the World Trade Organization (WTO): different international organizations thus pull in opposing directions. As in the case of the process of negotiation of the 2005 IHR (Rushton 2009: 61, 65), this example demonstrates the extent to which health regimes continue to be hostage to state interest and preference. It reminds us also that international society remains a field of action in which plural interests compete, at the same time as it reaches equilibrium points enabling occasional forms of collective action.

In any event, global health manifestly gets caught up in the routine business of international society in manifold ways. Most obviously, the regular conflicts that mar international life have pronounced impacts on health. War and violence are known vectors of disease (McInnes 2009; Iqbal 2010). The 20–40 million lives lost to the great influenza epidemic of 1918–19 substantially reflected the direct and indirect consequences of war, including the dislocation of health care wrought during its course (Lee 2003: 51–2). At the same time, a complex array of international organizations influences global health in a myriad of other ways (Zacher and Keefe 2008: 127). The WHO is one clear case in point, and it cannot convincingly be suggested that its activities escape the tutelage of powerful states. The manner in which its funding is organized means that its core budget is barely one-quarter of the total, the remainder coming from voluntary contributions, usually earmarked for specific projects, over which the donors exercise close scrutiny (Elbe 2010: 117).

Other international organizations wield great influence, even when their brief is not directed towards health as such. This is strikingly so in the case of the WTO, given that a multitude of trade instruments have manifest consequences for health, and that linkage became even more apparent after the WTO's creation (Fidler 2005: 389). What this emphasizes is that much health governance is produced by regimes that are not directly charged with responsibility for health (Labonté et al. 2011b vol. I: lii). Moreover, the general promotion of the role of the 'private' in the provision of global health has accompanied the greater weight given to international financial institutions such as the World Bank (Williams and Rushton 2011: 11–12). The World Bank had emerged as a very powerful actor on the health scene during the 1990s, to some degree stepping into the political void created by the relative ineffectiveness of the WHO at that time (Brown, Cueto, and Fee 2011: 74), although the Bank in turn contributed further to that demise (Labonté et al. 2011b vol. I: xxvii).

Through the auspices of these organizations, it was possible for international society to extend its programme of 'financial conditionality', by applying a broadened test of good governance that now reached into the area of the management of health (Fidler 2009b: 223; Elbe 2010: 175). In this way, international society established itself in a position not just to react to health vulnerability as it emerged on the ground, but to promote or demote alternative ideational conceptions of the nature of that vulnerability. Arguably, it has been in this area—through its prevailing concepts of global health—that it has exercised its most important influence. International organizations do not just impact the provision of health care, but are instrumental in 'transmitting the various understandings of what healthcare is all about' (Inoue and Drori 2011: 15; see also Kickbusch 2009: 397). It is this conceptual transmission that is the focus of the next section.

THE VULNERABLE IN GLOBAL HEALTH

Is vulnerability in global health universal, or does it display a more systemic variation? This section confronts how vulnerability has been understood—and acted upon—in the context of global health. Global health is assuredly a field that gives rise to the potential for great harm. As is often noted, its 'body count far surpasses . . . that from interstate war and civil conflict' (Kirton 2009b: xv). This gives some impression of its order of magnitude. However, this seemingly generic vulnerability has not itself been the proximate source of most of the remedial action undertaken to alleviate it. Instead, this has emerged from a contested terrain in which policymakers 'use science and epidemiology to synthesize and translate risks and opportunities between the worlds of hard power and normative values' (Fidler 2011: 347). This has been a complex process, to be sure, at least as much so as with similar processes of legitimation in any other political field. This should not be surprising, given the scale of the stakes. The complexity arises also from the fact that global health reflects the deep inequalities that pervade all global social, economic, and political structures (WHO CSDH 2008: 10), and, as such, its own inequities can scarcely be addressed in isolation from this wider environment.

The reason for this relates back to the very concept of vulnerability. On the one hand, it is a measure of exposure to hazard, and of the underlying condition of sensitivity. On the other, it is in turn affected by the resources available to adapt or respond. Maldistribution of social goods and resources results in inequity in remedial capacity, and this directly affects the resulting impact (Fidler 2007: 56; Price-Smith 2009: 92–3). If the capacity to adapt is such a powerful motif in the discourse of climate change, it has no less relevance to that of global health. Once again, potent international social rules and norms are at work in patterning those capacities.

As it stands, this suggests that vulnerability, even if socially conditioned, is finally tantamount to the resulting distribution of material resources to adapt. However, to counterbalance this conclusion, just as important to health outcomes are those powerful ideational vulnerabilities to which many populations are exposed. Accordingly, while the WHO does readily acknowledge the social determinants of health, it does not include among these its own concepts of health as a highly important influence in its own right. But it is precisely this social knowledge that is so decisive in framing the concept of vulnerability and how it comes to be operationalized. Major impacts arise from the fundamental way in which global health is conceived and put into practice.

In its historical development, the global health regime has assuredly advanced its own concepts. As we have seen, these have tended above all to prioritize the need to avoid the spread of infectious diseases. While certainly acknowledging human entitlements to health, these concepts have given weight to wider international social purposes, such as economic prosperity, and international peace and security (Inoue and Drori 2011: 12). To the extent that it stresses the latter, human health is presented as a means to an end, rather than as an end in itself. Moreover, in articulating its own visions from time to time, international society has again deployed its own categories. These have developed around the distinctly understood consequences of infectious versus chronic diseases, and around its alternating preferences for what has been called 'horizontal' versus 'vertical' approaches to the control and management of disease. Unlike in the other cases, the distribution of vulnerability is not produced by those categories directly. Instead, in the case of health, international society tends to reinforce existing categories drawn from elsewhere, given the striking correlation that is already present between the distribution of ill health and many other socio-economic categorizations.

There are, however, different approaches to dealing with health. For example, the distinction has been drawn between historical systems of 'horizontal' management of global health, in contrast to more recent forms of 'vertical' management (Fidler 2009b: 219): the former refers largely to instruments that operate between societies, whereas the latter operate within them. Intrusive vertical management bears the hallmarks of the traditional international societal practice of policing its own criteria of 'rightful membership' (Clark 2005). In the case of health, it has done so self-consciously—as noted in the Constitution of the WHO—by making internal health management a condition of responsible membership of international society. More recently, this has been further advanced by including health quite explicitly as part of the internationally prescribed test for 'good governance' (Fidler 2009b: 223).

This horizontal/vertical distinction can often be deceptive: rather than a stark alternative, the vertical approach is as likely to be a continuation of the horizontal by other interventionist means. Instead of the vertical—with the priority, in Fidler's terms, to 'reduce threats within states'—being wholly separate from the horizontal ('manage germ traffic between states') (Fidler 2009b: 219), the former can be construed as a means towards the latter end. That is to say that intervention in the health affairs of another country is as likely to be motivated by the wish to protect oneself from threat as by concern for the best interests of the other party. States with internal health problems likely to spill over adversely onto others are, in this sense, considered like rogue states, and similarly exposed to international action to quell the danger that they represent, even if this will sometimes be presented as humanitarian intervention (Ingram 2009: 97–8; Price-Smith 2009: 99–100).

The implications of these concepts and categories are widespread, but can be illustrated briefly in four areas: in the tension between biomedical and social understandings of health; in the respective priority accorded to dealing with infectious versus chronic disease; in the social production of the very scarcity that afflicts global health; and in the contrast between the seeming ubiquity of risk in theory, and its particular allocation in practice.

On the first, the criticism is widely made that the predominant approach to international and global health over most of its history has been an essentially biomedical one (Labonté et al. 2011b: xxviii; Lee 2009: 32). This may seem hardly controversial, and could indeed be regarded as laudable, as the only sensible way forward in a disparate international society containing many conflicting interests. However, such an approach is not without its costs. Too narrow a focus on the technicalities of medical science risks losing sight of other critical social parameters. For much of the period, this is in effect what the WHO primarily chose to do (Meier 2010: 163). There are now worries that some private foundations simply reinforce this very same tendency (MacLean and Brown 2009: 3). Their activities have been associated with a focus on tackling individual diseases, and this disaggregated approach may incidentally distort local health priorities in recipient countries (Garrett 2011: 17; Williams and Rushton 2011: 13).

Secondly, in general terms, there has been much greater attention paid to tackling infectious, as against chronic, disease (MacLean and Brown 2009: 3). While this choice may have been based on reasonable assessments of the prospects for effective treatment, the outcome has not been 'neutral' with regard to the relative incidence of the respective diseases in different sectors of international society, nor with respect to the incentives driving the priorities within the medical research effort.

Thirdly, while it is demonstrably true that global health faces the common issue of limited resources, the allocation of these resources does avowedly represent choices, and often these have been skewed in ways that reduce the vulnerability of some, while seemingly tolerating and legitimating the vulnerability of many others. Any such seeming 'naturalization' of exposure demands, as a response, a commensurate 'denaturalization' of scarcity (Schrecker 2011: 260). Some examples will be considered further below.

Finally, and most fundamentally of all, there is the underlying appreciation of risk and vulnerability. Risk can be thought to lie everywhere (WHO CSDH 2008: 110), such as in the emergence of new types of 'superbugs', seemingly resistant to all known antibiotics. On top of this, however, social vulnerability has recently been very unevenly distributed. What is most pronounced in the landscape of global health is, accordingly, 'differentiated profiles of risk and vulnerability' (Ingram 2009: 82). However, this occurs not simply because some risks 'elude the control of protective institutions of society' (Cockerham and Cockerham 2010: 33), but rather because action against other risks is prioritized, and the displacement of vulnerability is the inevitable consequence of that choice. It is in this light that the manipulation of risk has been described as 'a measure of social violence, capturing how power distributes unevenly down the social ladder' (Nguyen and Peschard 2011: 319). In this way, the allocation of health risks should be considered 'thoroughly *anthropogenic*'—not any part of nature (Berlinguer 2003: 60).

We can develop this theme further by reviewing the marked recent trend towards the 'securitization' of global health. What this demonstrates so starkly is the great discrepancy between the paramount discourse of global health and the actual risk to health on the ground. In this context, one pertinent question has been asked: 'Why have some health problems been associated with human security, while others have not?' (Chen and Narasimhan 2003: 3). It is no little irony that the increased focus on *global* health has been accompanied exactly by a more *localized*, rather than universal, set of priorities. The relevance of this is immediate, insofar as securitization for some appears necessarily associated with the enhanced vulnerability of others. Here the key point is not simply the preferences that are expressed through the means of international society, but how this effectively leads to the toleration and legitimation of these health outputs. In either case, what is the reason for this differentiation in degrees of acceptance for such sharply contrasting outcomes?

One answer has been provided by Jonathan Mann, a former senior official of the WHO, in his Preface to the high-impact book, *The Coming Plague*:

The world has rapidly become much more vulnerable to the eruption and, most critically, to the widespread and even global spread of both old and new infectious diseases. This new and heightened vulnerability is not mysterious. (quoted in Lee 2003: 18)

It may not be mysterious, but neither is it a response to some straightforwardly existing reality 'out there' that has somehow rendered 'people' more vulnerable. This is the key point made by McInnes: 'it is clear that it is not "health" that has been securitised, but rather a limited range of health issues . . . [I]t is not an agenda based on health needs, but on the sense of risk to the state, and in particular to Western states' (McInnes 2009: 54). The urge to securitize on the part of some simply draws attention to the cognate willingness to tolerate vulnerability with respect to others, and to this extent reinforces the applicability of Veitch's (2007) previously considered scheme of analysis: the legalization of responsibility in some ring-fenced areas creates, as a logical corollary, open spaces of irresponsibility elsewhere. In much the same way, proactive securitization in some defined areas leaves unaddressed those to whom that health regime remains inapplicable: it legitimates and deepens their vulnerability.

That vulnerability is now at the centre of thinking about global health is reflected in its pervasive imagery as a threat to security. In 2000, for the first time, the Security Council pronounced a health issue (HIV/AIDS) as a matter of concern to international security (MacLean and Brown 2009: 10). Security is the antidote to vulnerability. But is this vulnerability that is to be securitized genuinely universal, and is it to be counteracted uniformly across the board? In fact, securitization is being implemented in a fashion as skewed as the distribution of vulnerability to which it effectively responds (Rushton 2009: 75). In much the same way as in the earlier cases, those who might be thought 'objectively' to be the least vulnerable of all have become the principal subjects of a pronounced vulnerability discourse, and presented as the most pressing 'victims' of the effects of global change. This is just as apparent in the field of global health as it has been with respect to climate change and migration. This vision of the emerging health landscape has been devised largely 'through definitional fiat' (Elbe 2010: 131).

This actual practice is in stark contrast to officially declared objectives. In its *World Health Report 2007*, the WHO itself defined global health *security* as 'the activities required . . . to minimize vulnerability to acute public health events that endanger the collective health of populations living across geographical regions and international boundaries' (WHO 2007: ix). This appears to adopt both a global and an inclusive approach. At the same time, it manifestly objectifies the risk 'out there', and the extent of the exposure to it, and in so doing elides other international contributions to the problem. This wider practice is inconsistent with its declared intention, insofar as the push to securitize global health, as exemplified in the 2005 revisions of the IHR, has come principally from the developed world: 'One of the most powerful forces driving the evolution of a stronger regime is the increasing awareness that the health of peoples in the industrial world is profoundly influenced by the health conditions in the developing world' (Zacher and Keefe 2008: 74). At the same time, this has contributed to a highly contested politics of global health vulnerability, and a perception that 'rich countries require poor countries to comply in order to ensure biosecurity in rich countries, and that rich countries have less interest in the capacities, *and the states of health and vulnerability*, in poorer countries' (Koivusalo and Mackintosh 2008: 1165, emphasis added). How this all plays out in practice we can now see when we turn to the resulting distribution of vulnerability in global health.

THE DISTRIBUTION OF GLOBAL HEALTH VULNERABILITY

The recent prominence of a discourse about the health vulnerability of the global rich stands in uncomfortably sharp contrast to the seeming facts of risk on the ground as regards the global poor. Shortly after the formation of the WHO, it was recorded that there had been a great 'moral evolution' away from those early twentieth-century concepts of managing health that had sought to protect the 'favoured' nations from contamination by disease from the 'less-favoured' (Howard-Jones 2009 [orig. 1950]: 28). Has this really been so? On the contrary, there is ample evidence that the recent reinvigoration of interest in global health has been led by the concerns of the developed world, rather than by any immediate concern for the health problems experienced elsewhere: the priority remains to keep the problem at arm's length, by a combination of horizontal and vertical means.

In this respect, international society has had little need to invent its own separate categories for the management of health: these are already available in those other social stratifications that are fully reflected in the distribution of health. That is not to say that these correlations are by any means completely perfect. While it is clearly the case that the 'global *divergence* in life expectancy' coincides exactly with the 'global *divergence* in per capita incomes' in the mid-eighteenth century (Deaton 2011: 228), this correlation does not continue to pertain beyond a certain threshold (Segall 2010: 6–7). Nonetheless, the distributions of global health do mirror, for the most part, the variable distribution of other social and economic goods, including relative access to the institutions of international society.

What has become manifest in the demand for systems of global surveillance of disease (Weir and Mykhalovskiy 2010) is the seeming denial of precisely these connections. The rich countries have now determined to become more vigilant, and to encourage international society to take on this task with greater energy. The driving force behind this has unmistakably been the sense of vulnerability that has latterly emerged in the developed world (Weir and Mykhalovskiy 2010: 22–3). This irony is neatly captured in the summary judgement that what has contributed to the heightened role of the G8 in matters of global health has been the 'increasingly equal vulnerability of each G8 member to a new generation of infectious diseases' (Kirton and Mannell 2007: 126): this seems openly to acknowledge that it is the most developed sector of the globe that has now been placed most at risk. What it is most at risk to is the perception that the 'developing world is a reservoir of disease' (Aginam 2004: 298). However, this flies in the face of the startling statistic that only '1 per cent of the people in developed countries die of infectious diseases' (Zacher and Keefe 2008: 9). Far from such statistics alleviating any sense of vulnerability, it remains this underlying perception that has driven the policy prescriptions that feed on it: greater security is now demanded in the developed world because any increase in vulnerability is politically unaccept- able (Koivusalo and Mackintosh 2008: 1164). This echoes the politics that have recently surrounded human movement as well.

What is currently being securitized makes the contrast with what is simultan- eously rendered vulnerable all that much starker. Of the global health burden of death by infectious disease in the early 2000s, some 82 per cent occurred in Africa and Southeast Asia, and less than 5 per cent in Europe and the Americas (WHO figures, cited in Long 2011: 101). At the same time, the region of the Americas contains some 10 per cent of the total burden of disease, yet 31 per cent of the world's health workers. In comparison, Africa suffers 24 per cent of the global burden of disease, with only 3 per cent of the health workers (WHO 2011: 92). Clearly, there is a grotesque mismatch between need and the availability of resources to meet it. This situation is compounded by movement of trained health personnel towards high- and middle-income countries. On this, there has admittedly been recent action, in the form of the 2010 WHO Global Code of Practice on the Recruitment of Health Personnel (Taylor and Dhillon 2012), but this has been modest in intent. It establishes a voluntary code, and, whatever its long-term potential, can do little in the short term to deal with the increasing reliance of rich-country health services on poor-country trained personnel.

There are the widely remarked sharp contrasts in life expectancy: that in Japan is more than double that in Zambia, a statistic that is 'disturbing' if not automatically 'unjust' (Segall 2010: 153). While the developed world volubly voices its concerns about the spread of infectious disease, the developing world remains relatively powerless to staunch the inward flow of other diseases, such as those associated with smoking and diet, that now encroach upon its own populations (Barraclough 2009: 103). Estimates place the death burden associated with smoking as falling between 70–80 per cent upon developing countries by 2030 (Collin, Lee, and Bissell 2009: 369; Elbe 2010: 136).

The developing world thus faces the prospect of a 'double burden', simultaneously carrying a disproportionate share with respect to both infectious and non-infectious disease (T. Brown 2011: 322). If this is globalization, it is highly asymmetric, with the flow of harms in the one direction far surpassing the return traffic in the opposite. As a result, '[g]lobal income inequalities reinforce global health inequalities, adding (literal) injury to (material) insult' (Deaton 2011: 243–4). The picture is equally lamentable when viewed from the perspective of remedial action, particularly with respect to medical research and the availability of medicines (Pécoul et al. 1999). There are, of course, exceptions to this bleak overall picture, with some specific programmes directly geared towards reducing the incidence of disease in the developing world. These are, however, the exceptions to a stark general rule. In broad terms, we find the application of the crude, but suggestive, 10:90 ratio—a mere 10 per cent of research spending globally is devoted to addressing the health problems that account for 90 per cent of the global disease burden (Zacher and Keefe 2008: 108–9; Archibugi and Bizzarri 2009: 204; Labonté et al. 2011b vol. I: li).

The situation is particularly vexed as regards both research into medicines, and their availability (at an affordable price). The 80 per cent of the world's population in the developing world accounts for only some 20 per cent of global sales of pharmaceuticals (Zacher and Keefe 2008: 108). The reason is straightforwardly that the bulk of research and production is geared to those illnesses that afflict the developed world in particular, because that is where the effective economic demand is to be found. The pharmaceutical companies are loath to embark on costly R & D that will not deliver good returns on their investment (Baxi 2010: 19; Correa 2011: 256): this contrived distribution of medicines, in turn, reinforces the selective vulnerability of populations.

Indeed, it could be said that, even if there have been dramatic improvements in managing health overall, the specific distribution of exposure to health risk today is much more *discretionary* than at any previous moment in history. This is reflected, for example, in access to influenza vaccines, a potentially severe problem for the future. On this issue, it has been noted, states 'have not agreed to binding arrangements on more equitable access', but instead have responded in 'ad hoc, reactive and nonbinding' ways that 'preserve national freedom of action' (Fidler 2012: 166–7).

Of course, with regard to access to medicines, much of this discretion lies in the hands of private institutions, including major corporations. Accordingly, the objection could be raised that many of these deficiencies are down to global capitalism rather than international society. However, the rules by which these corporations play are determined by international society at large, and these rules have done little to rectify those problems. To this extent, the outcome can be reasonably attributed to a lack of effective regulation by international society's own institutions (Pécoul et al. 1999). It is at this point that the WTO, and particularly its arrangements governing intellectual property (TRIPs), has been so hugely influential. This has a major and distorting impact on the trade in pharmaceuticals, in ways that magnify the global health inequalities that already exist. That there was a TRIPs agreement at all was essentially down to the power differentials that allowed developed countries to insist on one in the first place (Roffe, Tansey, and Vivas-Eugui 2006). Thereafter, approaching TRIPs as essentially a trade matter, it was no part of the WTO's job description to give priority to its implications for the distribution of global health (Muzaka 2011: 3), but this scarcely makes it innocent of the consequences of those arrangements.

At first sight, this may appear an unfair charge to make. Even if the TRIPs as originally designed did have malign health effects, this was duly acknowledged later, and some changes have since been made in practice. The principal evidence against this criticism is, therefore, the high-profile WTO Doha Ministerial Declaration of 2001. This stated in part:

> We agree that the TRIPs Agreement does not and should not prevent Members from taking measures to protect public health. Accordingly, while reiterating our commitment to the TRIPs Agreement, we affirm that the Agreement can and should be interpreted and implemented in a manner supportive of the WTO member's right to protect public health and, in particular, to promote access to medicines for all. (quoted in Correa 2011: 259–60)

Far from aggravating the situation, this surely is persuasive evidence of international society's intent to mitigate it?

Unhappily, the outcome has not been quite so straightforward. Even if it is assuredly the case that the Declaration was a 'victory for developing countries and civil society actors' (Muzaka 2011: 84), its effects have been decidedly less dramatic overall (Roffe, Tansey, and Vivas-Eugui 2006). The very flexibility encouraged by the Declaration has been, in some large measure, circumvented by the action of some countries, including the United States, through bilateral free trade agreements that have remained highly restrictive (Correa 2011: 265–6). In any case, the WTO has itself rowed back from some of the intent of the Declaration in its subsequent decisions in 2003 and 2005 (Muzaka 2011: 133–4). In this light, there remains a valid concern about 'the tail of intellectual property wagging the dog of human health' (Tansey 2006: 265).

To be absolutely clear, the suggestion is not that international society has directly willed and intended the ill health of millions of people. What it does do, however, is to act in support of other priorities in such a way that it necessarily becomes acceptant of the consequences of its own actions. With reference back to Veitch's analysis, by tolerating one set of benign outcomes, international society in effect legitimizes its malign implications elsewhere, thus rendering them even more deeply entrenched. They become so because no one appears to bear any responsibility for such an outcome.

CONCLUSION

So exactly who are the vulnerable in the age of global health? It would seem at first glance that the WHO is in accord with much of the above analysis. It has of late set out its own critical account of the social determinants of health, in words that echo closely the main lines of the argument in this chapter:

> The unequal distribution of health-damaging experiences is not in any sense a 'natural' phenomenon but is the result of a toxic combination of poor social policies and programmes, unfair economic arrangements, and bad politics. Together, the structural determinants and conditions of daily life constitute the social determinants of health and are responsible for a major part of health inequities between and within countries. (WHO CSDH 2008: 1)

There is much to agree with in this statement. However, its analysis of these social determinants does not reach sufficiently far down. Had it done so, it would have discovered that international society, including the WHO, is complicit in many of these structures of daily life, through its own conceptions of what global health is, and by means of the operational categories through which it should be advanced.

In this particular case, the principal instrument of international society's distributive authority has been its basic concept of health and its implicit prioritization of particular values. While global health has therefore taken on the appearance of being a purely technical and medicalized realm, we should not be deceived into ignoring its essentially contested normative condition. Moreover, international society has evidenced powerful resources to transmit its concepts of health to its member states, through those norms that it seeks to diffuse. These include state obligations to manage health in certain ways within their borders, as part of the responsibilities of a 'modernized' state, and for the benefit of international society as a whole. This socialization function with regard to health has been a potent force, pressing for conformity to international expectations (Kickbusch 2009: 397).

In its own Constitution, the WHO explicitly affirmed its adherence to a principle of 'equity in health', and declared its own commitment to eliminating 'differences that are not necessary and that are avoidable, and at the same time unacceptable and unfair' (quoted in Berlinguer 2003: 59). Accordingly, the rhetoric of global health since 1945 has been one of universal entitlement: vulnerability should be reduced, and protection enhanced, on this basis alone. In practice, international society has instead contributed to a pattern of differential vulnerability that has contradicted this stated goal. Has international society then simply been devious, and acted in duplicitous ways? On the face of it, its routinely reiterated normative purpose would suggest otherwise. For example, in programme statements, such as those in the 2000 Millennium Development Goals, undertakings to improve human well-being, including in the health sphere, have been regularly restated (Labonté et al. 2011b: xxiv). Instead of seeing them as acts of dishonesty, we are invited to understand its shortcomings, and why its goals have remained unrealized, as the result of other practical obstacles that have simply impeded its most earnest efforts.

Does any such explanation of the shortfalls in global health suffice? In large measure, the distribution of vulnerability reflects the asymmetries of power that are endemic in this international society. Assuredly, there is a wider context of globalization of which international society is only one part. It is, for that reason, possible to claim that the 'global distribution of health risks' maps the social geography of globalization (Schrecker 2009a: 33).

However, international society does remain a significant part of these processes overall, and cannot be wholly exculpated by appeal to their autonomy: these are processes in which it is already deeply implicated at many levels. If the current distribution of vulnerability challenges 'the logic and authority of the dominant order' (MacLean and Brown 2009: 14), it would be naïve to imagine that international society can emerge from this reckoning with perfectly clean hands. Equally, if this maldistribution of vulnerability lies at the heart of the problem of global health, to that extent it must be understood as inescapably moral: as a contributor to those outcomes, it falls also to international society to address it in these terms. In the next chapter, we must confront more explicitly the nature of this moral challenge. Why, as previously set out in Carr's analysis of the 1930s and 1940s, is it so important that today's problems of international order are understood as primarily ethical in nature?

6

The Moral Problem of the Vulnerable

It is unlikely that any framework for managing complex global arrangements can eliminate the problem of vulnerability altogether: 'some vulnerabilities are inevitable and . . . will remain a feature of social life, even in an ideal world' (Goodin 1985: 203). This, however, does not mean that no choices remain about the degree to which its various distributions can be considered tolerable or not. Crucially, it certainly does not mean that contemporary problems can be addressed without any reference to their moral dimensions, as it is in these terms that they are seen by those caught up in them. All attempts to respond to vulnerability, within the remit of international society, are compelled to face up to this reality, and for that reason moral concerns are core to the complexity that it now confronts.

As we have already seen in the preceding cases, these moral dimensions emerge directly from the deployment of the concepts and categories by means of which those issues are defined and managed in international society. However, moral implications emerge not just from the categorization that is deployed *within* each issue area, but additionally from the compartmentalization *between* them. International society deals not only with each of those issues in its own preferred way, but it does so by treating them separately, as if each were wholly distinct from the others. This separation is itself artificial, and contrives to compound the deformities that already characterize them individually. It is this artifice that gives the resulting problems their particular complexion and intensity. In what sense, then, are these moral problems, and why are they moral problems *for* international society?

Normative IR theory has long searched for some plausible account of moral claims in the international context, and for some philosophical grounding for international justice. These debates have thrown up multiple dichotomies, such as between a 'morality of states' and a 'morality of people' (Beitz 1979), or between communitarian and cosmopolitan accounts (Brown 1992; Cochran 1999). In the face of interdependence/globalization, yet further arguments have been advanced for the emergence of a qualitatively new normative context, since 'human beings are now involved in interdependent and reciprocal relations with each other' (Hutchings 2010: 3). This, it is claimed, generates new social obligations that make national borders increasingly irrelevant. To the extent that such an interpretation of interdependence implies reciprocity among equal players, it is different from the position set out in this book: the vulnerability perspective adopted here acknowledges instead the salience of existing power differentials, and locates ethical claims in the impact that the decisions of the powerful have on the circumstances of those that are rendered vulnerable as a result. It is this perception that international society is implicated in those outcomes that generates the moral grounds for complaint. This highlights the essence of Carr's problem of reconciling power and morality, given that the moral problem emerges precisely from the power relationships that are in play.

Accordingly, any final resolution of those debates about the definitive content of global justice is not necessary for the present purpose: the focus here is on the really existing ethical disputes that inform international society's practice of the vulnerable, rather than on development of any exogenous moral theory in its own right (Jackson 2009: 29). In this respect, what is so interesting is the extent to which ideas of vulnerability play a role in seemingly quite different ethical theories. It is quite possible, of course, that in some substantial respects a cosmopolitan account of vulnerability will differ from one that is communitarian in inspiration: the latter may be more interested in the 'affectedness' of close kin and neighbours, while the cosmopolitan attaches much, if not equal, weight to those that are distantly affected. Many cosmopolitans would argue that these obligations now do have a global reach, because the patterns of 'affectedness', once found only among those in close proximity, are today replicated in the very real impacts produced at much greater distance.

What is nonetheless so highly revealing is that both do readily acknowledge the import of relationships of vulnerability. As a result, the key point is that these moral fault lines profoundly inform the politics of international society, and animate the struggles that occur within it. For that reason, these contending principles matter, however much or little any one interpretation of what justice means is self-consciously adopted, or held to be morally compelling: they constitute an important part of the ethical politics that surround the substance of international order.

Accordingly, just as my earlier studies of legitimacy in international society were not intended to set out any overarching account of the moral basis of legitimacy, so this book does not seek to elaborate any systematic position on global justice. Such a task can safely be left to others (Beitz 1979, 1999; Rawls 1999; Pogge 2002; Caney 2005; Fabre 2007; D. Miller 2007; R. W. Miller 2010; Sen 2010). Nonetheless, it is worth pausing briefly over the general contours of this debate—not in order to take sides on the substantive issues that divide the various protagonists, but simply to direct attention to the fact that issues of vulnerability are already highly visible in many of the arguments deployed on *both* sides. Whether or not any one of these theories amounts to a fully persuasive interpretation of global justice in the round, we can at the very least note a surprisingly broad area of agreement between them about the close connections between vulnerability and the core concerns of justice, in whichever version the latter is understood. For international society, the implications of its own behaviour with respect to vulnerability have the further effect of opening up an ethical dimension, whether or not it is considered fully to act as a moral agent.

Vulnerability has indeed become a common trope in writing on international ethics (O'Neill 1996: 166–74; Caney 2005: 117–19), and specifically in some feminist ethics (Butler 2004). It is cognate with Andrew Linklater's discussion of 'harm' in world politics (Linklater 2011). Elsewhere, there has been interesting sociological work that grounds human rights in vulnerability (Turner 2006), and international legal work that explores the nexus between vulnerability and human rights (Morawa 2003).

The prominence of this theme of vulnerability is evident in many cosmopolitan assessments of global justice, and—perhaps more surprisingly—is to be found equally among communitarian sceptics. Of the former, the most striking example is Andrew Linklater's work on harm. He is especially mindful of the scope of the constituency subject to any harm from the decisions of others, and maintains that this is a central strand in ethical thought. 'The condition of vulnerability to harm by others', he suggests, can be considered 'an intrinsic feature of every social morality' (Linklater 2011: 91). If so, there can scarcely be any more powerful acknowledgement of its moral significance: it is intuitively something that people respond to as moral agents.

Other cosmopolitan theorists likewise broach central concerns about the inequities of the current order, and the potential exposure to harm that these create, resulting from the institutionalized unfairness of the system: what violates justice is exactly the unequal exposure to vulnerability that results from that unfairness. Thomas Pogge has long been an ardent and vocal champion of this position, and the theme of vulnerability, derivative of poverty, runs consistently through his analysis. He laments the fact of continuing widespread poverty despite the existence now of more restrictive and effective 'moral norms protecting the weak and vulnerable' (Pogge 2002: 2), and blames this on the operations of a global economic order that 'exacerbates the vulnerability of the weaker national economies' (Pogge 2002: 116). With some 18 million people dying each year as a result of poverty, he concludes that they are 'impoverished and starved through our institutional order coercively imposed upon them' (Pogge 2002: 176). The resultant obligations to rectify this situation, he contests, arise not just from the fact that we do actually possess the capacity to take remedial action, but additionally from the acknowledgement that 'we are also and more significantly related to them as supporters of, and beneficiaries from, a global institutional order that substantively contributes to their destitution' (Pogge 2002: 117). In this way, poverty and starvation are not just some inevitable fact of life, but result from one form of vulnerability that is both tolerated and sanctioned by the practices of international society, and is simultaneously of direct benefit to other sections within it.

There are, of course, many dissenters from this view, and they tend in varying degrees to cleave towards a variety of communitarian positions: these are less convinced that all the ills can be blamed on international society in the first place, and much more sceptical that abstract principles of justice apply globally in any straightforward sense. David Miller captures well one such position in that, while rejecting the full-blown justice claims of the likes of Pogge, he nonetheless does accept the need for some universal moral minimum of basic human rights (Miller 2007: 231). Again, the point here is not to get drawn into the details of this particular debate, but instead to highlight the degree to which it already revolves around issues of vulnerability as its central concern. This is manifestly so in Miller's own rendition of the argument. While critical of Pogge, Miller nonetheless admits the necessity for a set of international economic rules that adheres to basic concepts of fairness. He acknowledges that this quality is demonstrably lacking in present arrangements. 'Many societies', he observes, 'are vulnerable to exploitation and other forms of injustice by powerful states, corporations, and other agencies' (Miller 2007: 251–2). In conclusion, he insists that poor countries can reasonably demand an 'international order in which they are sufficiently protected from such vulnerabilities' (Miller 2007: 253). This emerges powerfully also in his specific justification for observing a basic minimum of human needs. The reason why this is essential, he makes clear, is that these 'intrinsic needs are those items or conditions it is necessary for a person to have if she is to avoid being harmed' (Miller 2007: 179). Taken literally, with reference to our earlier definition, the conditions for the avoidance of harm are then exactly the same as those required for the reduction of vulnerability. In short, at the heart of Miller's exposition, we find a residual notion of justice that is as much framed by vulnerability as that found in rival cosmopolitan accounts. Accordingly, this is a concern that straddles both sides of the cosmopolitan–communitarian divide: what remains in dispute is the nature and extent of the constituency of the vulnerable that should be the object of our moral concern, rather than any disagreement about the moral significance of vulnerability as such.

Given all this, why is it that vulnerability generates its own distinctively moral problems, and why should these be thought to fall to international society to resolve? At heart is the notion of asymmetrical power that characterizes specific relationships, however extensive those relationships are conceived to be. Accordingly, in one such version, it has been argued that in conditions of globalization, developed countries (as well as corporations) 'take advantage' of developing countries, and make improper use of their 'desperate neediness' (R. W. Miller 2010: 59). They act in this way because they have the power to do so, and this is the source of the moral problem. Accordingly, immediately central to any such interpretation is the ethical approach that was pioneered by Robert Goodin (1985). Even more than those considered so far, his ethical argument is explicitly framed around the concept of vulnerability. His primary interest lies in explaining the source of social responsibilities, and he does so in terms of the '*vulnerability* of the beneficiary' (Goodin 1985: xi). As he further amplifies, 'what is crucial . . . is that others are depending upon us. They are particularly vulnerable to our actions and choices' (Goodin 1985: 11).

However, we must note the very precise formulation of his specific argument. 'The central argument of this book', he affirms, 'is that we bear special responsibilities for protecting those who are particularly vulnerable *to us*' (Goodin 1985: 109, emphasis added). What is it about vulnerability that gives rise to this moral relationship? It might mean either of two related, but distinct, things. The first is that recipients of our responsibilities are already vulnerable, and they are then additionally exposed to what we are prepared to undertake by way of remedial action to alleviate their condition. Secondly, and more profoundly, it could be suggested that it is their relationship to us that constitutes the entirety of their vulnerability in the first place. What both seem to allow to varying degrees is not some wholly objective and pre-existing condition of vulnerability, that ends up by placing moral obligations on us. Instead, this is a notion of vulnerability that inheres in the very relationship between other people and *us*, and in which it is the relationship itself that constitutes the vulnerability. In either specific version, the argument has major implications for international society, given that so many people are rendered vulnerable to international society's power to decide.

Goodin recognizes *both* elements as being present. He is happy to objectify some types of vulnerability, when he admits of them that they are 'natural, inevitable, and immutable'. For the most part, however, they possess a different quality: they are 'created, shaped, or sustained by current social arrangements' (Goodin 1985: xi). There remains an intriguing ambivalence about these two senses. However, of central significance to the following argument is Goodin's diagnosis of vulnerability as an inherently moral condition in either version. He explains the reasons for the essentially moral nature of vulnerability, and for his own moral disapproval of relationships that generate vulnerability: 'What is really wrong with them', he suggests, 'is that they necessarily create opportunities for the strong to exploit the weaknesses of those who are vulnerable and dependent' (Goodin 1985: 193). In short, the source of moral concern about vulnerability is precisely the asymmetrical power relationship in which it is inevitably embedded. What is less clear, given the above ambiguity, is whether his disapproval is directed against the asymmetrical power to assuage vulnerability, or the asymmetrical capacity to constitute it in the first instance—or indeed against both in equal measure.

This book does not replicate Goodin's account of vulnerability by deploying it as the basis of a stand-alone normative theory. What it does suggest is that such concerns about vulnerability, whether convincing or not as any overall normative position, nonetheless add considerable complexity and intensity—objectively speaking—to the already hard choices faced by international society in negotiating its own global arrangements: an ethics of the vulnerable is inherent in what international society is and does. This can be explained only because of the ethical purchase of vulnerability not as some deontological moral position, but as a conspicuous feature of the activities of international society itself.

Michael Freeman, drawing upon Goodin's account, has similarly emphasized the importance of this 'vulnerability principle', in terms of which there is a 'moral responsibility for the known and foreseeable consequences of our actions, and special obligations to those who have been harmed by what we have done, or are vulnerable to future harm from what we propose to do' (quoted in Linklater 2011: 106, fn. 57). For purposes of this study, when we speak of others being vulnerable *to us*, the specific object of our concern is how people are, in effect, made vulnerable by the norms and practices of international society, as this is the principal (but by no means exclusive) vehicle through which we act upon them. For the same reason, it therefore falls to international society to develop its own forms of redress, because it alone can change the framework that gives rise to these specific vulnerabilities in the first place. Whether or not people self-consciously adhere to any precise version of this normative principle, it is sufficiently widespread and intuitively appreciated as a moral idea that international society cannot choose to ignore it, even when some of its most powerful members may have a compelling interest in trying to do so.

Vulnerability acquires its political purchase precisely because competing ideas about justice are important to human behaviour, even in the absence of any full agreement about exactly what this norm might mean or entail (Sen 2010: 2). In this way, it is fundamental to the problems facing international society. Hedley Bull, albeit largely predisposed to attach priority to a principle of order, famously acknowledged as much. In his later writings, and particularly in his Hagey lectures, he worried that if Third World complaints about international economic justice were not addressed, the international order would soon be eroded (Bull 1984; Hoffmann 1990: 30; Reus-Smit 2005: 93). Accordingly, we do not need a fully developed theory of global justice here to point out that moral clashes deriving from disparate concerns about justice are, objectively speaking, already embedded in the problems now confronting international society. It is this infusion that gives them their very hard edge, and the concept of the vulnerable provides a ready means of access to them. Those moral problems, as accentuated by international society's imposition of its own concepts and categories, can now be re-examined in the context of the previous four case studies, beginning with that of political violence.

POLITICAL VIOLENCE AND THE MORAL CONDITION
OF THE VULNERABLE

Many of the recent debates about war and violence may seem to have been about practicalities rather than about normative preferences. Much of the debate has focused on the status of civilians, and how this category needs to be reconsidered in the light of contemporary military operations, the drift towards 'total' war, and today's technologies of violence. Since absolute respect for civilians would apparently make contemporary war no longer fightable, it is commonly suggested, we need pragmatically to question whether such categories retain their moral value. What is up for discussion is how practical limits can be made to hold, rather than what is the moral essence of those limits. This perspective overall, however, fundamentally misunderstands the nature of the problem. It is not the military practice that has unsettled the traditional categories of discrimination, but rather the challenges to the wider concept of violence in which they had hitherto enjoyed ideological protection.

What we have previously seen is that in setting out its position on discrimination, international society derived it from its more fundamental concept of political violence that made moral sense of it in the first place: categories of discrimination were located within an overarching concept, and it is this that has now become the principal site of moral contestation (Owens 2008). When other agents challenge its ideas of discrimination, what they in fact seek to undermine is that particular concept of violence that sustains them: the categories of discrimination are the means to change, but an alternative concept of violence is the desired end. At the same time, by behaving as it has, international society has opened up the space for other moral challenges to emerge. At stake is the paradigm of political violence that currently enjoys legitimacy, and international society's wish to sustain it is now subject to substantial pressure from other rival accounts.

However, in its own dealings with those issues of discrimination, international society appears now to have suffered a loss on its part of any convincing moral bearings. At the same time, disparate judgements about who might legitimately be regarded as vulnerable to the exercise of force make the practical everyday dealing with those issues highly contentious and problematic. For that reason, there can be no resolution that does not recognize the moral dilemmas and choices that these issues engage. Distinguishing between the vulnerable and invulnerable in the context of violence is not some wholly technical or legal matter, but addresses fundamental normative concerns about the acceptable contours of political violence. These cannot be sidestepped.

This is not a wholly novel concern. One of the prominent debates in just war theory has been exactly about whether or not the principle of non-combatant immunity should be considered an essential moral principle of warfare, or simply one type of discrimination (among possibly many others) that just happened to be favoured for contingent historical reasons: it seemed more plausible because it was more convenient to implement. This issue had been raised many years ago: 'there is certainly room for legitimate doubt as to whether the norm of civilian immunity enjoys the status of an absolute moral imperative' (Hartigan 1967, quoted in Clark 1988: 92–3; see also Bailey 1972: 14–15). If so, the categories of the vulnerable and invulnerable, understood to mean active combatants or not, can be considered as wholly 'conventional', and in some respects morally 'arbitrary' as well (Finlay 2010: 299; McKeogh 2011: 588). Their moral value lies in their utility, as taking a significant class of persons out of the combat (Primoratz 2007b: 25), rather than in the moral quality of non-combatancy per se. For the same reason, the greater the practical difficulty in separating the two (not least because many acts of violence are designed intentionally to obscure the distinction), the less their utility and moral worth becomes in practice (Johnson 2011: 96).

As we have seen, to this have now been added arguments about moral asymmetry that further challenge the traditional paradigm (McMahan 2010). There is a new insistence to the claim that the 'distinction between combatants and non-combatants in itself has no moral significance' (McMahan 2008: 27). As a result, it is conceded that 'it is not surprising that we should feel some discomfort with a regime, like symmetrical *jus in bello*, that allocates liability to attack simply on the basis of membership of the class of combatants' (Rodin and Shue 2008b: 5).

As against all this, Walzer's contrary intuition is that the moral essence of war, as one form of political violence, is to be discovered in its attempt to discriminate between targets. Albeit that there are many other important ways in which war can be regulated (restrictions on weapons, locations, timing, and so on), the moral nature of war does not stand or fall by adherence to them. In contrast, he regards differentiation in the targets of war as being 'more closely connected to universal notions of right and wrong' (Walzer 1977: 42). Accordingly, distinguishing between justifiable targets and those who deserve to remain invulnerable is what brings us closer to the moral issues that are raised by the use of political violence. It accords with the 'morally foundational "no-harm" principle' (Primoratz 2007b: 29).

Core to this discussion is the complex relationship between violence and the stipulation of the vulnerable. Walzer had rested his war convention on an under-articulated theory of human rights. These rights form the foundations of the entire edifice, albeit that little was said to establish what they are or where they come from, and he has been exposed to considerable criticism on this account (Bull 1979). It is useful to consider a telling footnote in Walzer's presentation, as it neatly captures one distinction that is highly important.

> But the theoretical problem is not to describe how immunity is gained, but how it is lost. We are all immune to start with; our right not to be attacked is a feature of normal human relationships. That right is lost by those who bear arms 'effectively' because they pose a danger to other people. It is retained by those who don't bear arms at all. (Walzer 1977: 145, footnote)

There are many important claims being made here. This idea translates most directly as the argument about the moral priority of the combatancy/non-combatancy distinction. However, its underlying proposition is that we are all endowed with a right to invulnerability, and this can be overridden only in very specific conditions: we become vulnerable because of something we do that makes us temporarily forfeit that right (Shapcott 2010: 169). Even so, the right remains only in abeyance, and is fully restored once those pertinent conditions have changed. What is so significant about the logical sequence of this argument is that it begins from the pole of absolute restriction, and argues for the gradual relaxation of that restriction only insofar as certain specified conditions are met; when they no longer are, the restriction automatically comes back into force.

It is fair to say that international society, for its part, has tended to operate on the opposite assumption of a theory of the vulnerable, rather than a theory of the invulnerable. That is to say that it has sought gradually to introduce restrictions on the scope of violence, narrowing down a universal category to one that is more limited. It has been more reluctant to adopt any position of universal invulnerability founded on the conception of human rights that informs Walzer's account of the war convention. In doing so, it has constrained the applicability of rights as a protection against violence, and it is only in recent decades, especially since 1945, that this ground has begun to shift in any significant way. At the same time, and again as a result of trying to meet the challenge of non-state use of force, international society has itself begun to squeeze human rights from yet another direction (Luban 2003). The net effect is that international society has displayed marked inconsistency in its own position, both in principle and in practice.

What is so noteworthy is the extent to which these debates about discrimination, theoretical and practical, are actually driven by underlying normative concepts about the form of violence in which they take place. 'Implicit in the definitional parameter "civilians"', in one such argument, 'are associations such as "uninvolved", "innocent" or "neutral", all of which suggest civilian targets to be illegitimate targets' (Armborst 2010: 423). 'Innocents', we are told, 'should not be dragged into the conflict since they have done no harm' (Van Engeland 2011: 20). Directly relevant to this analysis is then the contention that the 'principle of discrimination has in practice meant regarding combatants as guilty and non-combatants as innocent' (Bailey 1972: 15). The underlying reason why these choices are so problematic is that each is supported by a strong appeal to a type of innocence, and this is what brings out its full normative force. The notion of innocence has long been an important theme in the just war tradition (Bailey 1972: 12–13; Kaufman 2007: 99; Primoratz 2007b: 30). Walzer refers to it as a 'term of art' which is applicable to the civilian population, on the grounds that they have 'done nothing, and are doing nothing, that entails the loss of their rights' (Walzer 1977: 146). Others have made related distinctions between innocence as 'action' and as 'capacity' (Phillips 1984: 58).

But what might 'guilty' and 'innocent' convey in the context of violence? Developments in just war theory, as reflected in the laws of war, moved steadily towards a separation between the two ideas of moral guilt and non-combatancy. From the seventeenth century onwards, there was a progressive decline in 'punitive' concepts of war, whereby it was undertaken as a punishment against wrongdoers. Associated with this move, from Grotius onwards, was the need to dispense with the 'fiction' that the enemy was collectively 'guilty' (McKeogh 2007: 73). In its stead emerged an understanding of the innocent not as the opposite of the guilty, but as the opposite of those 'doing harm'. Progressively, this came to be understood objectively as a reflection of the degree of direct participation in war, and hence as a proxy for combatancy.

Obviously, what is so highly contested between the various concepts of political violence is exactly which claims to innocence are to be respected and which dismissed. However, it should be stressed that this is not a matter of 'practicalities', but instead of the concept of violence that governs its use. The case study emphasized the destabilization of categories that has resulted from important perceived inequalities between belligerents. This is what makes the point. 'In situations of extreme asymmetry', in one such argument, 'the distinction between combatants and noncombatants loses its value for moral discrimination' (Kahn 2003: 43). What determines this assessment, however, is its related claim that we can make moral sense of the distinction only within a particular conceptual frame. Asymmetry changes that frame, and its dependent categories as a result. On this basis, it follows that '[w]ithout the imposition of mutual risk, warfare is not war at all' (Kahn 2003: 41). If so, the war convention no longer applies, at least in the traditional understanding of it (Fabre 2008).

This is in stark contrast to Walzer's conclusion about another form of 'asymmetry', namely a situation in which one party faces a 'supreme emergency'. Even though Walzer condones, as a last resort, infringement of the relevant principle of discrimination in this circumstance, he does so reluctantly. Just as importantly, this infringement does not lead him to any reassessment of the moral value of the rule. To the absolute prohibition that '[i]nnocence is inviolable', he allows only the qualification that 'it is (almost) the whole of our duty to uphold the rights of the innocent' (Walzer 2004: 36, 50). The rule remains otherwise intact.

Underpinning the various concepts of political violence, then, is a profound normative orientation, not simply a reduction of the vulnerable to one empirical category, already in existence and awaiting discovery. In reaching their definition of the category of the vulnerable, some operate from a starting point of restriction, others from one of permission. When applied to the opposed categories of civilians and combatants, the question becomes whether either of these has any different 'liability' to be killed. Leaving aside the exact grounds for making this distinction, the additional question can be posed as to which is the more problematic status to justify. The restrictive position assumes that what requires justification is the suspension of the immunity from harm. In other words, it is the liability that is problematic, and not the immunity. 'The work that a discrimination principle does, on this view, is not to demonstrate the immunity of non-combatants—which is true in or out of war—but . . . to show why others are sometimes non-immune' (Finlay 2010: 300). Alternatively expressed, it 'is not civilians who are given a special status in war, but combatants' (McKeogh 2011: 589).

However, when the concept of war is itself challenged, both the status and the liability are subject to renegotiation. At that point, the applicability of any form of discrimination is up for grabs, and this is the problem that international society now confronts. What has contributed to this outcome is that international society's practices, in vindication of its own concept of violence, have actually infringed its own categories of the vulnerable. International society opens the issue of political violence to moral challenge by the imposition of its own concepts and categories, and by its own failure to respect them in practice. What it has so far been unwilling to acknowledge is that questions about the moral uses of violence apply to all of its forms, not just to war exclusively, and therefore there is a moral equivalence about the application of violence against 'civilians', regardless of the type of violence that is involved (McPherson 2007: 546; Nathanson 2010: 72–4; Estreicher 2011–12). These are some of the moral problems that international society displays marked reluctance to countenance, but which, if left unaddressed, now threaten its historical achievements in the regulation of violence.

CLIMATE CHANGE AND THE MORAL CONDITION OF THE VULNERABLE

Similar issues can be demonstrated with respect to the moral problem of vulnerability in the context of climate change. As a policy realm, climate change management proceeds on an implicit understanding that those vulnerable to it somehow exist as objective categories: the task is to measure and assess relative degrees of existential vulnerability (Füssel 2010: 601; Gough and Meadowcroft 2011: 494). Insofar as the social dimension is introduced, it is used simply to explain the differential sensitivity and exposure faced by distinct categories of people. What is not fully accepted, and is itself a matter of deep contestation, is the extent to which the categories of the vulnerable already inhere in international society's own concept of the climate change problem, and are created and distributed in accordance with its own attempts to address it (O'Brien, St Clair, and Kristoffersen 2010b).

In short, this is not simply a matter of some historic responsibility for causing the problem in the first place, with regard to past emissions, but is very much a result also of distributing vulnerability through current policy actions and non-actions. The international climate process creates 'definitions, notions, and categories that together give meaning to our current idea of what climate change "actually" is' (Hajer and Versteeg 2011: 83), and the distribution of vulnerability is implicit in the way this is all done. Its concept of climate change dictates the operative categories for dealing with it, and this has formally structured the international negotiations into binaries—principally the developed and developing countries, and latterly the big emitters and others. Either configuration has important implications for how the issue is addressed, and for the vulnerabilities that flow from it. International society already injects an ethical dimension by how it addresses the problem. It is common enough to depict those moral issues of climate change in distributive and retributive (or corrective) terms (Paterson 2001: 119–23; Baer 2011: 331). What now needs to be understood is that these two approaches to justice in the climate change context are above all alternative ways of framing this core issue of vulnerability.

In effect, international society opened the door to an ethical dialogue as soon as it incorporated into its Framework Convention in 1992 its key Purpose, namely that the 'Parties should protect the climate system . . . on the basis of equity' (UNFCCC 1992: Art 3, 1). The appeal to equity amounted to an invitation to a moral exchange, and this dimension has continued to be understood in relation to vulnerability (Mearns and Norton 2010). This is exactly the point that Gardiner makes so emphatically in his analysis of the challenge to 'innocence' that lies at its heart:

> One of the primary reasons to be concerned about climate change is that it has the potential to visit extreme suffering on innocent people. In my view, if we ignore such values, we neglect concerns *right at the heart* of the climate change problem, concerns that make it the kind of problem that it is . . . To neglect these concerns is to refuse to admit a central part of the challenge that faces us. (Gardiner 2011a: 121)

Such a moral assessment, it follows, is not some optional add-on, but constitutes the full force of the problem (Baskin 2009). Gardiner further elaborates on the nature of the climate threat: 'But the deepest challenge is ethical. What matters most is what we do to protect those vulnerable to our actions and unable to hold us accountable' (Gardiner 2011a: xii). One of the things that troubles Gardiner most, and creates the conditions for his 'perfect moral storm', is thus the 'skewed vulnerabilities' that arise, largely as a result of the asymmetry between past contributions to the problem and present and future capacity to deal with its consequences (Gardiner 2011a: 119). This is compounded by the other instance of asymmetry in that those most causally culpable 'also stand to benefit from it' (Gardiner 2011b: 311).

The moral nature of these issues is often elided by the way the problem is conceptualized. Above all, it is seen as one of international collective action, with an emphasis on both the international and the collective. Since it is international, it treats the state as a unitary actor, and conceals its internal disparities in terms of the sources of emissions: the population is regarded as homogenous for this purpose, and this already distorts the moral calculus. As a result, this configures the problem as one between international society as a collective on the one hand, and nature on the other, rather than as one that is endemic in international society itself: the internal problem is thus externalized.

Moreover, in its own dominant conceptions, international society understands climate change as fundamentally an aspect of economic policy and development, and essentially reducible to the quest for new forms of clean energy. From this starting point, the problem is simply about method: what is the best means of achieving those ends? Here, the emphasis shifts to a debate about the relative role of the market, as expressed through carbon trading schemes and the like (Paterson 2011). The cognate debates have then been about the appropriate scope of the international negotiations (universal versus restricted), as well as about whether to pursue top-down, as opposed to bottom-up, approaches to the search for a solution. It is within these broad concepts of the climate change problem that its operative categories of vulnerability have come into play. These have revolved essentially around the categories of developed and developing states, or large and small emitters, each with its associated kinds of responsibilities. Pushed down the agenda are the underlying moral concerns that animate those issues.

If these moral concerns are deeply embedded in the problem, they manifest themselves in the politics of negotiating means of redress, and at this point the manner in which morality compounds the complexity of the issue becomes abundantly clear (Roberts and Parks 2007: 4–5). While it is certainly the case that there has been an imbalance of power between developed and developing countries in confronting climate change, that balance is undergoing radical change as the power of the hitherto relatively weak to obstruct a solution has become that much more apparent. The balance of emissions power has now shifted to the extent that there can be no viable solution that does not co-opt those developing countries, since they are already the source of virtually all future growth in emissions (Harris 2010: 78–9). Politically, key to securing their co-option is then a set of arrangements that will address their sense that past emissions have, however unwittingly, had the effect of violating the rights of the innocent and vulnerable. Any acceptable future climate order cannot avoid confronting this ethical concern. If Carr was correct that the key challenge facing the interwar international order was a moral one, then his argument speaks just as powerfully to the problems of climate change at the present time. There can be no solution that does not recognize the inherently ethical nature of what it is that we are trying to achieve, and if there is to be some 'give and take', then this must be predicated on recognition of the moral claims that are intrinsic to that problem.

There is, accordingly, wide recognition that there can be no effective international solution to climate change without facing its moral dimensions. These are not something that can be sidestepped, or treated as peripheral. Importantly, the IPCC stressed that while science can 'support informed decisions ... by providing criteria for judging which vulnerabilities might be labelled "key"', at the same time it acknowledged that determinations of exactly what constitutes 'dangerous' anthropogenic change involves 'value judgments' (IPCC 2007 Synthesis Report: 64). In short, there is no hiding from the moral dimension in seeking solutions to climate change, as any evasion will result in an imposition, not an acceptable solution: the outcome will then reflect the balance of power, not any balance of fairness. The dilemmas of climate change are 'inescapably ethical' and give rise to challenging international politics because 'nation states will not sign up to an agreement they perceive to be unfair, and focusing exclusively on efficiency will do little to guarantee fairness or equity' (Hepburn and Stern 2009: 37–8; see also Harris 2010: 78–9).

Why are issues of climate change inherently so morally problematic? There are a number of reasons, but they come down to two perceived sets of asymmetries. The first is an asymmetry of power; the second is an asymmetry between causality and benefit on the one hand, and adverse impacts on the other. Both revolve around the vulnerabilities that climate change entails.

With respect to the first asymmetry, there are three features of climate change that yield its moral complexity: the power of the affluent over the poor; the power of today's generation over the future; and the power of humanity over nature (Gardiner 2011a: 7). All three categories are vulnerable to our collective actions (Gardiner 2011a: xii). Most obviously, climate change can be understood as the infliction of a form of harm, and as such to press upon core areas of human rights. The human rights directly threatened are those to life, health, and subsistence, and against forcible eviction (Caney 2009: 233). Climate change is, then, best transcribed as 'transnational harm', and this leads directly to an ethical agenda (Harris 2010: 36; Linklater 2011). If GHG emissions cause harm to others, it is hard to escape the moral logic of an obligation to desist from perpetrating it (Baer 2011: 326). Elsewhere, action on climate change directly raises the balance of interests between present and future generations (Page 2006), and this too requires 'moral judgment' (Gardiner 2011b: 317). This full complexity was brought out—but certainly not resolved—in the 1992 Rio Declaration's affirmation that 'the right to development must be fulfilled so as to equitably meet development and environmental needs of present and future generations' (quoted in DeSombre 2007: 67).

In practice, climate change is being responded to at the moment by a policy of limited or non-action that entrenches further the vulnerability of the weak, largely at the insistence of the strong. The 'global injustice' arises because the 'ongoing failure adequately to address the problem exacerbates the global inequality that is part and parcel of the problem itself' (Vanderheiden 2008: xiii–iv). For example, as argued previously, there is a direct correlation between temperature increase and likely increases in sea levels. For this reason, as the 'canaries in the coalmine', the AOSIS states have pressed for a commitment to restricting temperature increase to 1.5 degrees. This is implicitly premised on a moral claim, namely that 'the measure of dangerous climate change that climate mitigation should seek to avoid should be impacts on the most vulnerable people' (J. Barnett 2011: 272).

At the heart of this moral controversy has been the relationship between vulnerability and responsibility (Baer 2011: 323–4; Füssel 2010: 598), and this is the source of the second perceived gross asymmetry. The two asymmetries are, of course, closely interconnected, insofar as power disparities create the ability to transfer costs to others (Gardiner 2011b: 313). The outcome has been depicted as one of *skewed vulnerabilities* (Gardiner 2011a: 119). 'Tragically and unjustly', it is claimed, 'climate change will cause the most suffering among those least responsible for it' (Harris 2010: 17). That this is an acute ethical issue is acknowledged by the UNDP, with the added qualification that, while this might appear to be the product of 'physical processes', it must more appropriately be seen also as 'a consequence of human actions and choices' (UNDP 2008: 9–10).

This is the ethical nub of the matter, and is regarded as such by those who feel most at risk. This has been underpinned by a corollary 'moral logic' (Christoff 2006: 842), namely that those who have contributed most to, and benefited most from, emissions must bear the initial brunt of remedial action, both in terms of their own reductions and also in financial and technological transfers to promote the reduction of others. However, this moral logic has not been universally shared, and, in consequence, differences about basic principles have bedevilled the UNFCCC from the outset. International society has already been engaged in a long-term moral negotiation about climate change, however much it may have been in denial about this fact. The success of its efforts to combat climate change now depends on policies that acknowledge the moral condition of the vulnerable as central to any solution.

HUMAN MOVEMENT AND THE MORAL CONDITION OF THE VULNERABLE

Although the earlier discussion drew attention to the myriad legal and political issues that arise in the context of human movement, it is essential now to draw attention to the core ethical issues (see Shapcott 2010: ch. 4). As Mervyn Frost has insisted, 'the problems must be understood as essentially ethical and that in some profound sense we are missing the point if we continue to see the problem presented by migrants as merely technical, legal, political or administrative' (Frost 2003a: 109). Indeed, there are good reasons to believe that the widespread preference to speak of the 'management' of migration is itself just such an attempt to 'de-politicize' it (Geiger and Pécoud 2010b: 11), and certainly to drain it of ethical content.

Why are ethics so central to this issue? A number of particular arguments will be canvassed below, but we can open with two more general claims. The first is the asymmetry of power, such that in the absence of agreed multilateral arrangements 'it is the relatively powerful states that are able to determine the basis of global migration governance' (Betts 2011b: 26). To this extent, the problem with human movement seems to replicate that with climate change. Secondly, this plays out in the iniquitous division of labour between rich and poor with regard to human movement: desperate but unskilled migrants become bottled in host countries that read 'like a roll call of some of the world's poorest . . . states' (Gibney 2006: 161), while, conversely, developing countries are virtually powerless to prevent the migration to developed states of their own trained professionals (Betts and Cerna 2011: 63). As regards the distribution of responsibility for the protection of refugees, it has been held that 'burden-sharing' is a 'fundamental norm underpinning the international refugee regime' (Hurwitz 2009: 170). However, actual state practice has been mostly marked by 'burden-shifting' rather than 'burden-sharing' (Kneebone 2009b: 28).

Why should this create an ethical problem? Is there anything in the least surprising about this tendency? Much depends on the normative parameters against which this is judged, and here the optimists see the glass as half full while the pessimists see it as half empty. Some appeal to the refugee regime, albeit 'only a century old', as compelling evidence of the 'evolution, if not sheer revolution, in international ethics' (M. Barnett 2011: 106). Others, while presumably assessing the same information, conclude instead that it demonstrates the 'evident absence of solidarist progress in relation to refugees', and are resigned to the prospect that when 'it comes to refugees and to people movement in general we remain much closer to a pluralist world of Westphalian sovereignty' (Hurrell 2011: 101, 93).

This ambivalence as to how much progress has been achieved is compounded by equally uncertain judgements about how to advance the normative cause. Frost diagnoses the problem in the contradictory moral claims that exercise themselves upon members of civil society (Frost 2003a: 116), and tries to argue his way towards a solution from that basis. Chris Brown, in contrast, while absolutely accepting that there is a normative problem in play, is far from convinced that normative theory can help us to escape from it. Instead, he settles for the pragmatist's solution: the quest for a 'morally satisfying general theory', he concludes, 'is almost certainly a waste of time'. Instead, we should focus on the particular, and do 'something about *this* problem *here*' (C. Brown 2011: 166). The puzzle, in turn, is how to know what is best to do in the specific case, in the absence of any guidance from a general moral theory.

In fact, the optimistic and the pessimistic versions are possibly much more profoundly entangled with each other than either one of them recognizes. The suggestion here is that it is the very progress that has been achieved in some respects that contributes to the selfsame recidivism that states display elsewhere. This point has been ably set out by Dauvergne: it is not just that refugee law is randomly moving in directions contrary to general human rights law, but rather that the one is moving in one direction *exactly to counter* what is happening in the other. As she explains, 'the growth of human rights norms is paradoxically linked to states pulling away from refugee law commitments' (Dauvergne 2008: 64): state default is because of normative progress elsewhere, not because of its deficiency. As the costs of compliance with the law appear ever higher, so the incentives to avoid entrapment by them appear that much more compelling.

This may help us to explain state behaviour as rational action, but what does it tell us about the nature of the resulting ethical problem? To answer this, we need to turn to the specific ethical dilemmas associated with human movement. There is no single large problem, but an accumulation of smaller ones that finally contribute to its impressive scale overall. Unless these are addressed, however, there can be no broadly acceptable global governance of human movement as a whole.

The first aspect is the incompleteness of the protection that is afforded by the current system. That is true in several senses, as has already been pointed out: it results from the tyranny of the operative concepts and categories that apply to this particular issue. The regime for human movement is not a single integrated system of regulation and protection, but a patchwork, depending on which category the person is deemed to fall into: for some (refugees), levels of protection are ostensibly higher, but so now are the obstacles to securing recognition of that status (Shacknove 1985). This leaves many gaps through which others (internally displaced, irregular migrants, climate refugees) can fall. This incompleteness is not some inadvertent side effect of a design fault in a system intended to work better. Instead, the gaps are a direct consequence of the discretionary nature of the system, and this is integral to its design overall: it is something on which the state members palpably insisted. The incompleteness is symptomatic of the previously highlighted tension between universalism (human rights) and particularism (refugee law), and this has been consciously constructed as an inevitable part of the regime. As such, it lies at the heart of the ethical problem that needs to be confronted.

The second issue is one particular manifestation of that general point. It has been referred to as the normative clash between communitarian and cosmopolitan frameworks (C. Brown 2011), or that between partialism and impartialism (Gibney 2004). Arguably, the least contentious aspect of human movement has been with regard to a right to leave a country, and it could be argued that this is the terrain where cosmopolitan and impartialist positions enjoy their most considerable sway. The problem, as already noted, however, is that normatively 'the right to leave a country cannot be fully exercised without a corresponding right to enter another country' (Juss 2006: 8). It is at the point of entry that the full force of communitarian and partialist doctrines makes itself felt, and as a matter of ethical theory this is perhaps the issue that has dominated the debate.

In turn, it easily slides into the third aspect, which is the ethical dilemmas about exclusion that are implicit in giving free rein to any community to determine its own composition. Any such licence, however qualified, is a necessary part of a communitarian position (Walzer 1983; C. Brown 2011: 155–6). However, its implementation comes at a price. Some regard this as unacceptably high, and object that 'communitarians have rarely faced up to the daunting violence that occurs at the borders of the nation-state as governments seek to exclude unwanted migrants and to check the flow of those seeking asylum' (Hurrell 2011: 100). In short, the moral problem expresses itself in the straightforward proposition that self-determination for some means exclusion for others. In so doing, current practices of exclusion make 'a virtue of the contemporary international system' (Gibney 2004: 26–7), by conditioning the rights of migrants to the requirements of international society. If there is a moral fault, it lies in the very nature of international society, not in the need for some technical adjustment to its current regulations.

The practice of exclusion leads directly to the fourth dimension, namely the mode of control of migration as a possible source of harm perpetrated by international society. These practices have considerable impact on the quality of life of many, and perhaps call into question the 'moral immunity' (Gibney 2004: 54) of those states who do not consider themselves to be contributing to the problem. If states should avoid actions that potentially harm others beyond their borders, then it can be argued that there is a moral claim to be made against an international society that institutionalizes such harm through the human movement controls that it has done so much to set in place (Gibney 2004: 49).

If these issues refer to the contradictory principles that operate in the relationship between states and would-be migrants of various kinds, then the fifth issue moves the discussion instead towards the relationship between states. It picks up on the problem resulting from the lack of equity in the distribution of demands on potential host states. As we have seen, there is no correspondence between the distribution of refugees and the capacity of receiving states to deal with them. This assuredly gives rise to another major ethical concern.

This particular issue highlights some interesting parallels with the case of climate change: how are the responsibilities to be shared? Juss demands that the 'international community' accept its responsibility 'for causing the international disorder that is generating the refugee crisis' (Juss 2006: 246). This advances a notion of responsibility couched in terms of (past) causal culpability. However, allocating the responsibility to international society collectively does little to assist in developing principles for its further distribution to individual states. How, in turn, this is to be done remains a central, and extremely practical, ethical concern. Intriguingly, some have suggested that a principle of common but differentiated responsibilities—as developed in the climate change context—should be applied equally in the case of refugees (Juss 2006: 226). As things presently stand, the major burden falls instead on those states least able to cope with it. To the extent that human movement is further stimulated by changes in climate, there can of course be seen to be a direct correspondence between the two domains, insofar as the 'responsibility' of developed states to admit 'climate refugees' is regarded as one specific extension of their general 'responsibility' for the harm they have caused by their past emissions. So, while in many refugee cases it might be the country of origin that is the source of the problem (in instances of political persecution, for example), with regard to climate-induced movement it is possibly the potential host states that will tend to be considered the source of the problem (McAdam 2011: 165–6). Admission of those fleeing because of climate change could, in this case, be regarded as part of the price that can fairly be exacted by application of a polluter pays principle. The international politics of human movement is already powerfully influenced by exactly such concerns and considerations.

Inherent in the system set in place by international society to regulate the flow of people is a highly selective policy of inclusion and exclusion. Arguably, as soon as states entered seriously into the business of controlling this movement, that was an inevitable outcome. As we have seen, this selectivity occurs at the margins of a set of migratory fault lines that are as much conceptual as they are physical or geographical. These conceptual discriminations are the cost imposed by international society for applying a humanitarian policy in the first place.

As has been demonstrated, however, this selectivity reflects the various competing ethical principles that jostle for our attention in the crowded domain of human movement: in privileging the demands of some over others, international society is de facto making its own moral choices that, in turn, become deeply embedded in the practices of international society as a whole. If there are problems with these practices—and the above case study has surely demonstrated that there are many—then they cannot be addressed other than by facing up to their inherently normative nature. Application of existing categories inflicts harm, and in doing so generates its own distribution of the vulnerable. To this extent, those who are vulnerable in human movement are what states have made of them, and they have become so in a deeply normative way: the ensuing politics and quest for effective regulatory procedures are but a symptom of this profoundly troubled ethical condition.

GLOBAL HEALTH AND THE MORAL CONDITION OF THE VULNERABLE

Much the same can be said in the context of global health, where the assignment of priorities has been the paramount influence, and is the direct source of much of the harm that has been experienced. Once again, this book does not advance its own distinctive moral position on global health, as if its problems had any wholly prior existence and invited moral scrutiny only from an *ex posteriori* perspective. Instead, the argument is that the problems can be captured only in moral terms, and as viewed by the participants, because of what international society already contributes to them. They arise in part directly from issues of health but also in part as manifestations of other more general problems. As Sen has insisted, '[e]quity in the achievement and distribution of health gets . . . incorporated and embedded in a larger understanding of justice' (Sen 2004: 23). In this way, global health offers a 'window into broader questions of global justice and human rights' (O'Manique 2007: 208).

If the deficit in global health is defined as a matter of inequity, then it is precisely in those terms that it must also be addressed and resolved. This is why so many regard the problem as being essentially a normative one: it is so not just because of ill health per se, but because of inequities in its distribution. It is considered a violation of justice, and the problem will not be rectified until this is addressed, whatever other absolute improvements in human health might be achieved in the meantime. Accordingly, many insist, 'any debate about the future of GHG [global health governance] must begin with a critical analysis of the normative basis of its study and practice' (Lee 2009: 28; McInnes and Lee 2012).

Even more than in the other cases, the initial first step has to be some clarification of the substance of the global health around which those problems are thought to arise. What is it about health that is potentially problematic? We are reminded that egalitarian and redistributive approaches normally have in mind the issue of health *care* as the focus of attention, as being something 'society can distribute more or less equally'. What is not immediately so obvious is 'can we really redistribute health itself?' (Segall 2010: 4). If we seek to do so, what conception of 'health' do we have in mind, since it seems to cover a wide spectrum, from 'bare life' at the one end, to conceptions of the 'good life' at the other (Baxi 2010: 13)? At the same time, neither is it fully clear what exactly is problematic about the distribution of health. Is the relevant criterion one of equality, or should it instead be one of sufficiency (Segall 2010: 165–6)?

Much of this debate, both in normative IR theory and in international political practice, does indeed revolve around the question of inequalities of health outcome. Even if it might seem counter-intuitive to think in terms of a more just distribution of health (since ill health is 'natural' or perceived as a matter of 'luck', and hence not in the gift of any society to determine its precise distribution), issues of equity are still germane because health is so strongly related to other social outcomes that make a difference to it. Accordingly, even if it is true that health is a 'nondivisible and non-transferable good', the concern remains important because 'the distribution of other goods (that *are* divisible and transferable) can affect the way in which health is distributed across society' (Segall 2010: 5). This is particularly so because of the widespread perception that, in regard to global health, 'the challenge remains not one of scarcity of resources . . . but of equity in their distribution' (Labonté et al. 2011b: xxxi). This is as true of *international* society as of any other, while acknowledging that this is a feature of most domestic societies as well.

The reason this is seen to be so politically sensitive is a widespread appreciation that, in moral terms, there is something distinctive about health. It is not just any other social good, to be distributed at will or according to the dictates of the market. It is in an important sense widely regarded as a 'special good' (Anand 2004: 17). In this way, it enjoys a degree of moral priority, since it underpins the capacity of people to enjoy any other rights to which they might be entitled (Pogge 2005: 184). This places it at the centre of ideas about 'justice as fairness', even if health was not one of the concerns addressed by John Rawls. Typically, this is the note volubly struck by the WHO's Commission on the Social Determinants of Health:

> Where systematic differences in health are judged to be avoidable by reasonable action they are, quite simply, unfair. It is this that we label health inequality. Putting right these inequities—the huge and remediable differences in health between and within countries—is a matter of social justice. Reducing health inequalities is . . . an ethical imperative. (WHO CSDH 2008: Executive Summary)

The salient feature of this argument is the focus on inequalities that are 'avoidable by reasonable action'. This directs our attention back to the discretionary element in international society's tolerance of such conditions: they not only exist, but exist in a way that is deemed acceptable, as against exercising any political choice to reduce them by taking alternative courses of action. It is this point exactly, of course, that lies at the core of Pogge's complaint. He starts from his central claim that approximately 18 million people die annually 'from medical conditions we can cure' (Pogge 2005: 182). What these people are inherently vulnerable to, then, is not simply disease, nor gaps in medical science's knowledge, but much more directly the choices that are made not to make available even those medical interventions that are possible. These may not represent 'intentional' choices consciously made by individuals, but they flow inescapably from the framework that international society 'wills' into being. It is in this sense, Pogge insists, that the deaths are avoidable:

> Participation in the imposition of social rules constitutes a human-right violation only when those rules *foreseeably* and avoidably deprive human beings of secure access to the objects of their human rights...[At fault are] the rules of the international institutional order, whose design profoundly affects the fulfilment of human rights, especially in the poorer and weaker countries. (Pogge 2005: 195–7)

We have already encountered some measures of these impacts, and the inequalities they entail, in the case study. We are routinely reminded that these inequalities, such as in life expectancy, are 'vast' (Segall 2010: 153), and they have recently been charted in great detail (Labonté and Schrecker 2011). For Pogge, the best measure of the situation is the scale of the effort made to overcome common diseases, particularly those with highest incidence in tropical countries: 21 per cent of this global health burden attracts 0.31 per cent of all public and private health research (Pogge 2005: 190). What is so problematic about this is that it represents a social choice, even if no individual would consciously will it (or possibly defend it) if the choice were to be presented explicitly in these terms. It is the prime example of how the 'invisible hand' can sometimes be the source of social 'bads'. This is the most striking testimony to the vulnerability that international society, directly and indirectly, elects to distribute through its erection of domains of irresponsibility.

Such measures of inequality can, to be sure, often be misleading (Deaton 2011). In one respect certainly they seem to be so. As has been pointed out, 'what is ethically troubling about the poor health of the Zambian child is that it falls below some decent level of health, not that it is worse than the health of the Norwegian child. The problem, in short, is one of insufficiency, not of inequality' (Segall 2010: 165–6). But the whole point is that, in terms of the present argument about vulnerability, it does not matter which precise form the moral objection takes: what is generally at issue is that these allocations of vulnerability appear to be discretionary, and could be otherwise redistributed (i.e. other choices are available), *regardless* of whether it is inequality or insufficiency that underlies the objection. This is the source of the moral problem. A normative theory of global health in the round may be required to resolve these many complex issues. For an empirical theory of global health ethics, regarded as already grounded in the international politics of global health, it suffices to demonstrate that there can be no resolution of these deep-seated problems that does not entail international society's willingness to address this pressing normative dimension.

This fundamental perception is merely compounded by the practices of health securitization that have recently taken place. On top of an existing skewed distribution of resources, it now appears that the system is to be further geared towards addressing the concerns of those who are already most privileged by the existing arrangements: the concerns of the objectively least needy are to be further prioritized and made subject to the security practices of developed states. Not only does this further exacerbate the international politics of global health (because of the asymmetrical priorities that will become further embedded in global governance), but it potentially erodes any appeal to humanitarian instincts, by framing policy in terms of security and self-interest (Peterson 2009: 180; Elbe 2010: 13). If there were already a completely level playing field in terms of global health, this might be just about acceptable. What makes it so insidious in the present circumstances, as already argued, is that the securitization of health for some is the inescapable corollary of the entrenched health vulnerability for so many others.

CONCLUSION

Does any of this help to clarify the sense in which, if at all, international society might be regarded as a moral agent? The central point to emerge is the extent to which morality, and its contestation, is an inherent attribute of the practices of international society. In terms of Frost's constitutive theory, all actions in a social practice 'are constituted not just as actions but as ethical actions' (Frost 2009: 20). This seems particularly true with respect to international society's practice of the vulnerable. Not only is it unintelligible without this moral dimension, but its moral character emerges fully from the consequences of its own activities.

I have suggested previously that key to understanding international society is the sense of being 'bound' to it, and this is central to its practices of legitimacy in general (Clark 2005: 23–5). But to what exactly is it that its members are bound? In some accounts it is international law that is to be found at the heart of the social project, as in Terry Nardin's famous rendition that 'international society is not only regulated by international law but *constituted* by it' (Nardin 1998: 20). In these terms, the members are bound to nothing beyond adherence to a concept of law, regardless of its precise substance and content. This is a notion that has been challenged by others, on the general grounds that law does not enjoy such complete autonomy from other moral values. Those sceptics then further suggest that any claimed minimalist commitment to law actually serves as a cover to smuggle in other values at the same time. Whereas the essential pluralism of international society, as a composite of separate communities, is inscribed by Nardin in the notion that 'international society . . . must tolerate the existence of difference among those communities' (Nardin 1998: 32), others complain that 'there is nothing in legal positivism that specifically endorses diversity' (Whelan 1998: 50). Accordingly, other liberal values are concealed in his fabric of law. On a similar note, the suggestion is commonly made that ES support for the seemingly sparse legal code for coexistence actually incorporates additional values at the same time, since 'the connection between international society and *order* is pivotal to the English School's evaluative interpretation of international relations' (Keene 2009: 114, emphasis added). If so, this makes even less assured any affirmative answer to Brown's question whether 'an ethic of co-existence [is] the only possible ethic given the diversity of goals of the states that make up international society' (C. Brown 2010: 35).

What then emerges if we explore, as has been the task of this chapter, 'the ethics of an actually existing international society' (Jones 2010: 113)? This has shown that the members of international society frame and contest major policy issues in essentially moral terms. They do so because the aggregate activities of international society produce 'solutions' to those problems that necessarily generate moral consequences, and are perceived as such by the participants. In this way, even if regarded as a practical association that eschews 'distributive' justice (as its intended goal) (C. Brown 2010: 34), international society finds itself in the business of creating 'purposive' moral impacts (even if unwittingly) by dint of the distributions of vulnerability to which it contributes.

This chapter has not attempted to set out its own normative theory of vulnerability. What it has done instead is to chart the multiple ways in which the issue areas considered in this book are characterized by profound moral cleavages, occurring around the ways in which international society has itself acted to distribute vulnerability in these fields. These moral dimensions are central to the nature of the problems that now arise, and their resolution is crucial to any acceptable form of governance. In each, by the way international society has privileged a particular understanding of the issue, and has implemented its own operational categories, it has implicitly staked out its own preferred position, with significant moral consequences. These positions are now under substantial ethical challenge, and international society currently lacks the moral resources to defend its existing practices or to set out a road map for the achievement of any acceptable alternative. All four domains are seemingly characterized by a fundamental moral disequilibrium. In the Conclusion, we can now finally address the question of what international society can do for those made vulnerable in this way.

Conclusion: What Can International Society Do for the Vulnerable?

In light of the foregoing study, what can international society do for the vulnerable? In order to answer that question, this conclusion proceeds in three interlinked stages. First, who are the vulnerable and how has international society contributed to their condition? Secondly, what does this tell us about international society, both as a set of actual practices, and also as a theoretical concept? Finally, how does this help us to think about the moral challenges to international order?

THE VULNERABLE

The book set out with two different notions of the vulnerable: on the one hand, those who are exposed to the risks of harm presented by physical or natural phenomena; on the other, those who are in addition exposed to the risks resulting from the workings of international society. The core argument has focused on that second dimension, and has sought to demonstrate the multiple ways in which international society 'constructs' the vulnerable. It does so principally through the fundamental concepts it applies in dealing with various individual problems, and through its set of associated categories for their management. In each of the four cases, the book has demonstrated the powerful effect that these concepts and categories have had on the forms of vulnerability, and on its consequential distributions. While there remain natural risks, to be sure, none of their specific framings, or resulting allocations, can be considered wholly natural. Instead, in effect if not always in intent, international society has acted as a potent medium through which these distributions have been made.

For the most part, the argument has traced how these mechanisms operate within each of the individual issue areas. The vulnerable have emerged from the specific concepts, and their cognate micro-categories, deployed around each problem. It is easy enough to point to the evidence of how international society impacts on these various global issues. On political violence, it has scripted resort to it such that what appear initially as merely technical manuals for its application, such as the 1949 Geneva Conventions, are much more profoundly seen as 'part of a new international normative order' (Cardenas 2010: 5). This normative order infuses its basic concepts and categories, and has been used to sustain one specific scheme for the legitimate resort to force, albeit that this now finds itself under extreme pressure.

Similar connections have been established in the other cases. In that of climate change, its 'emerging risks and vulnerabilities' are a 'consequence of human actions and choices' (UNDP 2008: 10), and many of these are taken—or avoided—at the international level. Its results, it has been suggested, have the potential to 'cause harms of a type and scale that would clearly count as human rights violations' (Baer 2011: 326). On human movement, its most telling impact results from the choice not to manage the issue in any kind of aggregate international terms at all (Hurrell 2011: 93–4). As regards the specific category of refugees, we are left with the uncomfortable thought that they are 'the victims of an international system that brings them into being, then fails to take responsibility for them' (Haddad 2008: 69). With respect to global health, analysts routinely depict it as conforming to systemic patterns: it is presented as a 'global system of disease' (Kay and Williams 2009b: 5), within which vulnerability is distributed to categories of people in accordance with their '"place" in the global order' (Lee 2003: 102), and the dominant characteristic of which is its manifold inequities (WHO CSDH 2008; MacLean and Brown 2009: 14). The impact of international society has been profound upon each of these areas in turn.

In this way, as we have seen, certain forms of vulnerability are privileged and addressed at the expense of others. For example, the vulnerability of the developed world to migration from elsewhere is placed ahead of the vulnerability of those people, with no choice but to remain in poor countries, who continue to be exposed to the harmful impacts of violence, climate, and disease. The vulnerability of the developed world to infectious disease has become the stimulus for vigorous international preventative action, while in contrast there is marked toleration of the system remaining porous in the opposite direction to the spread of chronic diseases from lifestyle, such as those associated with processed food and smoking (T. Brown 2011: 322). In short, if ours is now a risk society, some risks are treated more equally than others: international society mobilizes energetically against certain risks, but remains impassive with regard to others (Clapton and Hameiri 2012: 67–8). The ground rules of human movement are heavily skewed towards keeping the most vulnerable in place, while permitting or encouraging the movement of others with desirable skills. If the distribution of vulnerability is essentially about 'moving' various things around—people, diseases, climate burdens, and the impacts of political violence—the prime feature of international society's regulation of these movements has been its inconsistent practices towards them. It is at the level of international society that these overall human accounts come to be settled: normative and material balances of power compete to generate particular surpluses and deficits of vulnerability.

Particular outcomes are engendered by its designated categories, albeit that these play subtly variable roles in the diverse social practices of the vulnerable. In the case of violence, international society assigns vulnerability to combatants, but by its permissive attitude towards military necessity has contributed to the heightened risk now borne by civilians, and hence to the subversion of its own categorical preferences. With respect to climate change, it has acknowledged the central categories of developed and developing countries that potentially draw attention to ethical principles of equity, but which actually have served to reinforce political stalemate, and it has only recently indicated willingness to move beyond this deeply entrenched scheme. Its categories for differentiating those humans engaged in movement are absolutely central to the variable degrees of protection it affords, while simultaneously the practicalities of assigning people to the appropriate categories have ensured that states enjoy broad latitude in that process. Finally, its categories of infectious and chronic disease, among others, enable international society to undertake policies that ostensibly advance collective interests in the promotion of health, while at the same time enabling more aggressive action to be taken to minimize the social vulnerability of those already exposed to the lesser 'natural' health risks in the first place.

What must now be stressed, over and above, is that international society's intervention does not stop at this point alone. We have shown the consequences of its micro-categorizations. However, possibly most potent of all has been its macro-categorization into these individual issue areas—violence, climate, movement, and health—as if each is separate and discrete. The book has traced the concepts that have structured the individual regimes. The powerful additional impact it has had is to present each as if it were self-contained, and to design it in virtual detachment from the self-evident mutual interdependencies that exist among those various regimes.

This is, of course, wholly artificial and the source of yet another layer of problems for the people who have to negotiate their way through them. It has been stressed throughout that there are intense linkages among all four. Political violence impacts human health and movement, and could be a further consequence of climate change. Climate change, in turn, is likely to be an increasingly major factor in migration and in the distribution of global health (WHO CSDH 2008: 1). Human movement is directly related to all of the other three. And global health can scarcely be approached as a problem separate from developments in any of those other three areas. They come 'naturally' as a combined package, but, for reasons of convenience and interest, have been managed by international society as if they were instead discrete types of potential harm. Through this artifice is created a second and social layer of liability to harm.

Nowhere is the hand of international society more visible than in this overall design, and the distortions that follow from it. There is nothing natural about dealing with these four issues in isolation, and the source of many problems is their wholly artificial disaggregation at the hands of international society. Not only do people slip through the categories that are deployed *within* each, but they demonstrably slip through the cracks that have been created *between* the distinct regimes. It is at those interstices and fault lines that the work of international society in making the vulnerable is most readily to be discerned. The extent of the overlap between the four cases has already become abundantly clear. However, the effect of international society's separate treatment of them is to create very deep and treacherous crevasses: people are made vulnerable to them within each regime, but doubly so to the yawning gaps in between.

For example, it has been suggested that in the areas of violence and refugees the system overall works to provide two safety nets, with regard to both IHL and refugee law:

> Refugees benefit first and foremost from the protection of refugee law and from the mandate of the Office of the UN High Commissioner for Refugees (UNHCR). If refugees are in a State involved in an armed conflict, they will also benefit from international humanitarian law. It will amount to a double protection . . . The reason refugees benefit from several layers of protection is to be found in their vulnerability and in the absence of protection by their State of nationality. (Van Engeland 2011: 82)

While this might indeed be so in some instances, there is a less encouraging perspective that could be adopted instead: the two layers compound the vulnerability, not just the protection. Van Engeland's comment is assuredly right in drawing our attention to the crucial factor of the 'absence of protection by their State of nationality'. What this confirms, however, is that the vulnerability of those people is not some primordial condition, but is already the artifice of the workings of international society, and of its chosen regimes. While these may occasionally work in tandem to reinforce protection, there are considerably more instances where they work against each other, and distribute vulnerability by their failure to afford protection at the margins of any one. Thus, the application of a category in one issue area has considerable import for categories in others. For instance, whether an occurrence of violence is classed as an armed conflict or not has a pronounced impact on the degree of protection that is to be afforded to internally displaced persons (Kleine-Ahlbrandt 2004: 13–14). If an outbreak of violence is not deemed to be an armed conflict, internally displaced civilians may not be covered by the IHL provisions of Geneva Protocol II, but instead fall through this gap (Cossor 2006: 19–20).

As further cases in point we should note, amongst many others: the absence of any common ground between the refugee and climate regimes, such that there can be no such thing as climate refugees, and no explicit connection made between the two domains (McAdam 2011: 165–6); the inconsistent regulation of various forms of movement, such that the most helpless of peoples can move, for the most part, only to other poor countries, while the best educated can move to rich countries, and the system of global health further exacerbates the disparities between the two (Garrett 2011: 13; WHO 2011: 92); that international society's regulatory schemes are designed to prevent the movement of diseases, but also have the effect of restricting the 'migration' of those medicines needed for their effective treatment; that the failures to respond adequately to the challenges of climate intensify the causes of violence, migration, and ill health, but the separate controls existing within each largely block any effective means of redress for those made vulnerable by international society's decisions across the board. By its incomplete regimes of management for each, and just as much by its mutually reinforcing inadequacies across the set as a whole, international society does less for the provision of multiple layers of protection, and contributes more to the multiplication of the sources of risk.

A prescription that seemingly requires the dismantling of those existing regimes of protection, and starting again from the bottom with something wholly new, is unlikely to find much favour, and is not what is proposed here. Short of this, what can international society do for the vulnerable? If the proximate sources of international society's distribution of vulnerability are to be found in its concepts and categories that operate within its specific regimes, and in the disaggregation that operates across the whole, small first steps must be made by recognizing those causal links and acting on them. The concepts and categories do matter, and have real-life consequences. Moreover, what is additionally required is a more holistic approach, as in what are now considered the necessary responses to complex emergencies (Macrae and Zwi 1994b), where several issues emerge simultaneously. For example, human movement needs to be integrated with those other issues, such as climate change, to avoid compounding the risks by any artificial separation. The same can be said for the approach to global health and the pervasive impact upon it of international society's activities in other areas, such as trade and global finance (Schrecker 2009b). The connections between those governance structures need to be much more robust than is currently the case.

Does this attribute too much efficacy to international society specifically? It is certainly not suggested here that all mediation between people and potentially harmful conditions is undertaken by international society alone. For instance, the implementation of the Refugee Convention falls to state Parties, and many of the regime's current ills are attributable to the ingenuity that particular states have displayed in circumventing its political inconveniences. If there is fault, on this reckoning it is to be found not in international society's overall construction, but in the lack of state will to comply with the Convention's fundamental principles. Alternatively, in another example, many of the obstacles to access to medicine are apparently to be found in the workings of global capitalism (Baer and Singer 2009). What kind of contribution to understanding do we make, it might reasonably be asked, by bundling all these issues together as simply the fault of international society?

The answer, in short, is twofold. First, to take the case of refugees, it is simply not tenable to make any complete distinction between the honourable intentions of international society and the woeful derelictions of the state members. They are too much of a single piece for this sharp separation to hold. The Convention was deliberately designed to leave considerable latitude to states in its implementation. If states have since behaved badly, where exactly has been the strong contrary international pressure—the positive 'socialization'—for them to do better? The contrast with the manner in which international society has actively intervened to promote the free movement of capital could not be any more striking. Secondly, with respect to the deformities in the global research, development, and distribution of medicines, these are certainly a reflection of the market incentives that dominate the structure of production and distribution in this area. However, to suggest that this is not international society's business to regulate—when it regulates so much in other areas—is profoundly unpersuasive. There is assuredly scope for more effective positive inducements to be introduced. Their absence bears witness to the kind of market system that international society condones in its stead. This is demonstrated, for example, by its ambivalence towards the tobacco industry: the differing priorities of the WHO and WTO reflect the competing pulls of its health and trade dimensions. International society cannot protest its complete innocence in relation to global capitalism, given its highly selective complicity in its workings.

INTERNATIONAL SOCIETY

International society, as one major architect of the vulnerable, holds in its own hands some possible means of redress. To assess what potential it displays for responding to these challenges leads us to reconsider the nature of this seemingly mythical beast. This returns the focus of analysis to international society itself. Andrew Linklater has indicated that the big theme of how best to protect societies 'from the forms of harm to which all are vulnerable, though unequally' is already very much a feature to be found in ES theory (Linklater 2011: 86). This points us towards one important dimension of international society, namely 'the role actually played by values and rules' within it (Bull 1969: 632-3). To emphasize this theme is not necessarily to subscribe to a cosmopolitan normative position, nor even to provide any solidarist account of international society. What it does stress, above all, is the moral character and consequences of those very concepts and categories through which international society chooses to work, even when it does so as seemingly no more than a 'practical', rather than a 'purposive', association (Nardin 1983). If international society means anything at all, its essence is to be found in its own internal source of obligation—that sense of being bound—arising out of the very relations that give international society such identity as it has. Its collective interventions are not those of some neutral arbitrator or referee: it is wholly a part of, not apart from, the political struggles that it is called upon to adjudge. It is simultaneously the rule book and the score sheet for the games that are in play. This renders it an inherently normative enterprise, in effect if not by design.

What has been stressed throughout is that it serves as a powerful conditioning structure, even when its socialization produces inherently negative effects. In large measure, the reason for this can be attributed to the pervasive inequalities that characterize international society. Even when it makes normatively consequential decisions about the regulatory mechanisms that it chooses to adopt, its process for doing so falls far short of perfect deliberative conditions. For this reason, the temptation is to view it as no more than the activities of its most powerful members.

To view it in this way alone is to miss a crucial point, and this is essential for a full understanding of the social practice of the vulnerable, as described in these pages. This is a practice about the vulnerable within international society, and not about their exclusion from it. In that way, while assuredly reflecting inequalities, it is a practice that has the potential for subsequent challenge and reconfiguration, precisely because of the legitimation that is an essential aspect of it. This brings us back to the concept of hierarchy. It has been said of hierarchies generally that they are 'authoritative relationships requiring the weaker party to recognise the legitimacy of its subordination' and that they are, as such, 'possible within international society' (Clapton and Hameiri 2012: 61, 64). In this way, we can regard 'the vulnerable' as one expression of hierarchy within international society. While this context does not explicitly concern a right to rule, it does at the very least issue in a socially sanctioned set of rules and procedures, even when they deliver highly contested outcomes on the ground. The hierarchy is tolerated within international society, at the same time as many of its specific outputs are not. In this respect, international society is not wholly unlike many other political systems, with considerably more consensus over 'process' than over individual 'outcomes'.

In these various ways, its practices of the vulnerable reflect its endemic deformities, and principally its pervasive inequalities. As has been shown, the concepts and categories through which it operates are themselves inherently derivative from those inequalities. They reveal themselves in international society's preference for dealing with a state-imposed equality of belligerents with regard to political violence, and its inability to sustain a sharp discrimination between combatants and civilians marks the challenges that 'asymmetric' conflict has increasingly presented to its dominant modes of action in this regard: inequality of belligerents has perversely contributed to an increasing equality in the targets of violence. In broadly similar ways, issues of inequality have shaped outcomes with regard to climate, movement, and health as well. The dominant concepts and categories hold a mirror to this characteristic of international society and underline the extent to which some states are (at any one time) its dominant norm-makers, while others have to settle for their role as norm-takers. This is testimony to how international society works, rather than evidence for its absence. However, international society is an iterative process, and its inequities and associated normative deformities are subject to reformation over time.

There is no escaping this fundamental tension in international society. As individual musicians, some states play much louder instruments than do others. As an orchestra, the sound that emerges overall still transcends the efforts of any of those individuals, even when the orchestra does accept some direction from its leader. The core puzzle then is to make sense of that fundamental tension between what international society enacts as an expression of a basic consensus among most of its members and what it otherwise enacts, mostly in response to its dominant players. Across time, the business of international society is to find stable periods of accommodation between those two components of its identity, even if it cannot wholly avoid recurrent tensions between them. As regards the construction of the vulnerable, it is simply impossible to reduce either one to the other, and so the specification of the vulnerable remains permanently suspended between its provisional acceptance as legitimate and its continuing exposure to moral contestation. There is unlikely to be any final resolution of this paradox, and in its treatment of the vulnerable we gain an important insight into the fragile ethical condition of international society as a whole. Given its basic propensity to pluralism, and at the same time the routine aspiration of its successive dominant states to push it in specific directions of their own choosing (Jones 2010: 119), there is little prospect of any disappearance of this tension. The unsettled normative condition of the vulnerable bears testimony to this situation.

This tension and ambivalence are deep-seated characteristics of the social practice of the vulnerable. In each of the areas reviewed in this study, the constitutional moments have displayed significant degrees of consensus. These have, to varying degrees, mirrored the collective interests of the state members. Accordingly, it is easy enough to discern the source of those interests, and their expression, in each of the regimes respectively. The consensus view of international society has been that international armed conflict is the preferred form, and that due allowance must be made for the 'exigencies of war'. Agreed conventions must not be 'prejudicial' to the State parties, and there should be no full or automatic application of the same rules in non-international armed conflict, or in conditions adjudged to fall short of armed conflict. With respect to climate, the UNFCCC epitomized a consensus around an emerging problem, but also of the need to approach it within the context of economic sovereignty, and a commitment to economic growth and openness.

The consensus elements around human movement were just as visible in 1951. While there should be no prohibition on exit, there equally must be no absolute entitlement to entry. States agreed a set of procedures that would maximize their own discretion, while setting bounds on their specific responsibilities under these arrangements. It was similarly so for the establishment of the WHO in 1948. The acknowledgement of shared interests in international procedures to deal with collective concerns about health accompanied the need to ensure that these were harmonized with other interests, such as the priorities of safeguarding international commerce and relatively free movement of people in support of it.

Each of these equilibrium points of consensus was accompanied, however, either at the time or subsequently, by prominent elements of contestation as well. Significant states, including the United States, protested some of the extensions accorded under the Geneva Protocols, believing they granted a licence to forms of armed conflict to which they took exception, and refused to ratify them as a result. While the UNFCCC parties accepted the principle of CBDR, they held widely diverging interpretations of its meaning and significance: some saw it as a charter of restorative justice, while others regarded it as no more than a pragmatic recognition of differential capabilities. The shared state interest in the Refugee Convention was accompanied by dissent from those states elsewhere that regarded it as a wholly European affair, and has subsequently been severely tested by the failure of one of its goals, namely to secure an acceptable degree of burden-sharing among host nations in dealing with its consequences. Finally, on matters of health, there have been sharp controversies over practices of securitization, whereby international action has been stimulated in order to deal with the vulnerability of the peoples seemingly least exposed to disease and most capable of dealing with the associated risks in any case.

What all these examples demonstrate is the dual nature of international society: it is a compound of two sets of internal tensions, focused on issues of *values* and *hierarchy*. The first centres on degrees of consensus and dissent around norms, and the perpetual ambivalence that reigns in this regard. The second is with respect to the inequalities of power and the normative contestation that surrounds privileging the view of international society as the orchestra, on the one hand, as against the wish of some of its members, on the other, to play only their own tunes instead. There is never an easy equilibrium between either of these elements, but some moments are more difficult than others. Nonetheless, the tenacity and durability of international society is confirmed in the surprisingly small number of players who choose to quit the stage altogether.

THE MORAL CHALLENGE TO INTERNATIONAL ORDER

At this point, therefore, the argument can finally revisit E. H. Carr's diagnosis of the fundamental problem of international order as essentially moral. This claim notwithstanding, his argument in *The Twenty Years' Crisis* has been criticized by Hedley Bull for losing sight of international society altogether (Bull 1969: 638). It did so, Bull suggested, because of Carr's methodological fixation on the idea that the rules exist only as an expression of the interests of the stronger. 'Conventions play an important part in all morality', Carr had written, 'and the essence of a convention is that it is binding so long as other people in fact abide by it' (Carr 2001: 146). On such a slippery surface, he was unable to get any reliable moral purchase. As a result, his problematic of the satisfied and dissatisfied powers, and his prescription for some give and take between them, lacked the moral substance that he wished to prescribe. This is apparent in his insistence on a moral equivalence between his two categories, in the sense that it is false to see 'the struggle between satisfied and dissatisfied Powers as a struggle between morality on one side and power on the other'. Instead, he was adamant that this 'is a clash in which, whatever the moral issue, power politics are equally predominant on both sides' (Carr 2001: 99). While this certainly says that neither side enjoys a monopoly on morality, its effect goes even deeper in seeming to negate the very possibility of any moral relationship between them at all. This is so since, unlike in the case of vulnerability, a moral dimension is not an intrinsic property of the relationship between the satisfied and dissatisfied. As such, his wolf of power ends up but flimsily disguised in sheep's moral clothing. Where is the moral problematic of international order to come from, when it is so effectively elided in this way?

In short, he was correct in his general diagnosis of the problem, but wrong in his specific solution to it. Approaching that same problem from the alternative perspective of vulnerability offers a more promising prospect. Elsewhere, Carr came close to acknowledging as much when he distinguished not between the satisfied and dissatisfied, but between the secure and insecure: 'secure and wealthy groups can better afford to behave altruistically', he attested, 'than groups which are continually preoccupied with the problem of their own security and solvency' (Carr 2001: 99). Why should that be?

This is not a conclusion that can readily be drawn from Carr's own premises elsewhere, but is a position that might reasonably be developed from the notion of international society as a really existing moral practice, despite its many failings in this regard. What Carr hints at, but does not pursue, is this notion of international order as inherently morally problematic, and as un-manageable without moral empathy. He was unable successfully to establish any such framework, starting as he did from the disparity in power, and action based on interest that seemed to reflect nothing beyond this disparity. In his version, there seemed no moral dimension in which the play of power could be automatically anchored.

As against this, the notion of vulnerability, understood as the defining property of a relationship, is much more readily commensurable with a concept of international society. Both are fundamentally relational in the same way: international society is 'bound' by the nature of its enterprise to address the vulnerable as it has made them. This is so, in Robert Goodin's terms, because there is a direct connection between the two: the vulnerability of some resides specifically in their relationships 'to us', at least insofar as it is mediated through international society. It is in the essential nature of international society that it must therefore confront the impact of its own designated terms of vulnerability, as part of its overall social purpose.

The problem is how it does so. Evidently, it does incorporate the normative preferences of the most powerful, and the specific international institutional orders that it constructs will generally reflect the wishes of the most recent 'victors' (Clark 2001, 2005). However, it is also much more than that, and would be of considerably less interest theoretically, and of consequence practically, if it were not so. The orders it establishes are never complete, but are instead provisional and subject to contestation, and undergo subtle transformations in response to dynamic shifts both in values and power. Of these, none are of greater import than the renegotiation of its terms of vulnerability. As such, as Finnemore suggests more generally, this perspective opens up a way to 'attend to the views of the weak, the marginalised, the "done to" in world politics' (Finnemore 2008: 220). This is so, in part, because international orders are not the wholly autonomous creations of powerful states, but are exposed to normative adaptations stimulated by non-state or 'world society' actors (Clark 2007). International society has impacts that are real enough, but is itself a shifting arena of norms and power. If that field of action is bereft of moral content, there would indeed remain little to salvage from the concept of international society.

This places it in some kind of halfway house with regard to its moral agency. There are compelling reasons to be sceptical that international society enjoys sufficient moral consensus to act in support of any homogenous moral agenda. To this extent, the pluralist argument is correct that states have 'different goals and international society provides for that fact'. However, it is much more problematic to conclude from this that it does so 'not by arbitrating amongst those goals itself, but by establishing arrangements that leave states free to pursue their own goals' (Jones 2010: 119). This is at best a partial truth: the regimes of international society are not fully as permissive as this would suggest. International society does indeed, at certain moments, 'arbitrate' amongst goals, with decisive consequences for the vulnerable, as has been shown. It does so, of course, without any complete or permanent moral consensus, but rather more on the basis of a 'modus vivendi', an agreement that 'does not involve a principled adherence to authoritative norms' (Charvet 1998: 127–8). This reflects its various deliberative deformities, and ensures that 'the ethical life of international society is built on fragile foundations' (Charvet 1998: 122–3). Nonetheless, any such modus vivendi has the capacity to develop beyond its original basis, and to become in turn the grounds for a challenge to that original set of norms (Crawford 2002: 100–1), precisely because of the impact on the distribution of vulnerability that has resulted from it. Ethical fragility, in this sense, is most certainly endemic in international society, but this is not tantamount to squeezing moral agency out of it altogether. Any such modus vivendi is the less to be disparaged if the members of international society display a commitment to being 'bound' by its moral dimensions over the longer term, even if not responding to them in every instance: it is an iterative moral game, not one played once and for all.

This study allows us to bring international society back in, but in a way that Carr was unable to do. Carr certainly believed that there was a problem with the 'have-nots' of this world, and Bull, following Carr, was to demand some essential 'give and take' as the basic element in his own appeal to justice (Hoffmann 1990: 30). However, these calls for remedial action scarcely went beyond prudential interest on the part of the strongest, and therefore did not depend upon any notion of international society for whatever merit they had: the weak should be appeased only because the strong had some self-interest in doing so.

Instead, an argument from vulnerability—in the terms set out in this study— is located necessarily *in* international society, and makes no sense outside, insofar as vulnerability is one of its own constructs. There can quite literally be no remedy outside its framework, even if other sources of risk will always remain. Its problems of *legitimated* exposure to those risks are for international society to address, neither because of appeals to altruism as such, nor even necessarily by reference to a common humanity, but because they take the form that they do as part of its own handiwork. For all these reasons, this advances a median position between prudential self-interest and cosmopolitanism. It calls on international society to respond to the vulnerable because it alone can.

This allows us to rescue some moral purchase, and hence to understand its problems in meaningfully moral terms, *as part of its own inherently moral practices*. What makes them so, above all, is the way in which its activities inescapably distribute vulnerability around. To this extent, international society stands or falls as a permanent moral dialogue, in the light of the moral consequences that result from its own activities. As soon as we recognize international society as a powerful instrument through which other people become vulnerable 'to us', we are committed to seeing its specific problems in objectively moral terms. International society is very much in the harm business, and does much to determine its resulting distributions. The vulnerable are constituted as a reflection of its espoused norms, and it is only within its own internal social relationships that something can be done to alleviate their condition: social vulnerability can be mitigated only by social adjustment. Not all the risks to the vulnerable will thereafter disappear, but international society may, in this piecemeal and incremental fashion, approach another temporary equilibrium point around agreement on different terms for their exposure.

To this extent, international society emerges as both the villain and the hero of this story. In much of the preceding account, its role as villain has been dominant: a multitude of human ills and harms have been laid at its door. This has been a necessary first step in correcting any one-sided view of the vulnerable as a wholly natural or pre-existing category. It is in those terms that international society itself prefers to present them. However, in the many respects documented in this study, the vulnerable are largely what international society has made of them. Paradoxically, however, this perspective opens up the possibility of the vindication of international society, rather than just its vilification. In the claim that its own practices of the vulnerable are inherently moral, there emerges also the prospect of confronting the consequences of its own actions. This comes with no guarantees, but attests at the very least that there can be no sustainable international order without acknowledgement of that basic reality of international society's own politics. Putting the vulnerable *in* international society in this way makes practical sense of the vulnerable, while also making moral sense of international society.

References

Adelman, H. and Barkan, E. (2011), *No Return, No Refuge: Rites and Rights in Minority Repatriation*. Columbia University Press, New York.

Adger, W. N. (2006), 'Vulnerability', *Global Environmental Change*, 16 (3): 268–81.

——Brown, K., and Waters, J. (2011), 'Resilience', in Dryzek, Norgaard, and Schlosberg (2011a): 696–710.

Afifi, T. and Jager, J. (eds) (2010), *Environment, Forced Migration and Social Vulnerability*. Springer, Berlin.

Aginam, O. (2004), 'Between Isolationism and Mutual Vulnerability: A North–South Perspective on Global Governance of Epidemics in an Age of Globalization', *Temple Law Review*, 77: 297–312.

Alderson, K. and Hurrell, A. (2000), *Hedley Bull on International Society*. Macmillan, Houndmills.

Altman, A. and Wellman, C. H. (2008), 'From Humanitarian Intervention to Assassination: Human Rights and Political Violence', *Ethics*, 118 (2): 228–57.

Anand, S. (2004), 'The Concern for Equity in Health', in Anand, Peter, and Sen (2004): 15–20.

——Peter, F., and Sen, A. (eds) (2004), *Public Health, Ethics, and Equity*. Oxford University Press, Oxford.

Archibugi, D. and Bizzarri, K. (2009), 'The Global Governance of Communicable Diseases: The Case for Vaccine R & D', in Kirton (2009a): 199–217.

Armborst, A. (2010), 'Modelling Terrorism and Political Violence', *International Relations*, 24 (4): 414–32.

Armstrong, J. D. (1993), *Revolution and World Order: The Revolutionary State in International Society*. Oxford University Press, Oxford.

Asad, T. (2010), 'Thinking about Terrorism and Just War', *Cambridge Review of International Affairs*, 23 (1): 3–24.

Assessments of Impacts and Adaptations for Climate Change Project (AIACC) (2007), *Climate Change Vulnerability and Adaptation in Developing Country Regions*, Draft Final Report. AIACC, Washington, DC. <http://www.aiaccproject.org>.

Backstrand, K. (2011), 'The Democratic Legitimacy of Global Governance after Copenhagen', in Dryzek, Norgaard, and Schlosberg (2011a): 669–84.

Baer, H. and Singer, M. (2009), *Global Warming and the Political Ecology of Health*. Left Coast Press, Walnut Creek, CA.

Baer, P. (2011), 'International Justice', in Dryzek, Norgaard, and Schlosberg (2011a): 323–37.

Bagshaw, S. (2005), *Developing a Normative Framework for the Protection of Internally Displaced Persons*. Transnational Publishers, Ardsley, NY.

Bailey, S. D. (1972), *Prohibitions and Restraints in War*. Oxford University Press, London.

Bankoff, G. (2003), *Cultures of Disaster: Society and Natural Hazard in the Philippines*. Routledge Curzon, London.

Barber, B. R. (2003), *Fear's Empire: War, Terrorism, and Democracy*. W. W. Norton, New York.

Barnett, J. (2011), 'Human Security', in Dryzek, Norgaard, and Schlosberg (2011a): 267–77.

——Matthew R. A., and O'Brien, K. L. (2010), 'Global Environmental Change and Human Security: An Introduction', in Matthew et al. (2010): 3–32.

Barnett, M. (2011), 'Humanitarianism, Paternalism, and the UNHCR', in Betts and Loescher (2011a): 105–32.

Barraclough, S. (2009), 'Chronic Diseases and Global Health Governance: The Contrasting Cases of Food and Tobacco', in Kay and Williams (2009a): 102–28.

Barrett, S. (2009), 'Climate Treaties and the Imperative of Enforcement', in Helm and Hepburn (2009): 58–80.

Barry, B. and Goodin, R. E. (eds) (1992), *Free Movement: Ethical Issues in the Transnational Migration of People and Money*. Harvester, Hemel Hempstead.

Baskin, J. (2009), 'The Impossible Necessity of Climate Justice?', *Melbourne Journal of International Law*, 10 (2): 424–38.

Basolo, V. (2010), 'Environmental Change, Disasters, and Vulnerability: The Case of Hurricane Katrina and New Orleans', in Matthew et al. (2010): 97–116.

Baxi, U. (2010), 'The Place of the Human Right to Health and Contemporary Approaches to Global Justice: Impertinent Interrogations', in Harrington and Stuttaford (2010): 12–27.

Beck, U. (1992), *Risk Society: Towards a New Modernity*. Sage, London.

Beitz, C. R. (1979) [rev. ed. 1999], *Political Theory and International Relations*. Princeton University Press, Princeton, NJ.

——and Goodin, R. E. (eds) (2009), *Global Basic Rights*. Oxford University Press, Oxford.

Bell, D. (ed.) (2009), *Political Thought and International Relations: Variations on a Realist Theme*. Oxford University Press, Oxford.

——(ed.) (2010), *Ethics and World Politics*. Oxford University Press, Oxford.

Bellamy, A. (ed.) (2005a), *International Society and its Critics*. Oxford University Press, Oxford.

——(2005b), 'Introduction: International Society and the English School', in Bellamy (2005a): 1–28.

Benatar, S. and Brock G. (eds) (2011), *Global Health and Global Health Ethics*. Cambridge University Press, Cambridge.

——and Upshur, R. (2011), 'What is Global Health?', in Benatar and Brock (2011): 13–23.

Benwell, R. (2011), 'The Canaries in the Coalmine: Small States as Climate Change Champions', *The Round Table*, 100 (413): 199–211.

Berger, P. L. and Luckman, T. (1966), *The Social Construction of Reality: A Treatise in the Sociology of Knowledge*. Doubleday, New York.

Berlinguer, G. (2003), 'Bioethics, Human Security, and Global Health', in Chen et al. (2003): 53–65.

Bernard, K. W. (2012), 'Negotiating the Framework Convention on Tobacco Control: Public Health Joins the Arcane World of Multilateral Diplomacy', in Rosskam and Kickbusch (2012): 47–76.

Betts, A. (2010), 'Towards a "Soft Law" Framework for the Protection of Vulnerable Irregular Migrants', *International Journal of Refugee Law*, 22 (2): 209–36.

—— (ed.) (2011a), *Global Migration Governance*. Oxford University Press, Oxford.

—— (2011b), 'Introduction: Global Migration Governance', in Betts (2011a): 1–33.

—— (2011c), 'Conclusion', in Betts (2011a): 307–27.

—— and Cerna, L. (2011), 'High-Skilled Labour Migration', in Betts (2011a): 60–77.

—— and Loescher, G. (eds) (2011a), *Refugees in International Relations*. Oxford University Press, Oxford.

—— —— (2011b), 'Refugees in International Relations', in Betts and Loescher (2011a): 1–27.

Blaikie, P., Cannon, T., Davis, I., and Wisner, B. (1994), *At Risk: Natural Hazards, People's Vulnerability, and Disasters*. Routledge, London.

Blum, G. and Heymann, P. B. (2010), *Laws, Outlaws, and Terrorists: Lessons from the War on Terrorism*. MIT Press, Cambridge.

Bobbitt, P. (2008), *Terror and Consent: The Wars for the Twenty-First Century*. Allen Lane, London.

—— Freedman, L., and Treverton, G. (eds) (1989), *US Nuclear Strategy: A Reader*. Macmillan, Houndmills.

Boykoff, M. T. (ed.) (2010), *The Politics of Climate Change: A Survey*. Routledge, London.

Brem, S. and Stiles, K. (eds) (2009), *Cooperating Without America: Theories and Case Studies of Non-Hegemonic Regimes*. Routledge, London.

Brennan, D. G. (1989), 'The Case for Population Defense', in Bobbitt, Freedman, and Treverton (1989): 237–62.

Brklacich, M., Chazan, M., and Bohle, H.-G. (2010), 'Human Security, Vulnerability, and Global Environmental Change', in Matthew et al. (2010): 35–51.

Brough, M. W., Lango, J. W., and van der Linden, H. (eds) (2007), *Rethinking the Just War Tradition*. State University of New York Press, Albany, NY.

Brown, C. (1992), *International Relations Theory: New Normative Approaches*. Columbia University Press, New York.

—— (2003), 'Moral Agency and International Society: Reflections on Norms, the UN, the Gulf War, and the Kosovo Campaign', in Erskine (2003a): 51–68.

—— (2010), *Practical Judgement in International Political Theory: Selected Essays*. Routledge, London.

—— (2011), 'The Only Thinkable Figure? Ethical and Normative Approaches to Refugees in International Relations', in Betts and Loescher (2011a): 151–68.

Brown, O., Hammill, A., and McLeman, R. (2007), 'Climate Change as the "New" Security Threat', *International Affairs*, 83 (6): 1141–54.

Brown, T. (2011), '"Vulnerability is Universal": Considering the Place of "Security" and "Vulnerability" within Contemporary Global Health Discourse', *Social Sciences and Medicine*, 72 (3): 319–26.

Brown, T. M., Cueto, M., and Fee, E. (2011), 'The World Health Organization and the Transition from "International" to "Global" Public Health', in Labonté et al. (2011a): 65–86.

Brown, W. (2010), *Walled States, Waning Sovereignty*. Zone Books, New York.

Bukovansky, M., Clark, I., Eckersley, R., Price, R., Reus-Smit, C., and Wheeler, N. J. (2012), *Special Responsibilities: Global Problems and American Power*. Cambridge University Press, Cambridge.

Bull, H. (1966), 'The Grotian Conception of International Society', in Butterfield and Wight (1966): 51–73.

—— (1969), 'The Twenty Years' Crisis Thirty Years On', *International Journal*, 24 (4): 625–38.

—— (1977), *The Anarchical Society: A Study of Order in World Politics*. Macmillan, London.

—— (1979), 'Recapturing the Just War for Political Theory', *World Politics*, 31 (4): 588–99.

—— (1984), *Justice in International Relations: 1983–84 Hagey Lectures*. University of Waterloo, Waterloo, Ontario.

—— (2011), 'Foreword', in Betts and Loescher (2011a): vii–xiii.

—— Kingsbury, B., and Roberts, A. (eds) (1992), *Hugo Grotius and International Relations*. Oxford University Press, Oxford.

Burke, A. (2004), 'Just War or Ethical Peace? Moral Discourses of Strategic Violence after 9/11', *International Affairs*, 80 (2): 329–53.

Burson, B. (2010), 'Environmentally Induced Displacement and the 1951 Refugee Convention: Pathways to Recognition', in Afifi and Jager (2010): 3–16.

Busby, J. (2009), 'The Hardest Problem in the World: Leadership in the Climate Regime', in Brem and Stiles (2009): 73–104.

Butler, J. (2004), *Precarious Life—the Powers of Mourning and Violence*. Verso, London.

Butterfield, H. and Wight, M. (eds) (1966), *Diplomatic Investigations: Essays in the Theory of International Politics*. Allen and Unwin, London.

Caney, S. (2005), *Justice Beyond Borders: A Global Political Theory*. Oxford University Press, Oxford.

—— (2009), 'Human Rights, Responsibilities, and Climate Change', in Beitz and Goodin (2009): 227–47.

Cannon, T. (1994), 'Vulnerability Analysis and the Explanation of "Natural" Disasters', in Varley (1994): 13–30.

Cardenas, S. (2010), 'The Geneva Conventions and the Normative Tenor of International Relations', in Perrigo and Whitman (2010): 1–17.

Carens, J. H. (1992), 'Migration and Morality: A Liberal Egalitarian Perspective', in Barry and Goodin (1992): 25–47.

Carr, E. H. (1942), *Conditions of Peace*. Macmillan, London.

—— (2001) [orig. 1939], *The Twenty Years' Crisis 1919–39: An Introduction to International Relations*. Palgrave Macmillan, Houndmills (reissued with a new Introduction by Michael Cox).

Cerone, J. P. (2006), 'Status of Detainees in Non-International Armed Conflict, and their Protection in the Course of Criminal Proceedings: The Case of *Hamdan v. Rumsfeld*', *ASIL Insights* (American Society of International Law), 10 (17), 14 July. <http://www.asil.org/insights060714.cfm>.

Charvet, J. (1998), 'International Society from a Contractarian Perspective', in Mapel and Nardin (1998): 114–31.

Chen, L. and Narasimhan, V. (2003), 'A Human Security Agenda for Global Health', in Chen, Leaning, and Narasimhan (2003): 3–12.

—— Leaning, J., and Narasimhan, V. (eds) (2003), *Global Health Challenges for Human Security*. Harvard University Press, Cambridge, MA.

Childs, J. B. (ed.) (2005), *Hurricane Katrina: Response and Responsibilities*. New Pacific Press, Santa Cruz, CA.

Christoff, P. (2006), 'Post-Kyoto? Post-Bush? Towards an Effective "Climate Coalition of the Willing"', *International Affairs*, 82 (5): 831–60.

——(2010), 'Cold Climate in Copenhagen: China and the United States at COP15', *Environmental Politics*, 19 (4): 637–56.

——and Eckersley, R. (2011), 'Comparing State Responses', in Dryzek, Norgaard, and Schlosberg (2011a): 431–48.

Clapton, W. (2011), 'Risk in International Relations', *International Relations*, 25 (3): 280–95.

——and Hameiri, S. (2012), 'The Domestic Politics of International Hierarchy: Risk Management and the Reconstitution of International Society', *International Politics*, 49 (1): 59–77.

Clark, I. (1982), *Limited Nuclear War: Political Theory and War Conventions*. Princeton University Press, Princeton, NJ.

——(1988), *Waging War: A Philosophical Introduction*. Oxford University Press, Oxford.

——(1997), *Globalization and Fragmentation: International Relations in the Twentieth Century*. Oxford University Press, Oxford.

——(1999), *Globalization and the Theory of International Relations*. Oxford University Press, Oxford.

——(2001), *The Post-Cold War Order: The Spoils of Peace*. Oxford University Press, Oxford.

——(2005), *Legitimacy in International Society*. Oxford University Press, Oxford.

——(2007), *International Legitimacy and World Society*. Oxford University Press, Oxford.

——(2009), 'How Hierarchical Can International Society Be?', *International Relations*, 23 (3): 464–80.

——(2011), *Hegemony in International Society*. Oxford University Press, Oxford.

Coady, C. A. J. (2004), 'Terrorism and Innocence', *The Journal of Ethics*, 8 (1): 37–58.

——(2007), 'Collateral Immunity in War and Terrorism', in Primoratz (2007a): 136–57.

——(2008), *Morality and Political Violence*. Cambridge University Press, Cambridge.

Cochran, M. (1999), *Normative Theory in International Relations: A Pragmatic Approach*. Cambridge University Press, Cambridge.

Cockerham, G. B. and Cockerham, W. C. (2010), *Health and Globalization*. Polity, Cambridge.

Collier, P., Conway, G., and Venables, T. (2009), 'Climate Change and Africa', in Helm and Hepburn (2009): 125–41.

Collin, J., Lee, K., and Bissell, K. (2009), 'The Framework Convention on Tobacco Control: The Politics of Global Health Governance', in Kirton (2009a): 369–86.

Cooper, A. F., Kirton, J. J., and Schrecker, T. (eds) (2007a), *Governing Global Health: Challenge, Response, Innovation*. Ashgate, Aldershot.

————(2007b), 'Governing Global Health in the Twenty-First Century', in Cooper, Kirton, and Schrecker (2007a): 3–12.

Copeland, D. C. (2006), 'The Constructivist Challenge to Structural Realism: A Review Essay', in Guzzini and Leander (2006): 1–20.

Coppieters, B. (2008), 'Legitimate Authority', in Coppieters and Fotion (2008): 55–72.

——and Fotion, N. (eds) (2008), *Moral Constraints on War*. 2nd edn, Lexington Books, Lanham, MD.

Coronil, F. and Skurski, J. (eds) (2006), *States of Violence*. University of Michigan Press, Ann Arbor, MI.

Correa, C. M. (2011), 'Intellectual Property Rights and Inequalities in Health Outcomes', in Labonté et al. (2011a): vol. III, 249–73.

Cossor, E. (2006), *Protecting the Internally Displaced in Armed Conflict*. APCML, Law School, University of Melbourne, Melbourne.

Couto, R. A. (2010), 'The Politics of Terrorism: Power, Legitimacy, and Violence', *Integral Review*, 6 (1): 63–81.

Cox, M. (ed.) (2000), *E. H. Carr: A Critical Appraisal*. Palgrave, Houndmills.

Crawford, N. (2002), *Argument and Change in World Politics*. Cambridge University Press, Cambridge.

Cronin, B. (2003), *Institutions for the Common Good: International Protection Regimes in International Society*. Cambridge University Press, Cambridge.

Crothers, C. (1996), *Social Structure*. Routledge, London.

Cullen, A. (2010), *The Concept of Non-International Armed Conflict in International Humanitarian Law*. Cambridge University Press, Cambridge.

Daniels, R. J., Kettl, D. F., and Kunreuther, H. (eds) (2006), *On Risk and Disaster: Lessons from Hurricane Katrina*. University of Pennsylvania Press, Philadelphia, PA.

Dauvergne, C. (2008), *Making People Illegal: What Globalization Means for Migration and Law*. Cambridge University Press, Cambridge.

Davies, S. (2008), *Legitimising Rejection: International Refugee Law in Southeast Asia*. Martinus Nijhoff, Leiden.

——(2010), 'What Contribution can International Relations Make to the Global Health Agenda?', *International Affairs*, 86 (5): 1167–90.

——and Glanville, L. (2010a), *Protecting the Displaced: Deepening the Responsibility to Protect*. Martinus Nijhoff, Leiden.

————(2010b), introduction in Davies and Glanville (2010a): 1–12.

Deaton, A. (2011), 'Global Patterns of Income and Health: Facts, Interpretations, and Policies', in Labonté et al. (2011a): vol. III, 224–47.

Dembour, M.-D. and Kelly, T. (eds) (2011a), *Are Human Rights for Migrants? Critical Reflections on the Status of Irregular Migrants in Europe and the United States*. Routledge, Abingdon.

————(2011b), introduction in Dembour and Kelly (2011a): 1–22.

Depledge, J. and Yamin, F. (2009), 'The Global Climate-change Regime: A Defence', in Helm and Hepburn (2009): 433–53.

DeSombre, E. R. (2007), *The Global Environment and World Politics*. 2nd edn, Continuum, London.

Devetak, R. (2005), 'Violence, Order, and Terror', in Bellamy (2005): 229–46.

——(2008), 'Globalization's Shadow: An Introduction to the Globalization of Political Violence', in Devetak and Hughes (2008): 1–26.

——and Hughes, C. W. (eds) (2008), *The Globalization of Political Violence: Globalization's Shadow*. Routledge, London.

Dimitrov, R. (2010), 'Inside the UN Climate Change Negotiations: The Copenhagen Conference', *Review of Policy Research*, 27 (6): 795–822.

Dobriansky, P. J. and Turekian, V. C. (2009/10), 'Climate Change and Copenhagen: Many Paths Forward', *Survival*, 51 (6): 21–8.

Donnelly, J. (2006), 'Sovereign Inequalities and Hierarchy in Anarchy: American Power and International Society', *European Journal of International Relations*, 12 (2): 139–70.

Doyle, T. and Chaturvedi, S. (2011), 'Climate Refugees and Security: Conceptualisation, Categories, and Contestations', in Dryzek, Norgaard, and Schlosberg (2011a): 278–91.

Dryzek, J. S. (2005), *The Politics of the Earth: Environmental Discourses*. 2nd edn, Oxford University Press, Oxford.

——Norgaard, R. B., and Schlosberg, D. (eds) (2011a), *Oxford Handbook of Climate Change and Society*. Oxford University Press, Oxford.

————(2011b), introduction in Dryzek, Norgaard, and Schlosberg (2011a): 3–17.

Duffield, M. (2001), *Global Governance and the New Wars: The Merging of Development and Security*. Zed Books, London.

Duner, B. (2007), *The World Community and the 'Other' Terrorism*. Lexington Books, Lanham, MD.

Dunne, T. (1998), *Inventing International Society: A History of the English School*. Macmillan, Houndmills.

——(2000), 'Theories as Weapons: E. H. Carr and International Relations', in Cox (2000): 217–33.

——(2003), 'Society and Hierarchy in International Relations', *International Relations*, 17 (3): 303–20.

——(2005), 'The New Agenda', in Bellamy (2005a): 65–79.

——(2009), 'Liberalism, International Terrorism, and Democratic Wars', *International Relations*, 23 (1): 107–14.

Düvell, F. (2011), 'Irregular Migration', in Betts (2011a): 78–108.

Eckersley, R. (2012a), 'Does Leadership Make a Difference in International Climate Policy'. Paper presented at ISA Annual Meeting, San Diego, 1 April.

——(2012b), 'Moving Forward in the Climate Negotiations: Multilateralism or Minilateralism', *Global Environmental Politics*, 12 (2): 24–42.

Elbe, S. (2010), *Security and Global Health: Toward the Medicalization of Insecurity*. Polity, Cambridge.

Erskine, T. (ed.) (2003a), *Can Institutions have Responsibilities?: Collective Moral Agency and International Relations*. Palgrave, Houndmills.

——(2003b), 'Making Sense of "Responsibility" in International Relations: Key Concepts and Questions', in Erskine (2003a): 1–18.

Estreicher, S. (2011–12), 'Privileging Asymmetric Warfare (Part III)? The Intentional Killing of Civilians under International Humanitarian Law', *Chicago Journal of International Law*, 12 (2): 589–603.

Evangelista, M. (2008), *Law, Ethics, and the War on Terror*. Polity, Cambridge.

Evans, G. (1975), 'E. H. Carr and International Relations', *British Journal of International Studies*, 1 (2): 77–97.

Fabre, C. (2007), *Justice in a Changing World*. Polity, Cambridge.

Fabre, C. (2008), 'Cosmopolitanism, Just War Theory, and Legitimate Authority', *International Affairs*, 84 (5): 963–76.

Fabry, M. (2010), *Recognizing States: International Society and the Establishment of New States Since 1776*. Oxford University Press, Oxford.

Falkner, R. (2012), 'Global Environmentalism and the Greening of International Society', *International Affairs*, 88 (3): 503–22.

Fidler, D. P. (2005), 'From International Sanitary Conventions to Global Health Security: The New International Health Regulations', *The Chinese Journal of International Law*, 4 (2): 325–92.

——(2007), 'A Pathology of Public Health Securitisation: Approaching Pandemics as Security Threats', in Cooper, Kirton, and Schrecker (2007a): 41–64.

——(2009a), 'The Globalization of Public Health: The First 100 Years of International Health Diplomacy', in Kirton (2009a): 125–32.

——(2009b), 'Germs, Governance, and Global Public Health in the Wake of SARS', in Kirton (2009a): 219–23.

——(2011), 'After the Revolution: Global Health Politics in a Time of Economic Crisis and Threatening Future Trends', in Labonté et al. (2011a): 329–51.

——(2012), 'Negotiating Equitable Access to Influenza Vaccines: Global Health Diplomacy and the Controversies Surrounding Avian Influenza H5N1 and Pandemic Influenza H1N1', in Rosskam and Kickbusch (2012): 161–72.

Figueroa, R. F. (2011), 'Indigenous Peoples and Cultural Losses', in Dryzek, Norgaard, and Schlosberg (2011a): 232–47.

Finlay, C. J. (2010), 'Legitimacy and Non-State Political Violence', *The Journal of Political Philosophy*, 18 (3): 287–312.

Finnemore, M. (1996), *National Interests in International Society*. Cornell University Press, Ithaca, NY.

——(2008), 'Paradoxes in Humanitarian Intervention', in Price (2008): 197–224.

Foot, R. (2003), introduction in Foot, Gaddis, and Hurrell (2003): 1–23.

——(2004), *Human Rights and Counter-Terrorism in America's Asia Policy*, Adelphi Paper 363. Oxford University Press for the International Institute for Strategic Studies, Oxford.

——Gaddis, J. L., and Hurrell, A. (eds) (2003), *Order and Justice in International Relations*. Oxford University Press, Oxford.

Ford, J. D. and Pearce, T. (2012), 'Climate Change Vulnerability and Adaptation Research Focusing on the Inuit Subsistence Sector in Canada: Directions for Future Research', *The Canadian Geographer/Le Géographie canadien*, 56 (2): 275–87.

Frazer, E. and Hutchings, K. (2011), 'Virtuous Violence and the Politics of Statecraft in Machiavelli, Clausewitz, and Weber', *Political Studies*, 59 (1): 56–73.

Friedman, G. and Starr, H. (1997), *Agency, Structure and International Politics: From Ontology to Empirical Inquiry*. Routledge, London.

Frost, M. (2003a), 'Thinking Ethically about Refugees: A Case for the Transformation of Global Governance', in Newman and van Selm (2003): 109–29.

——(2003b), 'Constitutive Theory and Moral Accountability: Individuals, Institutions, and Dispersed Practices', in Erskine (2003a): 84–99.

——(2009), *Global Ethics: Anarchy, Freedom, and International Relations*. Routledge, London.

Fullinwider, R. K. (2003), 'Terrorism, Innocence, and War', in Gehring (2003): 21–36.

Füssel, H.-M. (2010), 'How Inequitable is the Global Distribution of Responsibility, Capability, and Vulnerability to Climate Change?: A Comprehensive Indicator-based Assessment', *Global Environmental Change*, 20 (4): 597–611.

Gammeltoft-Hansen, T. (2011), *Access to Asylum: International Refugee Law and the Globalisation of Migration Control*. Cambridge University Press, Cambridge.

Gardiner, S. M. (2011a), *A Perfect Moral Storm: The Ethical Tragedy of Climate Change*. Oxford University Press, New York.

——(2011b), 'Climate Justice', in Dryzek, Norgaard, and Schlosberg (2011a): 309–22.

Garnaut, R. (2008), *The Garnaut Climate Change Review*. Cambridge University Press, Melbourne.

——Jutzo, F., and Howes, S. (2008), 'China's Rapid Emissions Growth and Global Climate Change Policy', in Song and Woo (2008): 170–89.

Garrett, L. (2011), 'The Challenge of Global Health', in Labonté et al. (2011a): 3–22.

Gaskarth, J. (2012), 'The Virtues in International Society', *European Journal of International Relations*, 18 (3): 431–53.

Gehring, V. V. (ed.) (2003), *War After September 11*. Rowman and Littlefield, Lanham, MD.

Geiger, M. and Pécoud, A. (eds) (2010a), *The Politics of International Migration Management*. Palgrave, Houndmills.

——— (2010b), 'The Politics of International Migration Management', in Geiger and Pécoud (2010a): 1–20.

Gemenne, F. (2010), 'What's in a Name: Social Vulnerabilities and the Refugee Controversy in the Wake of Hurricane Katrina', in Afifi and Jager (2010): 29–40.

Gibney, M. J. (2004), *The Ethics and Politics of Asylum: Liberal Democracy and the Response to Refugees*. Cambridge University Press, Cambridge.

——(2006), '"A Thousand Little Guantanamos": Western States and Measures to Prevent the Arrival of Refugees', in Tunstall (2006): 139–69.

Giddens, A. (1987), *Social Theory and Modern Sociology*. Polity, Cambridge.

Gong, G. (1984), *The Standard of 'Civilization' in International Society*. Oxford University Press, Oxford.

Goodin, R. E. (1985), *Protecting the Vulnerable: A Reanalysis of our Social Responsibilities*. University of Chicago Press, Chicago.

Goodman, N. M. (1952), *International Health Organizations and Their Work*. Blakiston, Philadelphia, PA.

Goodwin-Gill, G. S. and McAdam, J. (2007), *The Refugee in International Law*. 3rd edn, Oxford University Press, Oxford.

Gough, I. and Meadowcroft, J. (2011), 'Decarbonizing the Welfare State', in Dryzek, Norgaard, and Schlosberg (2011a): 490–503.

Grant, S. (2011a), 'The Recognition of Migrants' Rights within the UN Human Rights System', in Dembour and Kelly (2011a): 25–47.

——(2011b), 'Irregular Migration and Frontier Deaths: Acknowledging a Right to Identity', in Dembour and Kelly (2011a): 48–70.

Gray, H. (2005), 'Katrina: Where the Natural and the Social Meet', in Childs (2005): 87–91.

Greenhill, K. M. (2010), *Weapons of Mass Migration: Forced Displacement, Coercion, and Foreign Policy*. Cornell University Press, Ithaca, NY.

Gross, M. L. (2010), *Moral Dilemmas of Modern War: Torture, Assassination, and Blackmail in an Age of Asymmetric Conflict*. Cambridge University Press, Cambridge.

Guzzini, S. and Leander, A. (eds) (2006), *Constructivism and International Relations: Alexander Wendt and his Critics*. Routledge, Abingdon.

Haddad, E. (2008), *The Refugee in International Society: Between Sovereigns*. Cambridge University Press, Cambridge.

Hajer, M. and Versteeg, W. (2011), 'Voices of Vulnerability: The Reconfiguration of Policy Discourses', in Dryzek, Norgaard, and Schlosberg (2011a): 82–95.

Halliday, F. (1992), 'International Society as Homogeneity: Burke, Marx, Fukuyama', *Millennium*, 21 (3): 435–61.

Hanna, E. C. (2011), 'Health Hazards', in Dryzek, Norgaard, and Schlosberg (2011a): 217–31.

Harbour, F. V. (2003), 'Collective Moral Agency and the Political Process', in Erskine (2003a): 69–83.

Harrington, J. and Stuttaford, M. (eds) (2010), *Global Health and Human Rights: Legal and Philosophical Perspectives*. Routledge, Abingdon.

Harris, J. (1980), *Violence and Responsibility*. Routledge and Kegan Paul, London.

Harris, P. G. (2010), *World Ethics and Climate Change: From International to Global Justice*. Edinburgh University Press, Edinburgh.

—— (2011), 'Reconceptualising Global Governance', in Dryzek, Norgaard, and Schlosberg (2011a): 639–52.

Harrison, M. (2009), 'Disease, Diplomacy and International Commerce: The Origins of International Sanitary Regulation in the Nineteenth Century', in Kirton (2009a): 3–23.

Hartigan, R. S. (1967), 'Noncombatant Immunity: Reflections on its Origins and Present Status', *Review of Politics*, 29 (2): 204–20.

Hartle, A. (2008), 'Discrimination', in Coppieters and Fotion (2008): 171–91.

Havercroft, J. (2008), 'Sovereignty, Recognition, and Indigenous Peoples', in Price (2008): 112–37.

Hawkes, C. (2011), 'Uneven Dietary Development: Linking the Policies and Processes of Globalization with the Nutrition Transition, Obesity and Diet-Related Chronic Diseases', in Labonté et al. (2011a): 275–305.

Hayashi, M. N. (2007), 'The Principle of Civilian Protection and Contemporary Armed Conflict', in Hensel (2007): 105–29.

Heinze, E. A. (2009), *Waging Humanitarian War: The Ethics, Law, and Politics of Humanitarian Intervention*. State University of New York Press, Albany, NY.

—— (2011), 'The Evolution of International Law in Light of the "Global War on Terror"', *Review of International Studies*, 37 (3): 1069–94.

Helm, D. (2009a), 'Climate-change Policy: Why has so Little been Achieved?', in Helm and Hepburn (2009): 9–35.

—— (2009b), 'EU Climate-change Policy—A Critique', in Helm and Hepburn (2009): 222–44.

—— and Hepburn, C. (eds) (2009), *The Economics and Politics of Climate Change*. Oxford University Press, Oxford.

Hendrickson, D. C. (1992), 'Migration in Law and Ethics: A Realist Perspective', in Barry and Goodin (1992): 213–31.

Hensel, H. M. (ed.) (2007), *The Law of Armed Conflict: Constraints on the Contemporary Use of Military Force*. Ashgate, Aldershot.

Hepburn, C. and Stern, N. (2009), 'The Global Deal in Climate Change', in Helm and Hepburn (2009): 36–57.

Hewitt, K. (ed.) (1983), *Interpretations of Calamity from the Viewpoint of Human Ecology*. Allen and Unwin, Boston.

—— (1997), *Regions at Risk: A Geographical Introduction to Disasters*. Longman, Harlow.

Hobson, J. M. and Sharman, J. C. (2005), 'The Enduring Place of Hierarchy in World Politics: Tracing the Social Logics of Hierarchy and Political Change', *European Journal of International Relations*, 11 (1): 63–98.

Hoffmann, S. (1990), 'International Society', in Miller and Vincent (1990): 13–37.

Howard, M. (ed.) (1979a), *Restraints on War: Studies in the Limitation of Armed Conflict*. Oxford University Press, Oxford.

—— (1979b), 'Temperamenta Belli: Can War be Controlled?', in Howard (1979a): 1–15.

Howard-Jones, N. (2009) [orig. 1950], 'Origins of International Health Work', in Kirton (2009a): 25–30.

Hurd, I. (2007), *After Anarchy: Legitimacy and Power in the United Nations Security Council*. Princeton University Press, Princeton, NJ.

Hurrell, A. (2003), 'Order and Justice: What is at Stake?', in Foot, Gaddis, and Hurrell (2003): 24–48.

—— (2007), *On Global Order: Power, Values, and the Constitution of International Security*. Oxford University Press, Oxford.

—— (2011), 'Refugees, International Society, and Global Order', in Betts and Loescher (2011a): 85–104.

Hurwitz, A. G. (2009), *The Collective Responsibility of States to Protect Refugees*. Oxford University Press, Oxford.

Hutchings, K. (2010), *Global Ethics: An Introduction*. Polity, Cambridge.

Inder, C. (2010), 'International Refugee Law, "Hyper-Legalism", and Migration Management: The Pacific Solution', in Geiger and Pécoud (2010a): 220–51.

Ingram, A. (2009), 'The International Political Economy of Global Responses to HIV/AIDS', in Kay and Williams (2009a): 81–101.

Inoue, K. and Drori, G. (2011), 'The Global Institutionalization of Health as a Social Concern: Organizational and Discursive Trends', in Labonté et al. (2011a): 3–20.

IPCC (2001), *Climate Change 2001, Working Group II: Impacts, Adaptation and Vulnerability*. Cambridge University Press, Cambridge. <http://www.ipcc.ch/>.

—— [Parry, M. L. et al. (eds)] (2007), *Climate Change 2007: Impacts, Adaptation and Vulnerability: Contribution of Working Group II to the Fourth Assessment Report of the Intergovernmental Panel on Climate Change*. Cambridge University Press, Cambridge.

Iqbal, Z. (2010), *War and the Health of Nations*. Stanford University Press, Stanford, CA.

Jackson, R. H. (2009), 'International Relations as a Craft Discipline', in Navari (2009a): 21–38.

Johnson, J. T. (2006), 'Humanitarian Intervention after Iraq: Just War and International Law Perspectives', *Journal of Military Ethics*, 5 (2): 114–27.

Johnson, J. T. (2011), *Ethics and the Use of Force: Just War in Historical Perspective.* Ashgate, Farnham.

Johnston, B. R. (ed.) (1994a), *Who Pays the Price? The Sociocultural Context of Environmental Crisis.* Island Press, Washington, DC.

——(1994b), 'Environmental Degradation and Human Rights Abuse', in Johnston (1994a): 7–15.

Johnstone, I. (2008), 'Legislation and Adjudication in the UN Security Council: Bringing Down the Deliberative Deficit', *American Journal of International Law,* 102 (2): 275–308.

Jones, C. (1998), *E. H. Carr and International Relations: A Duty to Lie.* Cambridge University Press, Cambridge.

Jones, P. (2010), 'The Ethics of International Society', in Bell (2010): 111–29.

Juss, S. S. (2006), *International Migration and Global Justice.* Ashgate, Aldershot.

Kahn, P. W. (2003), 'The Paradox of Riskless Warfare', in Gehring (2003): 37–49.

Kälin, W. (2009), 'Climate Change, Natural Disasters, and Internal Displacement', speech to Committee on Migration, Refugees and Population of the Parliamentary Assembly, Council of Europe, 24 June. <http://www.brookings.edu/research/speeches/2009/06/24-internal-displacement-kalin>.

Kalshoven, F. (1973), *The Law of Warfare: A Summary of its Recent History and Trends in Development.* Sijthoff, Leiden.

Kamm, F. M. (2004), 'Failures of Just War Theory: Terror, Harm, and Justice', *Ethics,* 114 (4): 650–92.

Kamrad-Scott, A. (2010), 'The WHO Secretariat, Norm Entrepreneurship, and Global Disease Outbreak Control', *Journal of International Organization Studies,* 1 (1): 72–89.

Karlsson, C., Parker, C., Hjerpe, M., and Linnér, B.-O. (2011), 'Looking for Leaders: Perceptions of Climate Change Leadership among Climate Change Negotiation Participants', *Global Environmental Politics,* 11 (1): 89–107.

Kartha, S. (2011), 'Discourses of the Global South', in Dryzek, Norgaard, and Schlosberg (2011a): 504–18.

Kashnikov, B. (2008), 'NATO's Intervention in the Kosovo Crisis', in Coppieters and Fotion (2008): 219–35.

Katz, R. and Muldoon, A. (2012), 'Negotiating the Revised International Health Regulations (IHR)', in Rosskam and Kickbusch (2012): 77–99.

Kaufman, F. (2007), 'Just War Theory and Killing the Innocent', in Brough, Lango, and van der Linden (2007): 99–114.

Kay, A. and Williams, O. (eds) (2009a), *Global Health Governance: Crisis, Institutions and Political Economy.* Palgrave, Houndmills.

——— (2009b), 'Introduction: The International Political Economy of Global Health Governance', in Kay and Williams (2009a): 1–23.

Keal, P. (2003), *European Conquest and the Rights of Indigenous Peoples: The Moral Backwardness of International Society.* Cambridge University Press, Cambridge.

Keane, J. (1996), *Reflections on Violence.* Verso, London.

Keene, E. (2002), *Beyond the Anarchical Society: Grotius, Colonialism and Order in World Politics.* Cambridge University Press, Cambridge.

——(2009), 'International Society as an Ideal Type', in Navari (2009a): 104–24.

Keohane, R. O. and Nye, J. S. (1977), *Power and Interdependence: World Politics in Transition*. Little, Brown, Boston.

Kickbusch, I. (2009), 'The Development of International Health Policies—Accountability Intact?', in Kirton (2009a): 395–405.

Kirton, J. J. (ed.) (2009a), *Global Health*. Ashgate, Farnham.

——(2009b), introduction in Kirton (2009a): xv–xxxv.

——and Mannell, J. (2007), 'The G8 and Global Health Governance', in Cooper, Kirton, and Schrecker (2007a): 115–46.

Kleine-Ahlbrandt, S. T. (2004), *The Protection Gap in the International Protection of Internally Displaced Persons: The Case of Rwanda*. Geneva Institute of International Studies, Geneva.

Kneebone, S. (ed.) (2009a), *Refugees, Asylum Seekers and the Rule of Law*. Cambridge University Press, Cambridge.

——(2009b), 'Introduction: Refugees and Asylum Seekers in the International Context: Rights and Realities', in Kneebone (2009a): 1–31.

Koivusalo, M. and Mackintosh, M. (2008), 'Global Public Health Security: Inequality, Vulnerability and Public Health System Capabilities', *Development and Change*, 39 (6): 1163–9.

Koser, K. (2007), *International Migration: A Very Short Introduction*. Oxford University Press, Oxford.

——(2011), 'Internally Displaced Persons', in Betts (2011a): 210–23.

Kunreuther, H. and Useem, M. (eds) (2010), *Learning from Catastrophes: Strategies for Reaction and Response*. Pearson, Upper Saddle River, NJ.

Labonté, R., Mohindra, K. S., Schrecker, T., and Stoebenau, K. (eds) (2011a), *Global Health*, 4 vols. Sage, London.

————————(2011b), 'Editors' Introduction: Global Health in an Interconnected World', in Labonté et al. (2011a): xxiii–lxii.

Labonté, R. and Schrecker, T. (2011), 'The State of Global Health in a Radically Unequal World: Patterns and Prospects', in Benatar and Brock (2011): 24–36.

Lake, D. A. (2007), 'Escape from the State of Nature: Anarchy and Hierarchy in World Politics', *International Security*, 32 (1): 47–79.

——(2009), *Hierarchy in International Relations*. Cornell University Press, Ithaca, NY.

Lang, A. (2003), 'The United Nations and the Fall of Srebrenica: Meaningful Responsibility and International Society', in Erskine (2003a): 183–206.

Lassman, P. and Speirs, R. (eds) (1994), *Weber: Political Writings*. Cambridge University Press, Cambridge.

Lee, K. (2003), *Globalization and Health: An Introduction*. Palgrave, Houndmills.

——(2009), 'Understandings of Global Health Governance: The Contested Landscape', in Kay and Williams (2009a): 27–41.

——and Dodgson, R. (2011), 'Globalization and Cholera: Implications for Global Governance', in Labonté et al. (2011a): 109–29.

Linklater, A. (2011), *The Problem of Harm in World Politics*. Cambridge University Press, Cambridge.

——and Suganami, H. (2006), *The English School of International Relations: A Contemporary Reassessment*. Cambridge University Press, Cambridge.

Loescher, G. (2003), 'Refugees as Grounds for International Action', in Newman and van Selm (2003): 31–49.

——and Milner, J. (2011), 'UNHCR and the Global Governance of Refugees', in Betts (2011a): 189–209.

Long, W. J. (2011), *Pandemics and Peace*. United States Institute of Peace, Washington, DC.

Luban, D. (2003), 'The War on Terrorism and the End of Human Rights', in Gehring (2003): 51–62.

Luterbacher, U. and Sprinz, D. F. (eds) (2001), *International Relations and Global Climate Change*. MIT Press, Cambridge, MA.

McAdam, J. (2011), 'Environmental Migration', in Betts (2011a): 153–88.

——(2012), *Climate Change, Forced Migration, and International Law*. Oxford University Press, Oxford.

McEvoy, P. (2011), 'Law at the Operational Level', in Whetham (2011a): 108–34.

McInnes, C. (2009), 'National Security and Global Health Governance', in Kay and Williams (2009a): 42–59.

——and Lee, K. (2006), 'Health, Security and Foreign Policy', *Review of International Studies*, 32 (1): 5–23.

————(2012), *Global Health and International Relations*. Polity, Cambridge.

McKeogh, C. (2007), 'Civilian Immunity in War: From Augustine to Vattel', in Primoratz (2007a): 62–83.

——(2011), 'Are the Citizens of a Democracy a Just Target for Terrorists', *Irish Political Studies*, 26 (4): 579–92.

McKeown, R. (2009), 'Norm Regress: US Revisionism and the Slow Death of the Torture Norm', *International Relations*, 23 (1): 5–25.

McKibben, W. J., Morris, A. C., and Wilcoxen, P. J. (2010), 'Comparing Climate Commitments: A Model-Based Analysis of the Copenhagen Accord'. The Brookings Institution, Washington, DC, 27 May.

MacLean, S. J. and Brown, S. A. (2009), 'Introduction: The Social Determinants of Global Health: Confronting Inequities', in MacLean, Brown, and Fourie (2009): 3–17.

————and Fourie, P. (eds) (2009), *Health for Some: The Political Economy of Global Health Governance*. Palgrave, Houndmills.

McMahan, J. (2008), 'The Morality of War and the Law of War', in Rodin and Shue (2008a): 19–43.

——(2010), 'The Just Distribution of Harm Between Combatants and Noncombatants', *Philosophy and Public Affairs*, 38 (4): 342–79.

McPherson, L. K. (2007), 'Is Terrorism Distinctively Wrong?', *Ethics*, 117 (3): 524–46.

Macrae, J. and Zwi, A. (1994a), *War and Hunger: Rethinking International Responses to Complex Emergencies*. Zed Books, London.

————(1994b), 'Famine, Complex Emergencies and International Policy in Africa: An Overview', in Macrae and Zwi (1994a): 6–36.

Mansell, W. and Openshaw, K. (2010), 'The History and Status of the Geneva Conventions', in Perrigo and Whitman (2010): 18–41.

Mapel, D. R. and Nardin, T. (eds) (1998), *International Society: Diverse Ethical Perspectives*. Princeton University Press, Princeton, NJ.

Martin, S. (2010), 'Forced Migration, the Refugee Regime and the Responsibility to Protect', in Davies and Glanville (2010a): 13–34.

——and Calloway, A. (2011), 'Human Trafficking and Smuggling', in Betts (2011a): 224–41.

Matthew, R. A., Barnett, J., McDonald, B., and O'Brien, K. (eds) (2010), *Global Environmental Change and Human Security*. MIT Press, Cambridge.

Mearns, R. and Norton, A. (2010), *Social Dimensions of Climate Change: Equity and Vulnerability in a Warming World*. World Bank, Washington, DC.

Médecins Sans Frontières (MSF) (2012), 'Mali: Refugees in a Vulnerable Situation', 26 June. <http://www.doctorswithoutborders.org/news/article.cfm?id=6091&cat=field-news>.

Meier, B. M. (2010), 'The World Health Organization, the Evolution of Human Rights, and the Failure to Achieve Health for All', in Harrington and Stuttaford (2010): 163–89.

Meyer, M. A. and McCoubrey, H. (eds) (1998), *Reflections on Law and Armed Conflicts: The Selected Works on the Laws of War by the Late Professor Colonel G. I. A. D. Draper, OBE*. Kluwer Law International, The Hague.

Miller, D. (2007), *National Responsibility and Global Justice*. Oxford University Press, Oxford.

Miller, J. D. B. and Vincent, R. J. (eds) (1990), *Order and Violence: Hedley Bull and International Relations*. Clarendon Press, Oxford.

Miller, R. W. (2010), *Globalizing Justice: The Ethics of Poverty and Power*. Oxford University Press, Oxford.

Miller, S. (2010), *The Moral Foundations of Social Institutions: A Philosophical Study*. Cambridge University Press, Cambridge.

Molloy, S. (2003), 'Dialectics and Transformation: Exploring the International Theory of E. H. Carr', *International Journal of Politics, Culture and Society*, 17 (2): 279–306.

——(2009), 'Hans J. Morgenthau versus E. H. Carr: Conflicting Concepts of Ethics in Realism', in Bell (2009): 83–104.

Morawa, A. H. E. (2003), 'Vulnerability as a Concept in International Human Rights Law', *Journal of International Relations and Development*, 6 (2): 139–55.

Morris, J. (2005), 'Normative Innovation and the Great Powers', in Bellamy (2005a): 265–82.

Moser, S. C. (2010), 'Now More than Ever: The Need for Some Societally Relevant Research on Vulnerability and Adaptation to Climate Change', *Applied Geography*, 30 (4): 464–74.

Muzaka, V. (2011), *The Politics of Intellectual Property Rights and Access to Medicines*. Palgrave, Houndmills.

Nanda, V. P. (ed.) (2011a), *Climate Change and Environmental Ethics*. Transaction Publishers, New Bruswick, NJ.

——(2011b), introduction in Nanda (2011a): 1–13.

Nardin, T. (1983), *Law, Morality and the Relations of States*. Princeton University Press, Princeton, NJ.

——(1998), 'Legal Positivism as a Theory of International Society', in Mapel and Nardin (1998): 17–35.

Nathanson, S. (2010), *Terrorism and the Ethics of War*. Cambridge University Press, Cambridge.

Navari, C. (ed.) (2009a), *Theorising International Society: English School Methods*. Palgrave, Houndmills.

——(2009b), 'Introduction: Methods and Methodology in the English School', in Navari (2009a): 1–18.

Newman, E. (2003), 'Refugees, International Security, and Human Vulnerability: Introduction and Survey', in Newman and van Selm (2003): 3–30.

——and van Selm, J. (eds) (2003), *Refugees and Forced Displacement: International Security, Human Vulnerability and the State*. United Nations University Press, New York.

Nguyen, V.-K. and Peschard, K. (2011), 'Anthropology, Inequality, and Disease: A Review', in Labonté et al. (2011a), vol. III: 309–37.

Nishimura, K. (2010), 'Transcending Sinnlosigkeit: E. H. Carr on International Morality'. Paper presented at Annual Meeting of the International Studies Association, New Orleans.

Noll, G. (2003), 'Securitizing Sovereignty? States, Refugees, and the Regionalization of International Law', in Newman and van Selm (2003): 277–305.

O'Brien, K., St Clair, A. L., and Kristoffersen, B. (eds) (2010a), *Climate Change, Ethics and Human Security*. Cambridge University Press, Cambridge.

——————(2010b), 'The Framing of Climate Change: Why it Matters', in O'Brien, St Clair, and Kristoffersen (2010a): 3–22.

Okereke, C. (2010), 'The Politics of Interstate Climate Negotiations', in Boykoff (2010): 42–61.

Olmas, S. (2001), 'Vulnerability and Adaptation to Climate Change: Concepts, Issues, Assessment Methods'. Climate Change Knowledge Network. <http://www.cckn.net>.

O'Manique, C. (2007), 'Global Health and Universal Human Rights: The Case for G8 Accountability', in Cooper, Kirton, and Schrecker (2007a): 207–26.

O'Neill, O. (1996), *Towards Justice and Virtue*. Cambridge University Press, Cambridge.

Owens, P. (2008), 'Distinctions, Distinctions: "Public" and "Private" Force?', *International Affairs*, 84 (5): 977–90.

——(2011), 'Beyond "Bare Life": Refugees and the "Right to Have Rights"', in Betts and Loescher (2011a): 133–50.

Page, E. A. (2006), *Climate Change, Justice and Future Generations*. Edward Elgar, Cheltenham.

Pan, J., Phillips, J., and Chen, Y. (2009), 'China's Balance of Emissions Embodied in Trade: Approaches to Measurement and Allocating International Responsibility', in Helm and Hepburn (2009): 142–66.

Panayi, P. (2011), 'Imperial Collapse and the Creation of Refugees in Twentieth-Century Europe', in Panayi and Virdee (2011a): 3–27.

——and Virdee, P. (eds) (2011a), *Refugees and the End of Empire: Imperial Collapse and Forced Migration in the Twentieth Century*. Palgrave, Houndmills.

——————(2011b), 'Preface: Key Themes, Concepts and Rationale', in Panayi and Virdee (2011a): vii–xxiv.

Paterson, M. (2001), 'Principles of Justice in the Context of Global Climate Change', in Luterbacher and Sprinz (2001): 119–26.

——(2011), 'Selling Carbon: From International Climate Regime to Global Carbon Markets', in Dryzek, Norgaard, and Schlosberg (2011a): 611–24.

Pattison, J. (2008), 'Just War Theory and the Privatization of Military Force', *Ethics and International Affairs*, 22 (2): 143–62.

Pécoul, B., Chirac, P., Trouiller, P., and Pinel, J. (1999), 'Access to Essential Drugs in Poor Countries: A Lost Battle?', *Journal of American Medical Association*, 281 (4): 361–7.

Perrigo, S. and Whitman, J. (eds) (2010), *The Geneva Conventions Under Assault*. Pluto Press, London.

Peterson, S. (2009), 'Epidemic Disease and National Security', in Kirton (2009a): 143–81.

Phillips, R. L. (1984), *War and Justice*. University of Oklahoma Press, Norman.

Phuong, C. (2004), *The International Protection of Internally Displaced Persons*. Cambridge University Press, Cambridge.

Pickering, S. (2008), 'The Globalization of Violence against Refugees', in Devetak and Hughes (2008): 104–24.

Pogge, T. W. (2002), *World Poverty and Human Rights*. Polity, Cambridge.

——(2005), 'Human Rights and Global Health: A Research Program', *Metaphilosophy*, 36 (1/2): 182–209.

Polsky, C. and Eakin, H. (2011), 'Global Change Vulnerability Assessments: Definitions, Challenges, and Opportunities', in Dryzek, Norgaard, and Schlosberg (2011a): 205–16.

Price, R. M. (ed.) (2008), *Moral Limit and Possibility in World Politics*. Cambridge University Press, Cambridge.

Price-Smith, A. T. (2009), 'Ghosts of Kigali: Infectious Disease and Global Stability at the Turn of the Century', in Kirton (2009a): 85–101.

Primoratz, I. (ed.) (2007a), *Civilian Immunity in War*. Oxford University Press, Oxford.

——(2007b), 'Civilian Immunity in War: Its Grounds, Scope, and Weight', in Primoratz (2007a): 21–41.

——(2011), 'Civilian Immunity, Supreme Emergency, and Moral Disaster', *Journal of Ethics*, 15 (4): 371–86.

Rasmussen, M. (2006), *The Risk Society at War: Terror, Technology and Strategy in the Twenty-First Century*. Cambridge University Press, Cambridge.

Rawls, J. (1999), *The Law of Peoples*. Harvard University Press, Cambridge, MA.

Reus-Smit, C. (1997), 'The Constitutional Structure of International Society and the Nature of Fundamental Institutions', *International Organization*, 51 (4): 555–89.

——(1999), *The Moral Purpose of the State: Culture, Social Identity, and Institutional Rationality in International Relations*. Princeton University Press, Princeton, NJ.

——(2005), 'The Constructivist Challenge after September 11', in Bellamy (2005a): 81–94.

——(2008), 'Constructivism and the Structure of Ethical Reasoning', in Price (2008): 53–82.

——and Snidal, D. (eds) (2008), *The Oxford Handbook of International Relations*. Oxford University Press, Oxford.

Rich, P. (2000), 'E. H. Carr and the Quest for Moral Revolution in International Relations', in Cox (2000): 198–216.

Richardson, K., Steffen, W., and Liverman, D. (2011), *Climate Change: Global Risks, Challenges and Decisions*. Cambridge University Press, Cambridge.

Roberts, A. (2008), 'The Principle of Equal Application of the Laws of War', in Rodin and Shue (2008a): 226–54.

——and Guelff, R. (2000), *Documents on the Laws of War*. 3rd edn, Oxford University Press, Oxford.

Roberts, J. and Parks, B. C. (2007), *A Climate of Injustice: Global Inequality, North–South Politics, and Climate Policy*. MIT Press, Cambridge, MA.

Rodin, D. (2008), 'The Moral Inequality of Soldiers: Why *jus in bello* Asymmetry is Half Right', in Rodin and Shue (2008a): 44–68.

——and Shue, H. (eds) (2008a), *Just and Unjust Warriors: The Moral and Legal Status of Soldiers*. Oxford University Press, Oxford.

————(2008b), 'Introduction', in Rodin and Shue (2008a): 1–18.

Roffe, P., Tansey, G., and Vivas-Eugui, D. (eds) (2006), *Negotiating Health: Intellectual Property and Access to Medicines*. Earthscan, London.

Rosskam, E. and Kickbusch, I. (eds) (2012), *Negotiating and Navigating Global Health: Case Studies in Global Health Diplomacy*. World Scientific, Hackensack, NJ.

Roy, M. and Venema, H. D. (2002), 'Reducing Risk and Vulnerability to Climate Change in India: The Capabilities Approach', *Gender and Development*, 10 (2): 78–83.

Ruina, J. P. and Gell-Mann, M. (1989), 'Ballistic Missile Defense and the Arms Race', in Bobbitt, Freedman, and Treverton (1989): 263–6.

Rushton, S. (2009), 'Global Governance Capacities in Health: WHO and Infectious Diseases', in Kay and Williams (2009a): 60–80.

——and Williams, O. D. (eds) (2011), *Partnerships and Foundations in Global Health Governance*. Palgrave, Houndmills.

Saker, L., Lee, K., Cannito, B., Gilmore, A., and Campbell-Lendrum, D. (2004), *Globalization and Infectious Diseases: A Review of the Linkages*. WHO, Geneva.

Salter, M. B. (2003), *Rights of Passage: The Passport in International Relations*. Rienner, Boulder, CO.

Scheipers, S. (2009), *Negotiating Sovereignty and Human Rights: International Society and the International Criminal Court*. Manchester University Press, Manchester.

Schelling, T. C. (1989), 'Controlled Response and Strategic Warfare', in Bobbitt, Freedman, and Treverton (1989): 223–36.

Schneider, S. H. (2007), 'Assessing Key Vulnerabilities and the Risk from Climate Change', in IPCC (2007): 779–810.

Schrecker, T. (2009a), 'The G8, Globalization, and the Need for a Global Health Ethic', in MacLean, Brown, and Fourie (2009): 21–38.

——(2009b), 'The Power of Money: Global Financial Markets, National Politics, and Social Determinants of Health', in Kay and Williams (2009a): 160–81.

——(2011), 'Denaturalizing Scarcity: A Strategy of Enquiry for Public-Health Ethics', in Labonté et al. (2011a): 255–64.

Segall, S. (2010), *Health, Luck, and Justice*. Princeton University Press, Princeton, NJ.

Sen, A. (1981), *Poverty and Famines: An Essay on Entitlement and Deprivation*. Oxford University Press, Oxford.

——(2004), 'Why Health Equity?', in Anand, Peter, and Sen (2004): 21–33.

——(2010), *The Idea of Justice*. Penguin Books, London.

Shacknove, A. (1985), 'Who is a Refugee?', *Ethics*, 95 (2): 274–84.

Shapcott, R. (2010), *International Ethics: A Critical Introduction*. Polity, Cambridge.

Shearer, C. (2012), 'The Social Construction of Alaskan Native Vulnerability to Climate Change', *Race, Gender & Class*, 19 (1–2): 61–79.

Shue, H. (2008), 'Do We need a "Morality of War"?', in Rodin and Shue (2008a): 87–111.

——(2011), 'Civilian Protection and Force Protection', in Whetham (2011a): 135–47.

Skurski, J. and Coronil, F. (2006), 'Introduction: States of Violence and the Violence of States', in Coronil and Skurski (2006): 1–32.

Slim, H. (2007), *Killing Civilians: Method, Madness and Morality in War*. Hurst, London.

Smith School of Enterprise and the Environment, University of Oxford (2011), *International Climate Change Negotiations: Key Lessons and Next Steps*. SSEE, Oxford. <http://www.smithschool.ox.ac.uk/wp-content/uploads/2011/03/Climate-Negotiations-report_Final.pdf>.

Soares, M. B., Gagnon, A. S., and Doherty, R. M. (2012), 'Conceptual Elements of Climate Change Vulnerability Assessments: A Review', *International Journal of Climate Change Strategies and Management*, 4 (1): 6–35.

Solis, G. D. (2010), *The Law of Armed Conflict: International Humanitarian Law in War*. Cambridge University Press, Cambridge.

Song, L. and Woo, W. T. (eds) (2008), *China's Dilemma: Economic Growth, the Environment and Climate Change*. Brookings Institution, New York.

Steele, B. and Heinze, E. (eds) (2009), *Ethics, Authority, and War: Non-State Actors and the Just War Tradition*. Palgrave, Houndmills.

Steffek, J. (2006), *Embedded Liberalism and its Critics: Justifying Global Governance in the American Century*. Palgrave, New York.

Steffen, W. (2011), 'A Truly Complex and Diabolical Policy Problem', in Dryzek, Norgaard, and Schlosberg (2011a): 21–37.

Steinhoff, U. (2007), *On the Ethics of War and Terrorism*. Oxford University Press, Oxford.

Stern, G. (2000), *The Structure of International Society*. 2nd edn, Pinter, London.

Stern, T. and Antholis, W. (2007/8), 'A Changing Climate: The Road Ahead for the United States', *The Washington Quarterly*, 31 (1), 175–88.

Suhike, A. (2003), 'Human Security and the Protection of Refugees', in Newman and van Selm (2003): 93–108.

Tansey, G. (2006), 'Expanding Policy Options for Access to Medicines for All', in Roffe, Tansey, and Vivas-Eugui (2006): 257–68.

Taylor, A. L. and Dhillon, I. S. (2012), 'Transnational Diplomacy: Negotiation of the WHO Global Code of Practice on the International Recruitment of Health Personnel', in Rosskam and Kickbusch (2012): 101–27.

Taylor, M. (2005), ' "The Society of States under Siege?" An English School Perspective on the Emergence of Global Civil Society', *Australasian Journal of Human Security*, 1 (3): 5–25.

Thomas, C. and Weber, M. (2009), 'The Politics of Global Health Governance: Whatever Happened to "Health for All by the Year 2000"?', in Kirton (2009a): 103–21.

Tierney, K. (2006), 'Social Inequality, Hazards, and Disasters', in Daniels, Kettl, and Kunreuther (2006): 109–28.

Towns, A. E. (2010), *Women and States: Norms and Hierarchies in International Society*. Cambridge University Press, Cambridge.

Treverton, G. F. (1989), 'From No Cities to Stable Vulnerability', in Bobbitt, Freedman, and Treverton (1989): 190–204.

Tunstall, K. E. (ed.) (2006), *Displacement, Asylum, Migration: The Oxford Amnesty Lectures 2004*. Oxford University Press, Oxford.

Turner, B. S. (2006), *Vulnerability and Human Rights*. Pennsylvania State University Press, Pennsylvania.

UK Parliament (2012), 'Durban Climate Conference', Standard Note SN/SC/6140. House of Commons Library, London. <http://www.parliament.uk/briefing-papers/SN06140.pdf>.

UNDP (2008), *Human Development Report 2007/2008: Fighting Climate Change: Human Solidarity in a Divided World*. UNDP/Palgrave Macmillan, New York. <http://hdr.undp.org/en/reports/global/hdr2007-8/>.

——(2011), *Human Development Report 2011: Sustainability and Equity: A Better Future for All*. UNDP/Palgrave Macmillan, New York. <http://hdr.undp.org/en/reports/global/hdr2011/>.

UNFCCC (1992), (Durban). <http://www.unfccc.int/key-documents/the_convention/items/2853.php>.

——(1998), (Kyoto). <http://www.unfccc.int/kyoto_protocol/items/2830.php>.

——(2007), Decision 1/CP13, Bali Action Plan. <http://www.unfccc.int/key-documents/bali_road_map/items/6447.php>.

——(2010), (Cancún). <http://www.unfccc.int/meetings/cancun_nov_2010/items/6005.php>.

——(2011), (Durban). <http://www.unfccc.int/files/press/news_room/statements/application/pdf/111206_cop17_hls_cf.pdf>.

UNHCR (1978), *Convention and Protocol Relating to the Status of Refugees*. UN, Geneva.

Van Engeland, A. (2011), *Civilian or Combatant? A Challenge for the 21st Century*. Oxford University Press, Oxford.

van Selm, J. (2003), 'Refugee Protection Policies and Security Issues', in Newman and van Selm (2003): 66–92.

Vanderheiden, S. (2008), *Atmospheric Justice: A Political Theory of Climate Change*. Oxford University Press, Oxford.

Varley, A. (ed.) (1994), *Disasters, Development and the Environment*. John Wiley, Chichester.

Veitch, S. (2007), *Law and Irresponsibility: On the Legitimation of Human Suffering*. Routledge, Abingdon.

Vihma, A., Mulugetta, Y., and Karlsson-Vinkhuyzen, S. (2011), 'Negotiating Solidarity? The G77 Through the Prism of Climate Change Negotiations', *Global Change, Peace, and Security*, 23 (3): 315–34.

Vincent, R. J. (1990), 'Order in International Politics', in Miller and Vincent (1990): 38–64.

Vlassopoulos, C. A. (2010), 'Institutional Barriers to the Recognition and Assistance of Environmentally Forced Migrants', in Afifi and Jager (2010): 17–27.

Vos, J. A. (2011), 'World Legislation as Deliberation about the Common Good of International Society', *International Organizations Law Review*, 8 (1): 241–51.

Walzer, M. (1977), *Just and Unjust Wars: A Moral Argument with Historical Illustrations*. Basic Books, New York.

—— (1983), *Spheres of Justice: In Defense of Equality and Pluralism*. Basic Books, New York.

—— (2004), *Arguing about War*. Yale University Press, New Haven, CT.

—— (2008), 'Mercenary Impulse: Is there an Ethics that Justifies Blackwater?', *The New Republic*, 12 March: 20–1.

Weir, L. and Mykhalovskiy, E. (2010), *Global Public Health Vigilance: Creating a World on Alert*. Routledge, New York.

Wendt, A. (1999), *Social Theory of International Politics*. Cambridge University Press, Cambridge.

Wheeler, N. J. (2000), *Saving Strangers: Humanitarian Intervention in International Society*. Oxford University Press, Oxford.

Whelan, F. G. (1998), 'Legal Positivism and International Society', in Mapel and Nardin (1998): 36–53.

Whetham, D. (ed.) (2011a), *Ethics, Law and Military Operations*. Palgrave, Houndmills.

—— (2011b), 'Ethics, Law and Conflict', in Whetham (2011a): 10–28.

WHO (1946), 'Proceedings and Final Acts of the International Health Conference', New York, 19 June–22 July. UN WHO Interim Commission, New York/Geneva. <http://www.who.int/>.

—— (2007), *The World Health Report 2007: A Safer Future, Global Public Health Security in the 21st Century*. WHO, Geneva.

—— (2011), 'A Global Profile', in Labonté et al. (2011a): 85–102.

WHO, Commission on Social Determinants of Health (CSDH) (2008), *Closing the Gap in a Generation: Health Equity through Action on the Social Determinants of Health*, Final Report. WHO, Geneva, reprinted in Labonté et al. (2011a): 81–113. <http://www.who.int/social_determinants/thecommission/finalreport/en/index.html>.

Wight, C. (2006), *Agents, Structures and International Relations: Politics as Ontology*. Cambridge University Press, Cambridge.

—— (2009), 'Theorising Terrorism: The State, Structure and History', *International Relations*, 23 (1): 99–106.

Williams, O. D. and Rushton, S. (2011), 'Private Actors in Global Health Governance', in Rushton and Williams (2011): 1–28.

Xinran, Q. (2011), 'The Rise of BASIC in UN Climate Change Negotiations', *South African Journal of International Affairs*, 18 (3): 295–318.

Yoo, J. (2006), *War by Any Other Means: An Insider's Account of the War on Terror*. Atlantic Monthly Press, New York.

Youde, J. (2010), *Biopolitical Surveillance and Public Health in International Politics*. Palgrave, New York.

Young, O. R. (2011), 'Improving the Performance of the Climate Regime: Insights from Regime Analysis', in Dryzek, Norgaard, and Schlosberg (2011a): 625–38.

Zacher, M. (2007), 'The Transformation of Global Health Collaboration since the 1990s', in Cooper, Kirton, and Schrecker (2007a): 15–27.

—— and Keefe, T. J. (2008), *The Politics of Global Health Governance: United by Contagion*. Palgrave, New York.

Zimmermann, A. (ed.) (2011), *The 1951 Convention Relating to the Status of Refugees and its 1967 Protocol*. Oxford University Press, Oxford.

Index

9/11 35, 51
  and national security 94

ABM Treaty (1972) 49
Afghanistan 51
Africa 77, 82, 87, 122
  African Union 101
  Organization of African Unity 94
air strikes 53
Al-Qaeda 51–2
AOSIS 74–5, 142
armed conflict
  international 41, 44–6
  laws of 41
  non-international 41, 43, 45–6
  see also Geneva Conventions; international
    humanitarian law; political violence
asymmetric conflicts 39, 54–5
Australia 99–100, 109, 116

Barber, B. 35
BASIC countries 71, 73, 79, 82
Beck, U. 10, 24
blockades 49
Bobbitt, P. 35
Brazil 78
Brown, C. 17, 104, 144, 151
Bull, H. 15, 33–4, 42, 48, 56, 96, 133, 161, 163
Butler, J. 35

Canada 79
Carr, E. H. 7–8, 31–4, 163
  critique of inter-war order 31–2, 73
  relativist 32
  status quo versus revisionist powers 32–3,
    161–2
Chan, M. 106
China 73, 78, 80
civilians 44–5, 136
  likelihood of being killed 38–9, 58
  see also non-combatants
civilization, standard of 20, 110
Clean Development Mechanism 72
climate change 10, 153
  adaptation 65, 67, 80–1
  categories 29, 64, 70–1, 139, 154
  causal responsibility 75, 88, 139
  CBDR 70–1, 75–7, 79, 146, 160
  concept 29, 64, 68–70, 139–40

developed countries 11, 65, 70–1, 75
developing countries 11, 65, 70–1, 75
  and economic development 69, 72, 76, 140
  equity 63, 80, 82, 139
  financial transfers 65, 67, 78–9
  GHG emissions 10, 30, 69, 73–4,
    78, 140–1
  as international issue 68, 80, 140
  intractable 63
  legitimacy crisis 82
  major emitters 71, 79
  market failure 80
  mitigation 80–1
  moral problem 29, 63, 83, 138–42
  and movement 101, 156
  and outsourcing 80
  sensitivity 66–7
  and sovereignty 69
  temperature increase 74, 77–8, 81, 142
  see also UNFCCC
collateral damage 53, 58–9
combatants 9, 38, 45, 54–5, 59, 135
  immunity from prosecution 39, 46
  liability to be killed 28, 38–9, 46, 55,
    57–8, 60
  moral equality 54
communitarianism 21, 128–9, 131, 145
complex emergencies 156
constructivism 5, 17
Convention on Biological Diversity 77
Copenhagen Accord 70, 74, 77–8, 80
  see also UNFCCC
cosmopolitanism 21, 128–30, 145

Dauvergne, C. 144
drones 55
Durban Platform 79
  see also UNFCCC

Egypt 71
English School (ES) 5, 14–22, 151, 157
Erskine, T. 17

famine 24
Fidler, D. 119
Figueres, C. 62
Finnemore, M. 162
Framework Convention on Tobacco Control
  (FCTC) 116

Freeman, M. 133
Frost, M. 143, 150

G8 123
G77 71, 82
Gardiner, S. 31, 139–40
Geneva Conventions (1949) 9, 45, 47, 153
  Common Article 3 45–6, 51–2
  Protocols (1977) 9, 45–6, 155, 160
Gentili, A. 57
global capitalism 10, 124, 157
global health 11–12, 85, 153
  access to medicines 124, 157
  biomedical approach 12, 119
  burden of disease 122
  categories 30, 118, 154
  cholera 110
  chronic disease 118–20
  concepts 12, 29–30, 106–7, 113,
    117–20, 126
  cordon sanitaire 109
  crisis 107–8
  disease transmission 107, 109
  distribution of health personnel 122
  and globalization 113–14, 127
  and global economy 12, 113
  governance (GHG) 113, 116, 147
  HIV/AIDS 113, 121
  horizontal approach 118–19
  infectious disease 118–20, 123, 153
  influenza vaccines 124
  inequities 147–8
  International Health Regulations
    (IHR) 111–14, 116, 121
  international sanitary conferences 109–10
  and international trade 109–10
  life expectancy 108, 122, 149
  life styles 113, 153
  malaria 107
  medical research 120, 124
  moral problem 30, 147–50
  positive achievements 108
  and private foundations 108
  quarantines 109–10
  SARS outbreak 112–13
  and scarcity 120
  securitization 113, 120–2, 150, 160
  smoking 116, 123–4, 153
  social determinants 117–20, 126, 148
  system of notification 113
  vertical management 112, 118–19
  and war 107, 116
Goodin, R. 132, 162
Green Climate Fund 79
Grenada 74–5

Haddad, E. 98
Hague Conferences 44
Hamdan case 51–2
Hart, H. L. A. 42
hierarchy 18, 158, 160
Howard, M. 47
Huhne, C. 71
human movement 11, 153
  and borders 11, 88, 96, 102–4
  categories 11, 21, 84, 90, 95–6, 98–103
  concepts 29, 85, 104
  forced 89, 90–1
  gaps in protection 85–6, 98–9, 102, 105,
    144–5
  and international politics 87–8
  legalization of 89–90, 102, 104–5
  moral problem 96–7, 104–5, 143–7
  multilateral management 86, 91
  and power asymmetry 84, 89, 143
human rights 21, 35, 47, 53, 90, 92–3, 98–100,
    112, 130, 135, 144
humanitarian intervention 18, 52–4
Hurrell, A. 20–1, 95
Hurricane Katrina 23, 67, 97

India 73, 78
indigenous peoples 11, 77, 107
innocence 30–1, 137, 139
interdependence 25–6, 128–9
Inter-governmental Panel on Climate Change
    (IPCC) 25–6, 63, 66, 141
internally displaced persons (IDPs) 102–3,
    155
  Guiding Principles 103
international humanitarian law (IHL) 52, 155
  compliance gap 58
  equal application 54
  legal capacity to enforce 42–3, 55
  and non-state actors 42, 51–2, 55
  see also Geneva Conventions
international society 4–5, 157–60
  as agent 5, 14–15
  bifurcated order 19–20
  being bound 150, 158, 162
  consensus 14, 18, 84, 159–60, 162–3
  constitutive 5, 16, 19
  deformity 18, 158
  diversity 17–19, 95
  and Europe 20
ideal type 15
institutions 19–20
  and law 150–1
  loss of moral bearing 61, 134
  as moral agent 16–17, 146–7, 150–1, 162–3
  pluralism 20–1, 159

and powerful 15, 34–5, 127, 158–9
  practical association 151, 158
  purposive association 151, 158
  and refuge 91, 95
  regulation by 124–5, 153–4, 157
  reification 14
  self-determination 90, 96, 145
  socialization 5, 15–16, 19
  solidarism 21
  sovereignty 91, 105
  toleration 20
  unity 17, 95
  see also vulnerable
irregular migrants 90, 101–2, 104
  additional hazards 90, 102
  soft law 102

Japan 79, 122
just war theory 42, 54–5, 59–60,
  134–5, 137

Kampala Convention 101
Keene, E. 20
Keohane, R. 25–6
Kosovo 53
Kyoto Protocol 72–3, 77, 79–80
  see also UNFCCC

Lauterpacht, H. 45
League of Nations 92
legitimacy 13, 19, 129
Libya 53, 87
Lieber, F. 44
Linklater, A. 130, 157

Maldives 75
Mali 1
Mann, J. 120–1
Médecins Sans Frontières (MSF) 1
Millennium Development Goals (2000) 127
Miller, D. 131
morality 2, 5, 12, 32, 161–4
  and IR theory 128–33
  see also climate change; global health;
    human movement; political violence;
    vulnerability
Morgenthau, H. 32

Nardin, T. 150–1
nature, state of 41–2, 97
New International Economic Order 21
non-combatants 30
  immunity 45, 53, 134–5
  see also civilians
nuclear weapons 49–50
Nye, J. 25–6

Obama, B. 67–8
Owens, P. 57

passports 90–1
  Nansen 92, 96
Pogge, T. 130, 149
political violence 9, 153
  categories 9, 29, 39, 41, 43–54, 134,
    138, 154
  concepts 9, 29, 40–1, 43–6, 54–60,
    134, 136–7
  challenges to state monopoly 48
  equality of belligerents 38, 43, 45–6, 54,
    57, 59, 139
  moral problem 43, 61, 134–8
public/private 40, 48, 55–7, 60
state monopoly 44, 48, 56, 61
  see also armed conflict; terrorism; war

Quirin case 51

Rawls, J. 148
refugees 11, 84, 91–2, 95–6, 98–101, 104,
  153, 155–7
  burden-sharing 93, 99, 143, 146
  environmental 93, 98, 101
  non-arrival practices 99–100
Refugee Convention (1951) 9, 93–5, 100,
  114, 156–7, 160
  and Cold War 93–4
  and inter-war practice 92–3
  Protocol (1967) 4, 94
  specific definition 93, 99, 101
responsibility 10, 17, 146
  irresponsibility 26–7
Responsibility to Protect 18, 85, 102
  special 18, 132
risk 10, 24–5, 27, 67
  society 24, 58, 153
Roosevelt, F. D. R. 111
Rousseau, J-J. 42, 57–8
Russia 79

SALT 1 49
Saudi Arabia 71
Sen, A. 24
sieges 49
slavery 19
Smith, A. 27
South Africa 78
Southeast Asia 95
Steiner, A. 75
Stern, G. 15
Stern, T. 78
Sudan 74
sustainable development 76

Taliban 51
terrorism 38, 50–1, 61
 counter-terrorism 51–2
 proper authority 56
 resistance to state power 56
 substitutability of victims 48
 war on 51–2
torture 52

United Nations 108
 Security Council 15, 18, 71, 121
UNDP 62, 142
UNEP 75
UNFCCC 9, 62, 64, 69–70, 72, 75, 77, 91,
 139, 160
 Rio Declaration 68–9, 72, 142
 Kyoto COP 76–7
 Bali COP 70, 72
 Cancun COP 72, 75
 Copenhagen COP 70, 74, 82
 Durban COP 62, 75
UNHCR 92–3, 99, 155
United States 35, 51–2, 73, 76–7, 116, 125, 160
 Byrd-Hagel Resolution (1997) 65
 National Research Council 63

Van Engeland, A. 155
Vattel, E. de 59
Veitch, S. 26–7
vulnerability
 adaptability 25–6
 assessments 63–4
 assured 49
 categories 6, 27–8, 30–1, 98, 152–5
 concept 6–7, 28–9, 152–3
 condition 1, 6, 28
 in disasters 1, 4–5, 23
 distribution 5–6, 10–11, 21, 38, 63–4, 100
 domestic deformity 21
 gender dimension 67
 and material power 35–6, 142
 as moral condition 2, 4, 8, 34, 128–33, 163–4
 and norms 3, 6, 22–3, 84–5, 88, 105, 163

objective 3, 22–3, 33, 152
 and poverty 21
 sensitivity 25–6
 social 1, 3, 7, 14, 24, 67, 84
vulnerable
 definition 3, 27
 in IR 1, 4–5, 128–33
 relation to international society 2, 38,
 152–7, 162
 social practice of 2, 5, 7–8, 13–14, 17,
 20, 40, 158

Walzer, M. 38–9, 55, 60, 135–6
 supreme emergency 59, 137
war
 concept 38, 40–2, 44–5, 60–1
 convention 38, 47, 59
 crimes 55–6
 discrimination 43–5, 59, 134, 138
 as institution 6, 42
 moral reality 37
 see also global health
Weber, M. 40
Wen, J. 76
World Bank 117
World Health Organization (WHO) 9, 106,
 113, 116–17, 119, 121–2, 126,
 157, 160
 Alma-Ata Declaration 112
 competing principles 112
 Constitution 111–12, 119, 126
 Commission on the Social Determinants
 of Health (CSDH) 148
 Global Code of Practice on the Recruitment
 of Health Personnel 122
World Meteorological Organization
 (WMO) 70
world society 35
World Trade Organization (WTO) 116, 157
 TRIPs 125
World War I 47, 59, 116
 peace settlements 91
World War II 45, 49, 92, 112